A H[ZIONISM

1897 TO 2020

Politics

Religion

One Beast, Two Arms

THE TWO TENDENTIOUS AUTHORS ARE:
PETER ARNOLD & JORGEN LARS RASMUSSEN
BOTH AKUM (derogatory word for a
Christian) pg 119.

A History of Zionism
1897 to 2020

 Critical Thinking Institute

ISBN # 978-0-9856145-8-4

Library of Congress Control Number: 2019940714

Published in 2019

Jon Larsen Shudlick
Biographer / Author / Self Publisher
239-218-4028

Proof Read by: Phyllis Janet Marino
Cover Illustration: Phillip Amandro
Design and Layout: Linda Leppert

Printed in the United States of America 2019

For information concerning rights & permission or other questions contact the publisher.

Moral relevancy, the process now used in most Christian churches is a surrender of Western Ideology and Christian ethics and an act of Desertion by our religious leaders.

September 11, 2012 — Armed militants overwhelmed security at the US mission and killed Ambassador to Libya **J. Christopher Stevens**, State Department Information Management Officer **Sean Smith**, and diplomatic security agents **Tyrone Woods** and **Glen Doherty**.

Immediately afterwards, U.S. intelligence officials and the Obama Administration concluded that the attacks grew out of a nearby mob that was protesting an anti-Islam film, The Innocence of Muslims. This conclusion, the CIA later decided, was wrong: the people initially believed to be protesters were actually a loose group of Islamic militants who had shown up at the mission with the intent to attack it.

In the words of Hillary Clinton,

"What difference can it, at this time, possibly make?"

Dedication

This book is dedicated to the

66 million murdered Christian

martyrs and the 900 Christian

Churches and Monasteries

destroyed and the over

1,000 Russian Orthodox priests

killed at the hands of the Jew

Bolshevik Commissars.

The Real Holocaust!

As revisionist historians, basing their historic perceptions singularly on original documentation, without any references to other published history or academic consideration, we are disseminators of truth. **Truth is not in all circles cherished or even accepted. The victors, who are no more honest than the losers, write history. Sadly in this age Cultural Marxism now called PC or Political Correctness is the overriding academic philosophy relating to history. A large portion of late 20th and now 21st century mainstream "history" can only be regarded as fiction.**

"Nothing is more important than true history."

Willis Carto

This book is Revisionist history!

The Greatest Story Never Told

UNTIL NOW

A Book For The "TV Age"

This is the first book designed to attract the "Television Age" of Non-Readers; and to help Students who are functionally illiterate, but must learn our important message about true history.

Confucius, the Chinese philosopher said, 2,000 years ago, "One picture is worth a thousand words," and that is why television has prospered, while the Booksellers are dying. <u>This book is different</u>. This book is a walking, talking newspaper. We include hundreds of visuals to impact and entertain our mass non-reading population. In most books, you turn the page, and you see "a sea of print" facing you, and you say to yourself, subconsciously, "must I read all this?" You will not see such "seas of print" in this book, pages are broken up by humorous and provocative "grabber headlines." Additionally, we use bold type, for easy reading, instead of the faint "Casper Milquetoast" type seen in most books. The industry prints books as they were printed hundreds of years ago.

It may amaze you to know that only 10% of the population buys books on a regular basis, while 90% of mass America gets the little information they do get from radio and television. One third of our Students are functionally illiterate. And those "porno rock" radio stations hardly broadcast any news, and just may include one minute of "drug busts" per hour. Yet 100% of our Readers must understand our message, as true history is vital to everyone.

Author Jon Larsen Shudlick with mentor and friend Eustace Mullins. Mr. Mullins was designated the only authorized biographer of Ezra Pound by letter from him dated July 24, 1958. Four of Ezra Pound's protegés have previously been awarded the Nobel Prize for Literature, William Butler Yates, for his later poetry, James Joyce for "Ulysses", Ernest Hemingway for "The Sun Also Rises", and T.S. Elliot for "The Wasteland". Jon Larsen Shudlick produced three beautifully edited DVD's with Eustace Mullins; "Secrets of the Federal Reserve", "The New World Order", and "Murder by Injection", an expose of the Federal Drug Administration.

PUBLISHER'S STATEMENT

The publisher, Jon Larsen Shudlick, is a former Army Chief Investigator and former five term mayor of Ocean Ridge, Florida.

The author and publisher of this critical manuscript both realize the controversial nature of these topics. Therefore, we suggest and request that you research these subjects on your own with all due diligence.

A most important aspect of education that our government educational system is remiss from emphasizing is the concept of **thinking critically** or **critical thinking**. Critical thinking means you question what you hear and read. Teaching itself should help you understand **how to think**, not what to think. Asking questions like who, what, where, when, why or how after reading a subject and then interpreting on your own, leads you to **thinking critically** or **critical thinking**. Today with vast information available at your fingertips through the Internet, Wikipedia, CD's, books, magazines, a variety of newspapers, journals and so many different points of reference there is really no reason not to be knowledgeable about any topic you wish to pursue.

Unfortunately, the present social engineering educational agenda is **unacceptable, inferior and a complete failure**. Our government educational system has plunged our country into third world status, falling from a rank of **4th** among industrialized nations to **34th!!!** My friend, author, Jim Anderson states, "Our country has become nothing more than a third world country with the bomb." If you use your own ability to **think critically** and follow up on topics important to you and your future you can be much more confident in your own ideas and attitudes. With that knowledge and self-reliance you can achieve unlimited success.

About Jon Larsen Shudlick
"Believe it or Not"

INVESTIGATOR SHUDLICK

Born in Rice Lake, Wisconsin, a small rural community in the upper Midwest, Jon Larsen Shudlick's eclectic career includes being chosen as one of two Provost Marshal Investigators from his Company of Military Police that graduated from Fort Gordon, Georgia in the summer of 1965. His aptitude and dedication preceded his promotion to Chief Investigator of the 4th Missile Command in Chunchon, Korea.

He has been involved in real estate since 1972 when he obtained his Wisconsin broker's license. Moving to Florida in 1974 Jon became broker and president of Dutch Realty in Boynton Beach in the year 1980 where he was also founder of The Auction Man, Inc. in 1988.

Jon was a 5-term mayor of Ocean Ridge, Florida and a two-term Chairman of the South Palm Beach County Council of Governments.

Besides his many and varied business, educational, and international accomplishments Jon also hosted his radio program, "Conspiracy Facts" for 7 years from WTAN 1340 in Clearwater, Florida.

Jon's dynamic speaking ability and opportunities were epitomized when he gave "The Great Speech" before the American Bar Association in December of 1992 at Lake Buena Vista, Florida (appeared in the Perspective section of *St. Mary's Law Journal,* 1993, Vol. 24, Num. 4, page 1215).

Jon's culmination included a speech before the Florida Supreme Court in opposition to the Anti-Discrimination Proposal of the Florida Bar Anti-Discrimination hearing given in Tallahassee, Florida on Monday, April 5, 1993.

His brilliant career includes an appearance on *The Oprah Winfrey Show* on January 4, 1993 in reference to the criminal elements of the family divorce industry.

Presently, Jon has given every effort to **Truth in History** and to his continuous self-publications of books on the subject of **Conspiracy Dominated History**.

To read more about Jon's successes and triumphs go to www.leeelections.com.

The great enemy of the truth is
very often not the lie, deliberate, contrived
and dishonest, but the myth, persistent,
persuasive and unrealistic.

— John F. Kennedy

NATIONALISM

POPULISM

INDIVIDUALISM

ACKNOWLEDGEMENT

Reading most dedications I would question in my own mind if the person's wife or helpmate was truly as important to the completion of the publication as the author stated. In this instance there are few words that can describe the importance of **PHYLLIS JANET MARINO** to the completion of this writing. Her continuing criticism, enthusiasm, corrections, redrafting perseverance, encouragement and every imaginable secretarial skill were instrumental in bringing this book to its level of expertise. It is absolute to say that I could not have achieved this critical commentary without her help and devotion.

Publisher, Jon Larsen Shudlick

Index

Page #	Chapter Title

Part II

A Historic Relevancy

The "Great War" also called the First World War heralded the formation of the communist movement as a world force. The disastrous consequences of this war resulted in the Soviet State, in what had been Russia. The War pitted Czarist Russia and European Europe excluding Switzerland and Sweden against Germany. Germany acquiesced to American, Swiss, and Jewish influences, allowing Vladimir Lenin who had been sitting the war out in Zürich to travel by train from Zürich to Berlin to St. Petersburg with a large amount of gold, Ashkenazim, and armaments paid for by <<Jacob Schiff>>. The imperial German intent was to ferment a Russian revolution against the Czarist government (the cousin of the King of England) as a means of gaining access to grain and foodstuffs from the Ukraine, and to break the alliance of their opposition. <<Schiff>> had already financed Japan in the Sino-Russian Pacific war. They succeeded

Vladimir Lenin

Jacob Schiff

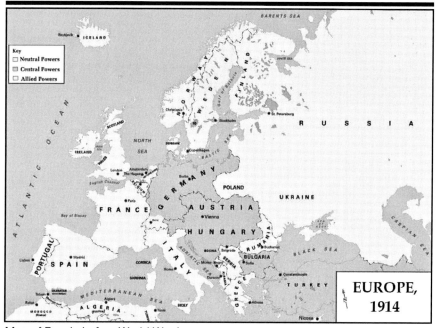

Map of Russia before World War I

Map of Russian Territorial Losses after WWI

White areas indicate nations that remained neutral throughout the course of World War I.

The territories noted in dark grey (above) along Russia's western boundary used World War I and its resulting chaos as a means to independence, including: Bessarabia (today occupying parts of Ukraine and Moldova), Estonia (the collapse of the Russian war effort in World War I was followed by the proclamation of Estonian independence in 1918). Red Army forces resisted and Soviet Russia did not recognize Estonia until 1920. The area was reoccupied by the U.S.S.R. in June 1940, later taken into the Soviet Union and then occupied by Germany in 1941, Finland, Lativa, Lithuania, Poland.

with terrible consequences that remained until the 1990's, with a considerable Russian presence in the Pacific Ocean.

Precipitation of events began in March 1917 when food riots relating to shortages in St. Petersburg forced the Czar to abdicate. This resulted in two parallel governments in Russia, the provincial democratic government of Alexander Kerensky, and the St. Petersburg Soviet Revolutionary Council. Real power however rested with the Mensheviks that were separated by two factions, those who wished to continue the war against Germany and those who desired withdrawal from the conflict. This schism ended with the arrival of <<Lenin>> and his millions in gold allowing him to pay his supporters, end the Russian war against Germany, and take control of the revolution. <<Lenin's>> first move was to shut down the Constitutional Assembly that was in the process of writing a Russian constitution, and upon that act to establish the dictatorship of the proletariat.[1]

The now established Soviet government (USSR)[2] then signed a peace treaty with Germany[3] in January 1918 ending hostilities between Russia and Germany thus releasing the German army's Eastern front. The historically called "Red Terror" began. The civil war in Russia resulted in brutal Jewish Commissars murdering their way across the landscape. Opposing Czarist government factions had produced the pogroms[4], which were short-lived and resulted in the Soviet state.

By 1919 the communists had gained control of Russia and were threatening most European nations including Germany and Hungary. Communist activists included <<Paul Levi, Leo Jogiches,

| Paul Levi | Leo Jogiches | Rosa Luxemburg | Gustav Landauer | Kurt Eisner |

| Ernst Toller | Hugo Haas | Béla Kun | Tibor Tzamuelly | Béla Vágó-Weisz |

Rosa Luxemburg, Gustav Landauer, Kurt Eisner, Ernst Toller, Hugo Haas, Béla Kun, Tibor Tzamuelly, Béla Vágó-Weis,>> all of them Ashkenazim Jews.

As revisionist historians, basing their historic perceptions singularly on original documentation, without any references to other published history or academic consideration, we are disseminators of truth. Truth is not in all circles cherished or even accepted. The victors, who are no more honest than the losers, write history. Sadly in this age Cultural Marxism[5] now called PC or Political Correctness is the overriding academic philosophy relating to history. Sadly a large portion of late 20th and now 21st century mainstream "history" can only be regarded as fiction.

The content of this writing has been arduously researched and may be considered a partial history of the Ashkenazim[6] in Western Europe. As such much of the information contradicts presently accepted academic dictums. People who oppose this will as they always do, commence with personal attacks on the authors. Those who refuse to face historic reality, or counter facts, will therefore commence attacking the messenger, which is counterproductive to honest debate, and serves little purpose.

Right at the beginning we state that we are not opposed to Hebrews who are in fact Semitic peoples just as are Arabs. We are disparate of zionism[7] a word we refuse to capitalize. Zionism has nothing to do with religion or race it is simply a political movement structured to gain territory through theft, in the Levant, by stealing it from Palestinian Arabs who have resided there for over 20 centuries.

While we are not theologians we have studied this issue for well over three decades and also extensively studied the Torah, Talmud, New Testament, and Koran—all of which support this writing.

Jesus Christ was a Hebrew as were his disciples. That however does not alter the fact as expressed in the Gospels that Christ became disenchanted with the Hebrews of his day. Combined Christ's associates opposed the teachings and practices of first century Hebrews, and the religious teachers of the time, or that of this century. The reader should be cognizant that zionism is a device of the latter 19th century, having no relationship with the religious teachings of Roman times or that of the first century and before. Concepts such as the one claiming that God gave the Levant to Jews are not based on historic or any realistic facts. Firstly, present day Jews are 97% Ashkenazim and only about 3% are Hebrews or have Hebrew extraction. Khazars only became Jews in the 6th to 8th centuries, and the espoused biblical promise was made pre AD. Secondly, Jews never in any recorded history represented more than 15% of the entire Levant population.[8] Thirdly is the concept based on the 19th century invention of victimhood, which has been used by Jews in their massive extortion campaign since WWII.[9]

In the latter 19th century, with the development of zionism, the ancient Hebrew teachings of the Torah[10] gradually took a backseat to the Talmud, which is the most egregious religious text of history. Today any Rabbi will advise that the Talmud is the primary instrument of Jewish teaching and that the Torah takes a backseat to it. Talmudic teaching is an abomination, the very concept of a secular unreligious philosophy. To expose the truth of that teaching is neither Nazi or anti-Semitic it simply represents truth about modern Judaism. Talmudic teaching is the backbone of zionist belief. It is a repugnant philosophy based on racism, hatred, racial and gender segregation, and apartheid societal geography. Zionism is

hegemony on a monumental scale. It is the greatest evil and is the embodiment of racial exclusion, "A People Apart", "The Chosen of God", "Never Again", and so forth. The text of this book will substantiate this beyond any reasonable doubt.

Just one paragraph about anti-Semitism; the word is an oxymoron: it was the creation of zionism. The Semitic race is a subgrouping of the Caucasian race and as such comprises the peoples of the Levant, both Arab as well as Hebrew. It does not however include any Ashkenazim who are not Semitic but of Indo-European stock actually Turkistan. They came from the Caucuses and the Khazarian Empire, which was at war with the Byzantine Empire on one side and the Islamic Caliphate on the other. Between the 6th and the 8th centuries AD the Khazars converted to Judaism. Today they represent over 90% of living Jews of the world.

Jews have for centuries mounted a systematic war against European Christian culture. Hatred of Christianity is emphasized in the Talmud. This war has expanded exponentially since WWI and is expressed in various means of enforcement and social directives such as; internationalism, globalism, Cultural Marxism, political correctness, multiculturalism, open borders, radical gun control, feminism, homosexuality, and pornography. Utilizing these means to undermine and destroy Christian culture and Western society has proven very successful for the Ashkenazim. The reason that they do this is their insecurity of living as a minority in all of Western societies.

Zionism is a conspiracy, any group of individuals seeking "change"—now where have we heard that word before, whose ultimate aim is the control of the society in which they live. This book will show in detail what this plan consists of, how it is to be implemented, and who and what is causing it to be executed.

There is one more issue relating to this introduction. Those opposed to this document will claim that our assertion that Jews (in fact Ashkenazim) were the agitators of the Russian Revolution is not verifiable. This manuscript completely verifies our position. Additionally, the US Ambassador to Russia in 1919, David Francis, reported to Washington that the Russian Revolution was more than 50% Jewish. The American State Department in July 1919 prepared and distributed a document titled: "The Powers and Aims of International Jewry" which explicitly blamed Jews for the Russian Revolution. A Dutch diplomat, Mr. Qudendyke likewise reported to his government that the Bolsheviks were controlled by Jews of no nationality who were not Russians, and whose only objective appears to be the destruction of the existing orders of governments. To this we can add the comments of Sir Winston Churchill that we will expand on in later text.

Peter Arnold
Tel Aviv   2015 February

---

1. Proletariat is a collectivity of the lower classes [Working Class as opposed to nobility]
2. Union of Soviet Socialist Republics
3. Brest-Litovsk Treaty
4. Conflict between the Jewish and Christian population resulting in Jews being repressed.
5. PC (Political Correctness) is a product of the Soviet Cultural Marxism.
6. Ashkenazim are the Jew converts from the Khazarian Empire of the 6th century who emigrated to what are now Russia, Poland, Prussia [Germany] and the Baltic States.
7. Zionism is a socio-political movement based on Ashkenazim desire to create a nation state in the Levant. Ashkenazim are Jewish converts from the Caucuses, are not Semitic peoples, are not related to Hebrews, and have no rights to anything in the Levant.
8. See Roman census first century [Census of Quirinius]
9. The Holocaust Industry by Prof. [Norman Finkelstein]
10. First five chapters of the Old Testament

Note: There are many types of Jews, all of which try their best to hide their identity. In general terms Jews can be separated into; Reformed, Conservative, Orthodox, Hasidim, and Atheist. Any of these can be zionists. Zionism is Jewish nationalism vested in a state located on stolen land in the Levant. Reformed Jews are leftist liberals. Orthodox Jews deny Jesus Christ. Conservative Jews like to play on the fence going with the flow—a little Talmud and a little tolerance. Hasidism is ultra-conservative awaiting the arrival of the Messiah (who actually arrived 2,000 years ago). Last is atheistic Judaism the largest branch of Judaism, from which sprang zionism and communism. They are radical secularists, many heavily involved in politics. They use Judaism as a crutch to support their anti-Christian agendas including the promotion of gay rights, homosexuality, protection against criticism, pornography, radical feminist, socialism, and communism. The largest homosexual community in the world is Tel Aviv, the largest in America is New York City.

Prelude

There are two and only two major forces that compete for man's attention in this world. No more just good and evil. The eyes of the beholder often dictate the variance. But in reality we all understand the difference between good and evil. In today's bumper sticker mentality many of our fellow travelers in life have little interest in differentiating between the two. Others claim our problems to be the result of our complex materialistic society, but human nature has in fact not changed in the past 10,000 years. A shorter attention span due to lax education and overuse of video games is the only real change that has taken place. It is the result of the planned dumbing down of the U.S. educational system by the 20th and 21st century propaganda machines. During WWII, Dr. Joseph Göbbels was the German Reich Minister of Propaganda from 1933 to 1945.

Dr. Joseph Göbbels

After WWII in 1947, the Tavistock Institute ✱ was founded as a social science organization for instituting change in society. The Tavistock Institute was funded largely by the Rockefeller Foundation and U.S. and British government intelligence agencies.

Today, 21st century man has become the instrument of those who control the debate. The Jewish controlled media[13] with the support of multiple government agencies[14] is the controller of dialogue. He who controls dialogue controls society.

Due to the deliberate Rabbinical[15] miss-interpretation of the Torah[16] and its replacement in modern Jewish tradition by the Talmud[17] the true meanings and laws of the Old Testament have been perverted. Reformed Judaism then went on to allow female rabbis (biblically illegal), homosexual allowance (severe violation of the Torah), homosexual marriage, the seating of males and females together in synagogue, and the allowance of suspension of all dietary laws. Jews in the 21st century lead and control the entire feminist, homosexual, pedophile, and pornography industries and organizations. Biblically there are the forces of Canaan (Evil and the Devil) and the forces of Shem (good and God). Modern Jews have made every effort to

✱ The Tavistok Institute Of Human Relations by Dr. John Coleman.

9

obstruct and confuse these issues. The decedents of Shem are called Semites, and the descendants of Canaan the anti-Semites. Thus through the reversal of language good and evil have been reversed. Language is the primary issue with which the Tavistock Institute concerns itself. Changing homosexual to puff, fag to gay, semi-automatic rifle to assault weapon (1980's), and jacketed ammunition to cop killer bullet (1980's) illustrates the success of Tavistock.

How do we recognize Evil (the Devil)? The Bible is clear on this issue; "By their deeds ye shall know them." As you progress in the Mishnah, Talmud, and the Protocols, evil will rapidly become a concept that you will be able to recognize. It is this cabal created by rabbinical scholars, which is referred to as "The Will of Canaan" that you will see permeates everything that these people do. The destruction of Western Civilization and the submergence of our society, the destruction of the individual, the creation of a socialist society, and finally a totalitarian zionist cabal controlling everything is the end plan. The New World Order is part and parcel of it all. All this will be demonstrated with proof provided in the following pages.

Jewish secret societies and their ritualistic practice of numerology (a heathen practice of foretelling the future, actually used to promote rabbinical claims will be shown). This is the Hasidic Qabbalist device used by rabbis to deceive and self-promote their importance. What they in reality do is to write their predictions after the fact. The six million claims is most certainly one of these. You will learn of the "Protocols of the Learned Elders of Zion" their master plan for world government and the Jewish Communist Manifesto that has almost totally been inculcated in the American IRS statutes.

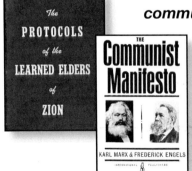

Neither the Protocols nor the communist manifesto can be ignored because they have both been made part of and incorporated into the legal structure of the United States.

Jorgen Lars Rasmussen
Trondheim, Feb. 2015

Know your enemy!

Perseus LLC is a private investment and merchant bank. They have offices in Washington DC, NYC, and Munich. They handle all Bilderberger accounts for America and Germany. All officers in Perseus are Ashkenazim. All listed depositors to the Bilderberger accounts are either Ashkenazim or corporations owned by Ashkenazim. American Friends of the Bilderbergers Inc. is a tax-exempt foundation that deposited over $200 million into the Perseus bank accounts in 2008.

The Tavistok Institute Of Human Relations by Dr. John Coleman. available from: Sacred Truth Publishing P.O. Box 18 Mountain City, TN 37683

The Tavistok Institute was founded in 1913 (not 1947)? pg; The Tavistok Institute Of Human Relations. Dr John Coleman

11. Dr. Joseph Göbbels, German Reichsminister of Propaganda 1933-45

12. The Tavistock Institute was founded in 1947 as a social science organization for instituting change in society. Funded largely by The Rockefeller Foundation and US and British government intelligence agencies.

13. Eight companies control over 90% of the American media. All are Jewish led: NBC/Universal Studios—<<Brian Roberts>>, CS/MTV/Paramount/ Viacom—<<Sumner Redstone>>, ABC/Disney—<<Robert Iger>>, CNN/Time mag—<<Jeff Zuker>>, FOX/Wall St. Journal/NY Post/21st Century Fox-<<Rupert Murdoch>>, NY Times <<Arthur Sulzberger>>, Washington Post etc.... *BEZOS,*

14. Between the NSA, CIA, military intelligence, and major American defense contractors over one billion dollars is spent on misinformation to the American public annually. "The System" ISBN # 978-1-937553-06-7, PP 1-32.

15. Rabbis are not priests, they are traditional lawyers that interpret the Talmud.

16. First five books of the Old Testament

17. Along with other books the legal interpretation of the Torah is based on rabbinical pronouncements beginning in the Babylonian Captivity.

Was Wellington House before. Pg 76 The Committee Of 300 by Dr John Coleman. 1947

In the first century of the Roman world under "Pax Romana"
the Levant was racked with continual religious turmoil
and violence caused by the 15% of the
population who were Jewish and who were unable to get along
with any of the other religions and cultures.

In 70 AD the Romans had had enough. Tiberius Julius
Caesar conquered Jerusalem, destroyed the Temple,
and banished all Jews to be dispersed throughout the
Empire, this was the Diaspora.
The second six million.[18]

This was not the first time.
The "Babylonian Captivity" was the result of the
Babylonian conquest of the Levant because the
Hebrews of the 6th century BC was also
unable to get along with anyone.

Nebuchadnezzar had had enough, and rounded up
the entire Hebrew population and relocated them to
Babylon, his capital.
The first six million.[19]

When the Babylonian empire released them after 70 years,
two thirds of them chose to stay in Babylon.
Those who returned brought
compound interest, the now developed
banking monopoly, and grand scale usury to the world.

WWII brought with it the third six million.

---

18. The entire population of the Levant in 68 AD was under six million (Roman census)
19. The entire Hebrew population of the Levant in 600 BC was unknown but Babylonian tablets indicate that 10,000 Hebrews (the entire population) were forced to move to Babylon.

History of the Hebrews
of the Levant

The Levant[20] is the region in which most 21st century European religions developed, with the exception of Islam[21] which originated on the Saudi Arabian peninsula around Mecca and Medina about 600 AD. In biblical and prebiblical times one of the groups inhabiting the Levant,[22] and there were many, were the 12 Hebrew tribes.[23] The Hebrews were primarily sheep and goat herders.[24] They were nomads who lived in tents and traveled throughout the Levant setting up their camps where they found fodder for their animals and water in this semi-arid region. A good understanding of climate, weather, and geography is a prerequisite for the survival of nomadic peoples.[25] Thus the development of a calendar, probably adapted from the Egyptians, was important as were the strict rules of nomadic societies in general. Historically we can view the present Bedouin society, as the model for whatever Hebrew society must have been like. Bedouins likewise live in tents, and have a very severe and fixed set of established laws and customs that are dictated by climate and geography. There are no records of any nomadic peoples developing architecture, technology, literature, or infrastructure and so it was with the Hebrews. There is much aggrandizement especially in the Torah about Hebrew accomplishments, but there is no supporting evidence for ✱

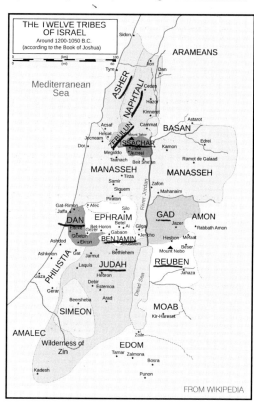

THE TWELVE TRIBES OF ISRAEL
Around 1200-1050 B.C.
(according to the Book of Joshua)

FROM WIKIPEDIA

✱ *The Egyptian Origins of King David and the Temple of Solomon.* by Ahmed Osman.

13

those claims. Nomadic peoples like the American Indians, peoples of the Asian Steppes, Hebrews, and Gypsies have not left a trail of great accomplishments. The Hebrews of the Levant did however produce voluminous tribal customs and laws that were eventually transcribed by Rabbis as the Talmud that was passed down as memorized law and eventually after and during the Babylonian Captivity written as the Talmuds.[26] It must be clearly understood that the Talmud is man's (the rabbis) interpretation of Biblical law and thus cannot be called the word of God; in fact it is the most evil intended religious document of history.[27] Furthermore, it must be understood that the Talmud is a work in progress, which began its life in Babylon in about 600 BC and has been added to and modified ever since.

A matter of language:

In the English-speaking world the most authoritative dictionary is the Oxford English Dictionary. It very clearly states that "Judaist" and "Judaic" are the correct and proper forms of the incorrect "Jews" and "Jewish" which are commonly used today. The use of language as a means of misrepresenting reality was briefly touched upon in the Prelude and has in the 21st century taken a prominent place in linguistics and societal change. To expand on this, today's Jews cannot truthfully call themselves Jews because they are in no way related to the Hebrews of ancient times and are certainly not Judeans. They can correctly identify themselves as Judaists or Ashkenazi or Ashkenazim, whichever they may be. A Judaist is a person who professes Judaism as his religion. The commonly used word Jew has no roots in the word Judaism. The adjective form of Judaist is Judaic. Jewish as an adjective, is just as incorrect as Jew as a noun. It has been an ongoing effort by zionists since the 1890's to muck up any clear understanding of who and what Jews of the present day are. If it becomes common knowledge that present day Jews are in no way or manner related to any Semitic Hebrew ancestry then their entire claims to the Levant become null and void. To clarify again Ashkenazim are not Semitic peoples they are Indo-Europeans (Turkistan) coming from the Caucuses and are not ✗ genetically related to Hebrews. The phrase "Of Jewish Blood" is one of the constructed misnomers; according to DNA tests[28] almost all professed Jews are in fact Ashkenazim.[29] The word Jewess (female) is another misnomer developed by zionists in order to pursue their

✗ DNA *Science and the Jewish Bloodline by Texe Marrs.*

"Jewish" "Racial Gender Purity"[30] another lie built on a house of lies. The very fact that no other religion in the world has a special name for its female members corroborates that statement.

Before the 20th Century:

The Hebrews of the Levant allied themselves with the Assyrians and following the death of their king Manasseh his son Amon ruled from 664 BC to 640 BC when he was assassinated. His son Josiah, aged 8, was then installed as King of Judah and ruled from 639 to 609 BC. By the 7th century BC the Assyrian empire was in rapid decline. The Egyptian Pharaoh of the 26th dynasty Psammetichus I, (644-610 BC) expanded Egypt's holdings to include the entire Levant and as far south as Phoenicia.[31] Assyria and Egypt made a treaty and Assyria withdrew from the Levant. This clearly demonstrates that contrary to Jewish pronouncements that the Hebrews were only a minor people of the Middle East and represented less than 15% of the overall population. When Psammetichus died in 610 BC his son Necho II ascended the Egyptian throne. The King of Judah, Josiah was to meet the Pharaoh but was assassinated at Megiddo, his son Jehoahaz replaced him in 609 BC but the Pharaoh exiled him. All this was the precursor to the Babylonian Captivity by which the people of Judah were captured en mass and transported to Babylon, the new super-power of the Middle East. Nebuchadnezzar of the Babylonian Empire besieged Jerusalem that was by this time a walled city and carried out the removal of its population.

The Babylonian Captivity began after the battle of Carchemish in 605 BC when Nebuchadnezzar defeated the allied armies of the Assyrian empire and Egypt, besieging Jerusalem and capturing the city. The Jewish support of the losing side resulted in their captivity. This was a huge event because it is a foundational argument of the Jews that 6 million were lost, the Babylonian Captivity was the first use of the 6 million fables. It is a total hoax; the entire Hebrew population of the Levant in 605 BC was about 10,000.[32] The probable number was about 6,000 not 6 million; the entire Levant including what is now Egypt, Lebanon, Jordan, and Syria did not contain 6 million people. Logic furthermore dictates that it would have been far beyond a Bronze Age civilization to move a population of six million individuals a distance of 650 km. Babylon's entire population in 605 BC has been estimated based on cruciform tablets to be 120,000. Today

Jerusalem has a population of 479,000 Jews and 281,000 Muslims and 14,000 Christians for a total of 774,000. (Less than 1 million) After the return, Hebrews in the Levant numbered about 4,000 and were the smallest religious minority in the entire Levant. The religions of the Levant were, Pharaoh worshipers, Assyrian Ball, Mot, Yam, and Greek Zeus, Hades, and Poseidon religions.[33]

While the Babylonian Captivity only lasted 70 years, it is of enormous importance to the history of Western Europe, as you shall learn later.[34] There are three factors of great impact. Firstly, is the fact that only one-third of the Jews chose to return to the Levant after they were released, the remainder chose to stay in Babylon. Secondly, those Jews that returned from Babylon brought with them the beginnings of the Babylonian Talmud and were now ingrained in Babylonian culture, banking, and business practices. Thirdly, the Babylonian banking system that included compound interest and other usury[35] practices became part of Jewish banking. The charging of compound interest only became a common practice in Europe after the Jews took over the banking industry there.[36]

It is very important to understand the difference between Jewish rabbis and priests. Priests, who can only be male, were all decedents of the tribe of Aaron. They were employed at the temple in Jerusalem. Priests were Sadducees, which might in today's understanding be considered a privileged upper class, almost a political party. Before the construction of the temple they were interpreters of the Law (Torah). By the time of Christ there were many of them. Rabbis are not priests, they are lawyers, who replaced the priests after the captivity, and they were called Pharisees. Rabbis, unlike priests were not paid; they were lawyers who had secular employment most commonly by Christ's time as tax collectors for Rome or as lawyers. Religiously the schism between the priests and the rabbis was that rabbis said that there would be resurrection of the dead while priests said that there was no afterlife.[37]

As mentioned above, the Babylonian Captivity had without question a great impact on Judaism. The Hebrews that returned from Babylon were a new generation. Life expectancy at this time averaged 40 years, and thus after 70 years of captivity almost two generations had elapsed. Those who returned were more Babylonian than Hebrew. Before The Captivity the only viable religious text of the Hebrews was the Torah. A few years after the return, the Talmud had become the primary religious text. Next the Jerusalem

Talmud appeared, probably written by Hebrews who had escaped the Captivity it has however been a minor instrument. Both texts are accompanied by Mishnah texts. Both the Christian New Testament and the Talmud have sprouted numerous variations over an extended period of time. This has continued from 600 BC to today for the Talmud and from the third century AD to today with the New Testament. However in Judaism all sects claim to conform to the Talmud, while in Christianity there are many texts, Bibles, and books. The Talmud is a rabbinical interpretation of the first five books of the Bible and has two accompanying texts called the Mishnah and the Gemara, which are further expansions. The reason for this is that the original Talmud is written in many languages and has extensive commentaries within the text. This has gone in some cases to the extreme of 75 pages of comments on just one phrase. Much of the Talmud is nothing but the bragging of Hebrews intended to expand the political and social power of the rabbis.

By the second Diaspora[38] the Torah had been diminished by rabbinical effort and was superseded by the Talmud, which became the prominent document and law of the Jews from that time to the present.

The second Diaspora was the banishment of all Hebrews from the Levant in 70 AD by order of the Roman Emperor Titus, son of Vespasian and his commander Tiberius Julius Alexander. (The second Diaspora and the second six million.) Due to excellent Roman recordkeeping, we know the exact population of Jerusalem in 70 AD. Based on the 1 AD Roman census, the Hebrew population of Jerusalem was 600,000. Just as they did under Babylonian rule, Hebrews continually caused trouble. This provoked the Romans since they had provided roads, water supplies, libraries, civil administration, safe travel, access to the entire known world, administration, sewerage, police, and in fact all the things Hebrews did not have before Rome came. Hebrews were allowed to practice their own religion without Roman interference, they had their own ruler king, <<Herod Agrippa>>, and they even had their own army. What they were rebelling against is a true mystery; after all before the Romans came they were simply a bunch of nomadic goat and sheep herders. In the first century <<Herod the Great>> (Agrippa) was ruler of Galilee, and Perea who was the Roman client king. Rome had a Procurator[39] who was appointed by the Roman emperor Caesar Tiberius who at the time of 26 AD was Pontius Pilot.[40] Pilot came from central Italy[41] and he allowed the Hebrews to crucify Jesus Christ. It was not the Romans who demanded the execution, it was the Jews and their <<King Herod>>. Pilot offered to release Christ stating, "I see no crime in this man" but the Jews insisted that he be crucified and that a brigand Barabbas be released for the holiday. Pilot then said, "I wash my hands of this deed." The Romans were not only benevolent rulers; they even granted Hebrews citizenship of Rome and allowed them to have Saturday off in accordance with Hebrew law.[42] Things were so bad that the Roman satirist Juvenal in a satire 13.96-106 makes fun of the peculiar habits and customs of Jews in the Levant.[43]

The impact on Western European civilization caused by the change in banking from the Knights Templar to the Jews that took place in the Middle Ages was monumental. Beginning about the First Crusade[44] and in the immediately following years, the Knights Templar established a Western Banking system.[45] The Templar system covered the known Caucasian world—essentially Europe and the Middle East. Prior to this, after Roman law had broken down, any traveler had to carry all his earthy goods and hard assets and was likely to be robbed and killed. The Templars developed a secret code and any traveler could deposit funds with any Templar office that would give the traveler a sealed coded message stipulating the amount, which could then be picked up in any other Templar office (bank). Templars being religious monks complied with Christian usury laws and did not charge interest; they worked strictly on a fee for service system. By the 12th century the Templars were the richest organization in Europe and the Levant. Kings, Dukes, and even the Pope were massively indebted to the Templars because they loaned out money for a flat fee. In the 12th century both king Philip IV of France and Pope Clement V (Rome) were severely indebted to the Templars. In 1250 AD the Grand Master of the Templars was Jacques de Molay. When King Philip IV demanded more money for another war Grand Master de Molay denied the loan. Philip IV and the Pope conspired to eliminate the Templars and made arrangements with Jewish bankers to take over European banking. Then they devised a scheme to accuse the Templars of heresy and every abomination they could think of, the pope then excommunicated the Templars. (The first and only time in Roman Catholic canon law history whereby an entire group and of monastic monks were excommunicates.) They eventually burned de Molay on the stake and murdered most of the Templars. Neither the pope nor the king repaid any funds, and from that time forward the Jews were the bankers of the king, the pope, and the people of Europe and usury was reinstalled.

---

20. The Levant in historic terms is the region of the Eastern Mediterranean coast located between Aleppo and Gaziantep in the north and Suez and Ababa to the south.
21. The religion professed by Muhammad (570-632 AD) as the prophet of Islam.
22. The geographic region now comprising Saudi Arabia, Yemen, Iraq, Oman, UAE, Qatar, Bahrain, and Kuwait: (The Caliphate!)
23. The 12 tribes were as listed in the Torah: Rubin, Levi, Judah, Dan, Naphtali, Gad, Asher, Issachar, Zebulon, Joseph, David, and Benjamin. Biblically Joseph had two sons Manasseh and Ephraim both of whom were adopted.
24. Ancient Hebrew Research Center.
25. A tribe is an extended family group never more than a few hundred.
26. There are two Talmuds, the Babylonian and the Jerusalem, this text works exclusively with the Babylonian Talmud.
27. This will be expanded on in following text.
28. Test done in Israel
29. Tests at Hebrew University, and scores of articles including in "The Scientist".
30. In order for acceptance by Jewish laws a child must have been born of a Jew female to be considered a Jew.
31. Phoenicia was a Semitic civilization that was centered in the "Fertile Crescent" that is now modern day Iraq Syria and Lebanon & the Caliphate.
32. Babylonian Chronicles & Oxford History of the biblical World Michael D. Coogan Oxford University press, PP 350
33. Holst Stanford 2008 Origins of the Phoenicians: Interaction of Early Mediterranean Religions.
34. British Museum London, Cuneiform Babylonian Chronicles 605-694 BC
35. Usury is the act of extracting a rate of interest beyond what is allowed by biblical law. In Europe this was administered by Canon law (church law) in Hebrew times by the Torah and its priests. In Islam (Sharia), Judaism, and Christianity (Torah) compound interest is illegal.
36. A capitol offence in violation of Canon Law. Jews took over European banking after the Knights Templar was eliminated by them through loans to the Pope and King of France.
37. Acts 18:2-3 and Corinthians 9:3-15
38. First Century AD
39. Roman concept of a military governor (not unlike the American systems in Iraq and then in Afghanistan)
40. Was the fifth Procurator of Judea, form 26 to 36 AD. (Pontius Pilatus)
41. Samnium
42. Philo Greek historian 40 AD (Embassy pp. 156-158)
43. Note: (About the second six million) The army of the Hebrew king in Jerusalem was under 30,000. The Roman Army in the Levant had a compliment of 70,000 the total population of Jerusalem in 70 AD was 611,000, only 42,000 had returned from the Babylonian Captivity. The six million claims of the Jews as lost in the Roman-forced diaspora was not possible.
44. 1127-AD
45. The Templar banking system was based on the same laws governing banking in Islamic nations today. Usury is considered a crime. Interest may not be charged. Compound interest is a felony. This is in fact why there is such animate opposition to Sharia law. The opposition is primarily from Jewish bankers who are robbing their customers.

Theodor Herzl addressing the First or Second Zionist Congress in Basel, Switzerland in 1897-98.

The First Zionist Congress
The beginning of it all.

Setting up the 20th century zionist domination of media and banking by reformed Jews was the goal of a meeting to be held in Munich, Germany by the World Zionist Congress. The Jews of Germany wanted no part of the zionists and blocked the meeting. Subsequently the World Zionist Congress was able to arrange the meeting in Basel Switzerland at the juncture of Switzerland, Germany, and France in 1897. The meeting was scheduled for the 29th of August to the 31st in 1897. <<Theodor Herzel>> called the meeting to order, it was a total Ashkenazim event.[46] One of the secret issues of the meeting was a reading of the "Protocols of the Learned Elders of Zion"—all 24 chapters.[47] The presence of the Protocols came to light when a fire alarm was triggered in the meeting building and the Protocols were stolen from the dais while everyone was outside. This copy now resides at the British Museum of History in London.[48] The copy was translated from Russian by Father Victor Madsen[49] from the original text in 1905.

The Protocols are of great importance because they outline the entire program for world domination by Jews. Regardless of disclaimers by Ashkenazim who assert that the Protocols were written by the Czar's secret police, those assertions can be put aside in view of the fact that almost the entire Protocol plans have been implemented in the last 100 years. The 24 chapters of the Protocols are a fast read. It is definitely worth your time to read and learn what the zionist plans are. Going back to the accusation that the Czar's secret police authored the Protocols, one can only say, as did Sir Winston Churchill that, "if the Protocols are indeed a forgery they are the most astounding historically correct predictions ever made in a forgery."[50]

Winston Churchill

---

46. M.R. Rilke, Eine Szene aus dem Ghetto (Argon Verlag Leibzig 1931)
47. Jewish virtual library (First zionist congress and Basel program)
48. The British Museum of History does not collect works of fiction.
49. Madsen was an English journalist who was fluent in Russian.
50. The Protocols can be downloaded from the Internet free of charge.

Israel has constructed and continues to expand an Apartheid Wall through the occupied West Bank. More than 85% of Israel's wall is illegally built on occupied Palestinian land. It often cuts through Palestinian villages, separating families from each other and farmers from their lands. A 2004 ruling of the International Court of Justice confirmed that the wall is illegal under international law.

FROM BDSMOVEMENT.NET

Is the cause of all wars in the Middle East.

Eretz Yisrael is the infamous "Greater Israel" plan also referred to as the "Oded Yinon Plan".[51] Greater Israel is the basis for the turmoil in the Middle East; it is the Likud[52] foreign policy of Israel. The present <<Netanyahu>> [Mileikowsky], Likud government strongly supports Eretz Yisrael as their foreign policy. The plan serves as guidelines for the Mossad[53] as well as the Israeli Defense Forces (IDF).[54] According to one of the originators of zionism, <<Theodor Herzel>>,[55] as well as numerous reviewed documents[51] "Greater Israel" comprises the following present day nations of the Levant; Jordan, Syria, Lebanon, Gaza, The West Bank, The Sinai, (of Egypt) Iraq to the Euphrates River, and North to the Turkish border, and the Saudi Arabian providence of An-Nafúd. Every Arab and Palestinian is cognizant of the plan and has seen its enactment in the genocide of Palestinians and the establishment of the world's largest concentration camp in Gaza as well as the construction of the apartheid walls. It was the Mossad-fabricated misinformation about "Weapons of Mass Destruction" that was used to "justify" America to attack Iraq in order to remove the largest Israeli opposing military in the Middle East. It is the continuation of the lies about Iran in an attempt to get

America to attack Iran. It is part of the turmoil in Turkey where the "Young Turks" of the Turkish army who are mostly Jews are in revolt against the civil government.

If we examine this zionist "Greater Israel" desire in context of the present Israeli foreign policy, the wars in Iraq, Libya, the Mossad managed civil wars in Syria now, and Lebanon in 2011, the continuous violations on UN brokered settlement expansions in the West Bank, the genocidal annihilation of the Palestinian population in Gaza, and the construction of the Apartheid walls, you will gain an immediate understanding of the cause of Middle East turmoil as well as the Oded Yinon Plan.

The foreign policy of Israel beyond and above any other issue is the systematic and unilateral plan to weaken, to destroy, and to annihilate all neighboring nations, and to remove all non-Jews from the West Bank and Gaza, so that "Greater Israel" may be realized. There can be no rational counter to this charge because the evidence is the present history of the Middle East. The Likud publicly and in Knesset[56] minutes clearly demonstrates those policies, which is the expulsion of all Christians, Muslims, and Palestinians from the territory of "Greater Israel" and to annex the West Bank and Gaza into Israel proper after all Arabs have been removed. (Outlined in the 9 page The Oded Yinon Plan)

The Yinon plan is a destabilization plan for all of Israel's neighboring states so as to insure Israel's hegemony of the entire Levant. The plan in detail outlines a regional reconfiguration through the Balkanization of all neighboring states to force those nations into smaller and weaker governments that Israel's IDF will be able to intimidate, or destroy.

The 9/11 attacks[57] were immediately followed by a flood of Mossad generated false information blaming Iraq's Hussein. Even though this disinformation was crudely constructed, it was sufficient to push the Bush administration and the Israeli congressional lobby into invading Iraq, clearly a war crime on the part of the US. The truth is that Hussein was a strong opponent of al Qaida and was managing a secular government. Hussein had no part in the 9/11 attacks, had no knowledge of them, did not approve of them, had no weapons of mass destruction, was not developing such weapons, had not threatened the US; and there was never any evidence Iraq ever considered attacking the US. The US attack on Iraq was a war crime, did enormous damage to the US, destabilized the Middle

East, largely destroyed Iraq's infrastructure and killed hundreds of thousands of Iraqi citizens in their cities and towns, all for the sole benefit of Israel.

The present civil war in Syria that has now expanded into Iraq and will soon be in Jordan has from day one been financed and militarily supported by the IDF and the Mossad. The Alawite ruler of Syria, Bashar al-Assad, manages a secular state that has protected Christians as well as Sunni and Shia Muslims. The civil war has produced over one million Christian refugees, and half a million Shia refugees. The Syrian refugees flooding into Europe and America are only 4% Christians, what does that tell you about the Obama administration? The Caliphate sometimes referred to as ISIL and ISIS is of the radical Wahhabi Sunni sect that is financed by Saudi Wahhabi religious fanatics and is more accurately named the Caliphate.

In Iraq the Eretz Yisrael plan is for the nation to split into three separate nations; Kurdistan, a Sunni and a Shia state, all of course weaker than the original Iraq, and with Kurdistan outside of the "Greater Israel" region eliminating one third of the opposition.[58] The Turks may have some objection to that.

51. Global Research article by Mahid Darius Nazemroaya (2011) Brittan's colonial design for the Levant, and Oded Yinon's plan is titled "A Strategy for Israel in the 80's" [ISBN 0-937694-56-8]
52. Likud (transit) founded in 1973 by terrorist <<Menachem Began>> it is the ultra-right wing of Israeli politics also known as the war party.
53. The Mossad (the institute) proper name is: Institute for Intelligence and Special Operations. (And that includes false flag operations all around the world)
54. IDF is Israeli Defense Force
55. Real name <<Theodor Benjamin Ze'ev Herzel>> was a Hungarian Ashkenazi and the father of modern zionism.
56. Knesset (the Meeting) is the unicameral Israeli legislative body
57. The authors, and thousands of professional pilots, civil engineers, architects, firemen, and professional investigators do not believe the government-produced 911 report (which, for example completely ignored the suspicious collapse of World Trade Tower Seven—and the previously scripted mainstream media report of its sudden collapse considerably before its actual collapse), or for that matter the Kennedy assassination one.
58. The "man" who said, "I am an Israeli" Joseph Biden actually called for Lebanon to be divided in similar manner as shown in the Yinon plan.

Babylonian Talmud

The Babylonian Talmud

The most evil religious document in the world's history

Because Jews have made it a crime for Jews to translate the Talmud, few copies are available. The first realistically good copies were translated into German in the 20s.[59] There are however many incomplete translations in French, English, Russian, and Latin. Many were made specifically for Christians and Muslims by having all disparaging information to them removed. Most good translations are in German because Yiddish is a German dialect spoken by most Ashkenazim and are very voluminous.[60] Due to its length and encyclopedia-like content it is not possible to make any reasonable comment on the entire Talmud. The German 19th century translation of the Babylonian copy seems the best and is the one used in this text. There are however other versions, the French version is simply called "The Talmud" it was then translated from the French into English.[61] In order to understand issues of zionism and Israel you must read this text.

Modern rabbinical comment relating to the Talmud and the Torah places the Talmud before the Torah in its importance to Jewish religious and social law. It is realistic to say that the study of the Talmud is the study of Judaism and Judaism is the study of the Talmud. This has been the case ever since the Ashkenazim displaced the Hebrews in Jewish society.[62] Ashkenazim are converts to Judaism and have no Hebrew bloodline. Definitive DNA tests of Jews in Israel, Europe, and America show a closer relationship between Palestinians and Hebrews than Ashkenazim and Hebrews. This is the ultimate resolution of the arguments about who is the proper owner of Levant real-estate.

The Talmud is horrendously complicated often with multiple page sub-commentary on every little detail and was originally written in many different languages. The accompanying commentaries of the Mishnah and Gomorrah are further expansions of the original Talmudic text: in some cases commentary on a sentence in the Talmud will have up to 75 pages of sub-commentary. Every rabbinical scholar injected his own opinions into the dialog consequently expanding, supporting, or diverging from the original content. The correct explanation of the Mishnah would be that it is a commentary of the Talmud encompassing the oral traditions and tribal laws of rabbis from the 6th to the 20th centuries. There is one other notable translation of the Talmud titled "The Talmud Unmasked" that was written by Rev. I. B. Pronates in 1893,[63] from Hebrew into Latin and then from Latin into English.

Passages from the Babylonian Talmud:

Location:	Quotation:
Sanhedrin 67a	Jesus is referred to as the son of Pandira[64]
Kallah 1b (18b)	(Jesus was) Illegitimate and conceived during menstruation[65]
Sanhedrin 43a	on the eve of Passover they hanged Jesus.
Zohar III (282)	[Jesus] Died like a beast and was buried in animal dirt heap.
Baba Media 114 a 11b	Only Jews are human (Gentiles) are animals
Sanhedrin 57a	for murder wither a Cuthean (derogatory name of Christian) by a Cuthean or an Israeli by a Cuthean, punishment is incurred, but of a Cuthean by an Israeli, there is no punishment.
Moed Kattan 17a	if a Jew is tempted to do evil he should go to a city where he is not known and do evil there.
Krthuboth (3b)	the seed of a Cuthean is as the seed of a beast.
Abhdash Zarah (15b)	Christians have sex with animals
Sanhedrin 58b	If a Heathen (Muslim or Christian) hits a Jew he must be killed. Hitting a Jew is like hitting God.

Masakkoth (7b)	(A Jew) is innocent of murder if he kills a Cuthean.
Baba Mezia 24a (Also confirmed in Baba Kamma (113b)	
	If a Jew finds an object lost by a Cuthean it does not have to be returned.
Sanhedrin 57a	What a Jew obtains by theft from a Cuthean he may keep
Baba Kamma 37b	Cuthean's are outside the protection of the law and God has exposed their money to Jews.
Choschen Ham (34-19)	Christians and servants cannot become witnesses in a trial against a Jew.
Yebamoth 98a	All Cuthean children are animals
Sanhedrin 59a	Murdering a Cuthean is like killing a wild animal
Abodah Zara 26b	Even the best Cuthean's should be killed
Yebbamoth 11b	Sexual intercourse with a little girl Cuthean is permitted if she is three years of age.
Hikkoth Akum X1	Show no mercy to the Goyim
Baba Necia 114,6	Jews are human beings but the nations of the world are not human beings but beasts.
Simon Haddarsen fol 56d	when the Messiah comes every Jew will have 2,500 slaves.
Zohar (1,25b)	those who do good to Christians never rise from the dead
Baba Kama (113b)	it is permitted to deceive Christians (Netanyahu's favorite passage)
lore Dea (159.1)	usury may be practiced upon Christians[66]

While this represents only 25 short excerpts from the Talmud it gives the reader a general idea of what is contained in the rest of the book. We must remain alert to the evil represented in this document whose principal target is Christianity and whose secondary target is Islam. There exists in America a large community[67] of Christian zionists lead by protestant media ministers who are part of the zionist support system. These religious perverts, who if they have studied scripture certainly know better, are employed in radio and TV most of which is owned by Jews. They all know that to stay on the air they must support the zionist line, as promulgated by the <<American Israeli Public Affairs Committee (AIPAC)>>.[68] There are, along with the ministers, a substantial number of media radio and TV shills for the Israeli lobby. Most of these people have become wealthy due to their support of Israel's policies. Major Ministers are; John Hagee, Gary Bower, Jerry Falwell*, Pat Robertson, major media people are; Glen Beck, Sarah Palin, Sean Hannity and Bill O'Reilly, almost all associated with FOX one way or another. It is a well-known fact in media circles that criticism of Israel, zionism, or for that fact anything Jewish will get you kicked off the air faster than you can imagine. The largest Christian zionist church groups in America are United Methodists, Reformed Church in America, Presbyterian Church, and United Church of Christ.

One of the primary tools developed by these organizations is the fallacy of a word coined in the latter 19th century in the Scofield Bible.[69] Judeo-Christianity is the falsely disseminated word invention of the 20th century. Almost Daily O'Reilly on his popular TV shows trots out the Judeo-Christian line. This is particularly egregious in respect to America. Jews were not part of this nation in its founding period. There were some small number of Sephardic Jews[70] that operated trading businesses in New Amsterdam, Providence, Philadelphia and Charleston, the numbers however were minuscule and none were involved in founding America.

Jews were on the other hand very active by the later 18th century especially in the slave trade. This issue has been cleverly hidden from public view, essentially to protect the Jewish community who were the primary slave traders of the American Colonies. Most operated out of Charleston and ports in Rhode Island and Providence Plantations. This issue fits in with the Talmud because it verifies the nature of the Jews.

Slave Ship Names	Owners of the Ships	Status of Owners
Abigail	<<Aaron Lopez Moses Levy Jacob Frank>>	Jews
Crown	<<Isaac Levy & Nathan Simpson>>	Jews
Nassau	<<Moses Levy>>	Jew
Four Sisters	<<Moses Levy>>	Jew
Anne & Eliza	<<Justus Bosh & John Adams>>	Jews
Prudent Betty	<<Harry Cruger & Jacob Phonix>>	Jews
Hester	<<Mordecai & David Gomez>>	Jews
Elizabeth	<<Mordecai & David Gomez>>	Jews
Antigua	<<Nathan Marston & Abraham Lyell>>	Jews
Betsy	<<Wlm. De Wolf>>	Jew
Polly	<<James De Wolf>>	Jew
White Horse	<<Jan de Sweevts>>	Jew
Expedition	<<John & David Roosevelt>>	Jews ←
Charlotte	<<Moses & Sam Levy & Jacob Franks>>	Jews
Caracoa	<<Moses & Sam Levy>>	Jews

Take note, that Jews owned every slave-trading ship. The 17th and18th century Christian communities did not accept slave trading as a legitimate enterprise and it was socially unacceptable.

59. Der Jerusalemische Talmud in seinen haggadischen Betanttreilen (Zürich 1880) and a second translation stems from <<W. L. Goldschmidt>> (1886-1888)
60. The Babylonian Talmud [Soncino edition] is 12,800 pages in length.
61. Translated in 1897 published by the Jewish Publications Society and translated by <<Henrietta Szold>>.
62. About 700 to 800 AD.
63. Master of Theology and Professor of Hebrew Languages at the Imperial Ecclesiastical Academy of St. Petersburg, Russia.
64. Pandira was a Roman Centurion who the Jews have claimed was the father of an illegitimately born Christ.
65. Jewish law and tradition prohibits intercourse during menstruation as a religious crime.
66. Usury is a crime when practiced against Jews.
67. About 40 million Christian zionists
68. AIPAC American Israeli Public Affairs Committee. The illegal Israeli lobby not registered FARA U.S. law 22 U.S.C. 611 (1938) requiring all foreign nation lobbies to register with the Department of State.
69. The Scofield Reference Bible was the product of the early 20th century. It was published in 1909 and revised in 1917. Cyrus I. Scofield was its author. It is the principal proponent of dispensationalist philosophy. It produces such fallacy as Rapture and other falsifications of biblical texts as propagated by John Nelson Darby (1800-82) basically what we today call fundamentalism.
70. Sephardic Jews Come from Spain and Portugal. Many either converted to Catholicism or fled the Spanish peninsula at the outset of the Inquisition which began in 1478, as established by Ferdinand II of Aragon & Isabella I of Castile. It was not abolished until 1834. Run by the Roman Catholic Dominican monastic order.

Ships on the Bosphorus in Istanbul, Turkey.

The Byzantine Empire

The Byzantine Empire was the Eastern Christian Empire comprising what are today the Levant, Turkey, Syria, Lebanon, part of Greece, Macedonia, Egypt, Jordan, and part of Iran. It was Christian.

In correct speech it would be called The Eastern Roman Christian Empire. Its capital was Constantinople whose name was changed by the Muslims after April, 1453, when Islam took the city as it fell to Mehmed II after a seven-year siege. He renamed the city Istanbul. The fall of the Eastern Empire was catastrophic for Christianity. Half of the entire European Christian world fell to Islam. Constantinople sits between the Black Sea and the Aegean Sea. The straight separates Europe from Asia and is called the Bosphorus. Today it is one of the most important sea straights in the world because whoever controls it can bottle-up the entire Russian warm water fleet in the Black Sea. Two languages were commonly spoken in Constantinople—Greek and Latin. The area was originally pagan,[71] but in 380 AD became Christian Eastern Orthodox.[72] There were numerous changes in the religious makeup of the empire, including the sacking of Constantinople by the fourth Crusade in the 12th century.[73] Constantinople was already weakened from decades of war with the Caliphate; this war had been ongoing since the 10th century. After the fall, Ottoman Turks became rulers of the Byzantine

Empire and continued to rule it until 1924 when the Caliphate was abolished. The empire had allied itself with Germany in WWI and when the armistice[74] was signed it collapsed. The Levant became a British protectorate, a condition that continued until the withdrawal of England from the Levant in the late1940s.

There is one more important consequence to these events. In WWI the British commander of the Egyptian expeditionary force was General Allenby. He

General Edmund Allenby

Amin al-Husseini
Grand Mufti of Jerusalem
In office 1921 – 1937

was stalemated by the Turks outside of Cairo. England was tapped out by the war and they were unable to supply any more troops because all were needed in France. Allenby met with the Grand Mufti of Cairo the titular head of the Palestine and concluded a treaty with the Palestinians stipulating that if they allied with England against the Turks they would be granted autonomy over the Palestine portion of the Levant. The treaty was consummated and the forces of Palestine and England defeated the Turks. Then came the greatest double-cross of 20th century history—the Balfour Declaration.[75] The population of the territory we now call Israel had the following population statistics in 1932: 91,398 Jews, 757,715 Palestinian Muslims, and 9,140 Christians.[76]

---

71. Roman Polytheism
72. Similar to present day Greek Orthodox.
73. 1202-1204, 4th Crusade.
74. The Armistice was not a military loss by Germany and its allies it was simply the end of hostilities.
75. The Belfour Declaration of 1917 made to the second <<Baron Rothschild>> as president of the World Zionist Conference it granted the Zionists the territory that had been granted to the Palestinians just months before. <<Chaim Weizmann and Nahum Sokolow>> had pushed the issue for some time.
76. Census Palestine 1931 Journal of the Royal Statistical society 1932 (PP 120)

The Khazars

**The Khazars are the Ashkenazim.
From the time of the 8th century they were known
as thieves, murderers, road bandits, users
of false identities, and worshipers of Baal.**

The Khazar Empire[77] was a group of European Turkish peoples who resided in the Volga-Caucuses of Eastern Russia and were prominent in the 4th to the 7th centuries AD. They were like the early Jews, nomadic, and were driven out of the Caucuses by the Eastern Christian Empire of Constantinople on one side and the (Islamic) Caliphate on the other after they converted to Judaism. It is assumed that they were part of the West Turkish Empire[78], which was allied to the Turks against the Sassanid (Persian)[79] Empire. Beginning in the 7th century AD the Khazars encountered difficulty with most neighboring nations. The Islamic Caliphate from one side and the Christians from the other side pressed them.[80] Their options were to either submit to Islam or to Christianity; they decided to convert to Judaism preventing their subservience to either Christianity or Islam. The Khazarian ruler died in 650 AD leaving five sons. According to tribal Baal law the eldest was inheritor of the crown, while the rest of the sons with their followers and families moved west toward the Danube.[81] The political motives for the conversion from paganism to Judaism were straightforward and based on geographic and political necessity. The other two options would have resulted in dependency and submission to the Caliphate or to Constantinople. As the Khazars lost territory they began a population migration toward what is now Poland, Prussia[82] the Western Baltic state[83] and western Russia. It is a clear and commonly accepted fact that the Ashkenazim[84] never resided anyplace in the Middle East and that the 97% of Israeli Jews living in Israel who are Ashkenazi have absolutely no ancestral rights to anything in the Levant. The capitol city of the Khazars in the Caucuses was named Atil and was found in the early 1950's.[85] The efforts to hide and obstruct the finding of Atil by Israeli academics are unprecedented. Genetic testing of Jews around the world clearly indicates that between 95 and 97% of all living Jews are in fact Khazar, not Hebrew descendants as they claim. It is therefore logical that claims by modern Jews that God gave them their ancestral lands of the Levant are nothing but a rabbinical fabrication because the covenant by God was with Hebrews and not with Khazars who came upon the scene some 3,000 years later. Another claimed "six million," the Khazars, now converted to Judaism, were forced of the out of their ancestral home in the Caucuses, between the Black Sea on the west, and the Caspian Sea to the east. This region is now Armenia, Georgia, Russia, and Azerbaijan.

---

77. A group of European Turk pagans who resided in the Caucuses of Eastern Russia that was prominent in the 6th to the 8th centuries AD who converted to Judaism in that time.
78. 522-AD
79. Persia is what Iran was called.
80. Persians, Huns, & Mommsen
81. Conversations with Arthur Koestler (The Thirteenth Tribe)
82. The German State on the Baltic and Berlin
83. Lithuania, Estonia, Latvia
84. Ashkenazi the word does not as is claimed by Jews come from Hebrew and has nothing whatever to do with the son of <<Noah or Japheth>>. The name stems from the name of the capital city of the Khazars named Atil.
85. By Russian Professor Yergeny Satonovski of the Middle East Institute of Moscow found Atil in the Caspian Sea.

DNA Testing on Ashkenazim

✗ DNA is the ultimate proof that Jews are not who they claim to be.

The primary zionist argument involving the entire issue of ancestry is the zionists dispute of Khazar past history, which they claim to be a myth. In fact they have often publicized that the Ashkenazim are a figment of anti-Semitism, a word that is a lie in itself. Semitic peoples are a sub-grouping of the Caucasian race comprising most original Middle East peoples, mostly Hebrews and Arabs, who share the same racial characteristics. Khazars do not share any similarity with Hebrews; they are also a Caucasian sub-grouping but are most closely related to Turks. All of this was difficult to prove until the 20th century when DNA testing was able to prove ancestry with 100% accuracy.[86] DNA tests in Israel, Europe, and America conclusively prove that between 96% and 97% of all living Jews today are direct descendants of the Khazars. Jewish scientists and doctors all over the Diaspora as well as in Israel administered these tests. The fact that the Khazars converted from paganism to Judaism between the 6th and 7th Centuries AD are now accepted everywhere. This has been widely publicized in Israel.[87]

It is a reasonable assumption that the entire repudiation of the history of the 6th to the 7th century AD of the Khazars has been scrabbled to allow zionists the opportunity to falsely claim untruthful ancestral land rights in the Levant. Israeli <<Dr. Frank Elhaik>> established absolute proof of this in December 2012 when he provided evidence countering previously falsified data by Israeli sources. The false information had been provided in order to substantiate the rights of now living Jews (actually ancestral Khazar converts) to land in the Levant. Thus the entire zionist hypothesis is ridiculous. By this logic, the Danes would own England, England would own half of France, Rome would own Europe and the Middle East, the Macedonians who under Alexander conquered much of Asia and the Indian sub-continent would own all of those. The established fact is, that Jews or Hebrews never once, including today, represented a plurality of the population in the Levant.[88]

In order to solidify Ashkenazi hold of Palestine[89] Israeli leaders have made continuous inflammatory statements relating to the

✗ DNA Science and The Jewish Bloodline — Tere Marrs.

Palestinian population of the Levant who have been residents of that region for all of recorded history. This began with <<Theodor Herzel>> in the 1890's who stated, "The removal of Palestinians must be carried out discreetly"...right to the presently sitting, Israeli Prime Minister <<Benjamin Netanyahu>> who stated, "They won't be able to face the war with us, which will include withholding food and water form Arab cities, preventing education, terminating electric power, and more." In every war between Israel and its neighbors, IDF air power was used exclusively to destroy civilian infrastructure including power plants, water sources, sewerage, schools, and food distribution. In fact Gaza has been turned into the world's largest concentration camp, worse than any the Nazis ever ran. When those non-Jews try to oppose the horrific conditions under which Israel keeps them they are labeled terrorists by America and Israel. Israeli foreign policy has been constant and uniform from 1948 onward to today. Every time they succeed in driving the indigenous population to revolt[90] they as their first act, destroy the entire infrastructure, using American provided[91] helicopters, bombers, missiles, rockets, bombs, artillery, and naval bombardment. And then America wonders why they have become a target for "terrorists." These Israeli wars of colonization of the entire Levant were expanded through the actions of the Mossad in supplying false information about Iraq,[92] provided to American intelligence through secondary sources to induce G. W. Bush and the Israeli-controlled US Congress to attack Iraq, thus eliminating the potentially largest barriers to Israeli aggression in the entire Middle East. All of this is in concert with Eretz Yisrael policies and the Oded Yinon Plan.

Now, its Iran [?]

---

86. The Missing Link of Jewish European Ancestry: Contrasting the Rhineland and Khazarian Hypothesis (Elhaik)
87. Haaretz
88. Arab Nationalism and Christianity in the Levant: The Politics of Religion in the Fag end of the Ottoman Empire (2006 Academia EDU)
89. Palestine comprises the land of Israel, and some of northern Syria, and some of Lebanon.
90. Lebanon three times, the Sinai peninsula, Egypt, Jordan, Syria, Gaza, and the West Bank
91. $3,000,000,000 in military aid per year and $3,000,000,000 in general aid, to the nation with the 33rd highest World economic rating. (2015 Index of Economic Freedom) out of 169 nations.
92. Weapons of Mass Destruction

The 20th Century

A violent century in which governments killed 240,000,000 more of their own citizens than were killed in wars.

Early European opposition to the Ashkenazim is readily understandable. The Ashkenazi spoke Yiddish, a German dialect, which the native populations did not understand. This was most pronounced in Russia and Poland where Yiddish was completely foreign. Peasants who were minimally educated and mostly illiterate, mistrusted trade people who spoke a language they could not understand. Most Ashkenazim could read and write and had basic educations. Mistrust of Jews became major factors in civil relations in the decades following the migration especially in Russia and Poland. The fact that by rabbinical decree, all Jews were required to live in ghettos (a people apart), the "chosen" of God created further animosity. In the 21st century the Mezuzah, which Jews hang on the right side of the entrance to Jewish homes, is displayed. Many Jews will not allow non-Jews to enter the door to their homes through the front door and many will not allow non-Jews to enter their domicile

Jewish Ghetto in Sighet.

at all. This is because non-Jews are considered animals having no souls and are unclean.

At the beginning of the 20th century at the New Year a Jewish prayer (Yom Kippur) called Kol Nidre became common knowledge among Christians.[93] This is an astounding prayer; it offers absolution for lies before and after the fact. It is why no one can trust any Jew; they have by Kol Nidre constituted lying to non-Jews as an accepted form of discourse. The prayer is an abomination and has in time caused the rift between Jews and non-Jews. The prayer is an open invitation to lie, cheat, and steal from non-Jews and be held ethically and morally innocent for doing so. It is an automatic absolution when Jews deal with non-Jews. Reformed Jews use the version of the modern representation while the Hasidim[94] still use the older version. It is obvious why indigenous peasant populations came to distrust them.

By the 8th century Ashkenazim were all located in Europe where they lived until WWII (that is 11 centuries). Jewish written history, which is the history taught in public education today, makes relentless claims of Jewish persecution, by everyone and anyone, but especially by Christians and Germans. Considering that the German Hanseatic League was the most Jew tolerant group in Europe, we find that peculiar. This is for the purpose of using victimhood as a political and social tool, in order to extort treasure from societies in which Jews live or have lived and do business. Jews embarked on this system of social control over 3,000 years ago and it continues to be the keystone of the Jewish financial condition today.[95] It is an absolute fact that the socialist theocracy of Israel would have financially collapsed by 1950 without massive extortion used as a financial instrument to keep their socialist theocracy economy operational. America, due to over 40 Jews in the legislative branch of government, provides Israel over $3 billion in military aid, over $3 billion in social aid, and hundreds of millions in tax benefits such as no American taxes on Israeli bonds. An excellent book on this issue is *The Holocaust Industry* by Jewish Professor <<Norman Finkelstein>> who lost his tenure and teaching position due to the publication of this book, which is in fact the ultimate Cultural Marxist event of the 20th century. Relevant to the issue is the GDP standing of Israel which is 25th in the world[96] of 193 nations. This would indicate that there are 168 more worthy nations for American largess. The bulk of the American zionist extortion racket, which is totally based on victimhood, is directed by AIPAC. In Europe not even neu-trals of WWII have been spared in this the greatest extortion racket in history. There are many forms to this venture, the Israeli company Elbit[97] obtains a research grant from the EU, Germany pays pen-sions to so-called holocaust survivors, American Jews are allowed to purchase Israeli bonds and not pay American taxes on paid div-idends, the IDF buys billions of dollars worth of military hardware parts and the cost is not repaid, Swiss Insurance carriers and Banks pay out over one billion dollars in reparations to Jews in Israel for unproven and impossible deposits never made. Further American military aid is separated into many differing categories, which are not listed in the foreign aid budgets; total accumulated US Israeli aid just in 2014 was well over $8,000,000,000. *Billion*.

---

93. Kol Nidre (All Vows prayer)
    Original version:
    He who wishes that his vows and oaths should have no value; stand up at the beginning of the year and say: "All vows which I shall make during the year shall be of no value."

    1919 new version: (Revised Festival Prayers)
    All vows, obligations, oaths or anathemas pledges of all names, which we have vowed, sworn, devoted, or bound ourselves to, from this day of atonement, until the next day of atonement (whose arrival we hope for in happiness) we repent beforehand, of them all, they shall be deemed absolved, forgiven, annulled, void and made of no effect; they shall not be binding, nor have any power; the vows shall not be reckoned vows, the obligations shall not be obligatory, nor the oaths considered oaths.

94. Hasidim are a strictly orthodox sect of Jews. Their history goes back to the 18th century in Poland. It is based on Baal Shem-Tov and incorporates mysticism, numerology, and ritual.

95. Total US foreign aid to Israel since 1948 is $234,000,000,000. Total German aid $3,000,000,000. Embezzled from Swiss banks and insurance companies, $1,250,000,000. (Note: these claims were all bogus, it was illegal under penalty of death for German citizens to deposit money in Swiss banks from 1938 to 1945.)

96. World Bank Statistics

97. Israeli Aerospace Industries

Note: You must understand the leading Bolsheviks who took over Russia. They hated Russians. They hated Christians. Driven by ethnic hatred they tortured and slaughtered millions of Russians without a shred of human remorse. It cannot be overstated. Bolshevism com-mitted the greatest human slaughter of all time. The fact that most of the world is ignorant and uncaring about this enormous crime is proof that the global media is in the hands of the perpetrators. [Jews]

Aleksandr Solzhenitsyn

Reichswehr units clash with Red Guard volunteers during the 1919 insurrection. The uprising cemented the Army's decision to control Germany's destiny by any means necessary, including an alliance with Hitler.

Nazi Persecution in Europe 1930 to 1945

The time between WWI and WWII is more accurately defined as the 2nd Thirty Years' War. (1914 to 1944). It was the British Empire's desire to destroy Germany which had become the major industrial, scientific, and economic power in Europe if not the world. This fact has been hidden by English and American Historians. The reason for this is that the entire post-war order depends on this lie. Revisionist historians universally acknowledge the fact that Germany was not the aggressor of WWII and did not start it.

The fact that Nazis persecuted Jews is historically accurate, but that is only a very small part of the issue, far greater is the reason for the persecution. In the 1930s Germany under the Weimar Republic was effectively an occupied nation. Jews controlled medicine, law, the media, and entertainment. A fair and just trial in the courts was not possible, unless you hired a Jewish lawyer, after all the judges were all Jews. Unemployment, suicide, crime, prostitution, and pornography were at record levels. The armistice treaty of the end of WWI had destroyed the moral fiber of Germany, its ethical backbone, and its industriousness. The treaty of Versailles was written by and established by Jews, which everyone in Europe was aware of. The American delegation was the only one opposed and the only one that did not directly benefit from the treaty. The Versailles Treaty, which was in fact an armistice, contained the following main points.

1) Germany was forced to admit and accept the blame for starting WWI,[98] which is a lie.
2) Germany was to pay £6,600 million for the damage of the war.[99]

3) Germany was forbidden to have submarines or an air force. She could have a navy but limited to six battleships, she could have an army but limited to 100,000 men. No German troops could be posted in the Rhineland or within 50 miles of the French border.

4) Germany was to lose all colonial property to France, Belgium, and England thereby expanding their already extensive control over third-world peoples.

5) Large portions of Germany were given to Poland, Czechoslovakia, and France, this included the Hanseatic League city of Danzig which was granted to Poland and whose population was over 90% German.

Paris Peace Conference, 1919: *The Paris Peace Conference was the meeting of the victorious Allied Powers following the end of World War I to set the peace terms for the defeated Central Powers. Involving diplomats from 32 countries and nationalities, the main result was the* **Treaty of Versailles,** *signed on 28 June 1919. The five major powers (France, Britain, Italy, Japan and the United States of America) controlled the Conference, the "Big Four" were the Prime Minister of France, Georges Clemenceau; the Prime Minister of the United Kingdom, David Lloyd George; the President of the United States, Woodrow Wilson; and the Prime Minister of Italy, Vittorio Emanuele Orlando.*

Separately German coal mines were now to be French owned and all coal had to be delivered to France, which refused to pay the miners a decent wage. The Alsace-Lorraine that had been German since the 30-year war, where German was the prime language, was granted to France. German West Africa (the most prosperous and self-managing colony in Africa) was given to England and was later renamed Kenya. The outrageous war reparations, part of the treaty caused the great German inflation that eventfully brought the Weimar Republic to an end.

The picture above shows the Weimar Republic in more troubled days. You can see that people began to find it difficult to feed themselves, and breadlines and souplines developed across the country. In the image above, the army is trying to help provide some food for the people.

About this time during the Weimar Republic labor unrest due to unemployment and Russian communist agitation in labor unions brought the German and Austrian economies to collapse. Labor unions called continuous strikes, especially by public service unions, eliminating public transport so citizens could not work if they wanted to, because there was no way to get to work. These communist unions were all managed and financed by Stalin and Soviet agents who were Bolshevik Jews. In Austria it reached the point where strikes lasted 60 to 90 days, food became scarce, travel impossible, and riots erupted in Austria and Germany.

By 1932 the National Socialist Party attained a majority in the Bundestag and in January of 1933 German president Paul v. Hindenburg, named Adolf Hitler Chancellor. It did not take the Jews of the diaspora in London long to react. Remember that Kristallnacht and the persecution of Jews (communists) only began on November 9, 1938, five years after Hitler came to power. The world diaspora was headquartered in London, England; the major news source for the Jewish community, *The Daily Telegraph,*[100] spearheaded a huge campaign against Germany. The headline on Friday March 24th 1933 was "Judea Declares War on Germany", the lead article was "Boycott of German Goods". Massive quantities of fliers and brochures were distributed, including, "Germany Must Perish!", "For Humanities Sake! Boycott German Industry", "Don't Buy German Goods", and many more.

The reason for the well-financed anti-German propaganda had nothing to do with the Jewish population of Germany; it had to do with banking. The financier of the anti-German diatribe was none other than <<Baron Rothschild>> head of the Rothschild banking consortium of Europe and president of the World Zionist Congress. Hjalmar Schacht was the Reichsminister of Economics and president of the Reichsbank from August 3, 1934 to November 1937. In the early 30's he had worked closely with Hitler to develop an alternate banking system not dependent upon the <<Rothschild>> banking monopoly, in order to refinance the German economy out of the worst depression of German history.

The Germans refused to borrow money to either issue bonds as backing for the Reichsmark from <<Rothschild>> in Frankfurt, Vienna, and London, or to borrow money to purchases raw materials. They instituted a barter system in which they traded produced goods for raw materials and they issued a new Reichsmark based on German mortgages. Germany had been trying to get out of the international banking conspiracy since 1918. The economies of all other nations of Europe were trapped in the <<Rothschild>> monopoly, with little hope of recovery. <<Baron Rothschild>> was livid that the Germans would have the nerve to circumvent his and his brothers banking empire and they established a war footing of the soon to be allied nations against what was to become the Axis. (All of the allied nations were in fact members of the banking cartel and greatly in debt to the cartel.) The German effort was so successful that money was readily available for business as well as private loans, interest rates fell, taxes were were lowered, and some were eliminated.[101] The exact opposite was happening in England and France whose interest rates were rising, money was tight, and the population was suffering. Germany had broken the usury credit ring of the banking monopoly by the simple force of rational economic policy; the <<Rothschild's>> were incensed. Hitler in 1937 made the following statement: "Germany will enter into no obligation to pay for her imports that she is not capable of fulfilling. The German government thus takes the standpoint of the respectable merchant who keeps his orders in harmony with his power to pay. We have come to learn that the value of a currency lies in the productive capacity of a nation."[102] [Not in the imaginary stored hard assets of that nation.]

It seems relevant at this time to list the members of the Axis as well the Alliance in 1940.

The Axis	**The Allies**
Germany	United Kingdom
Italy	United States
Japan	Soviet Union (an evil partnership)
Hungary	China
Romania	Canada (Commonwealth)
Bulgaria	Australia (Commonwealth)
Vichy France	New Zealand (Commonwealth)
	South Africa (Commonwealth)
Co partners	Greece (conquered by Germany)
Finland	Netherlands (conquered by Germany)
Iraq	Belgium (conquered by Germany)
Thailand	France in exile (conquered by Germany)
Slovakia	Luxemburg (conquered by Germany)
Albania	
Serbia	Colonial client states
Macedonia	India (as a colony)
Croatia	Rhodesia (Commonwealth)
	Philippines
Minor partners	Mongolia
San Marino	
Yugoslavia	
Burma	
India's provisional government (free India)	

Foreign Minister Vyacheslav Molotov signs the Molotov-Ribbentrop Pact. Behind him are Ribbentrop and Stalin.

We do not recall ever having seen such a list compiling all the members of the Allies and the Axis. The war winners always just list Germany, Italy, and Japan as the Axis nations, a dishonest over-sight. The winners of the war do not want you to gain any accurate concept of WWII; it runs counter to their politics. Nor do they want you to realize that six of their alliance had already been conquered by Germany and four were client states, leaving the allies with only six partners four of which were commonwealth nations.

This then brings us to the declaration of war by France and England against Germany and the beginning of WWII. England had concluded a mutual defense treaty with Poland in 1939 called the Anglo-Polish Military Alliance. Before we begin getting involved in this issue the reader must be aware that Germany and Russia had signed a treaty called the Molotov-Ribbentrop Pact on August 23, 1939. Neither the British nor the Poles were cognizant of this agree-ment. The Molotov-Ribbentrop Pact stipulated as follows:

1) A guarantee of non-belligerence by either party towards the other.

2) A commitment that neither party would ally itself to an enemy of the other.

3) The division of Romania, Poland, Lithuania, Estonia, and Finland into German and Russian spheres of influence.

The inevitable result was Germany invaded Poland on Sept. 1, 1939, Russia signed a Japanese cease-fire agreement on Sept 16th, 1939, and Stalin invaded his half of Poland on Sept. 17th, 1939. On September 3rd France and England declared war on Germany for invading Poland. So, the question that becomes prominent is why did France and England not declare war against Russia, the second belligerent in the Polish invasion? This is especially curious since Hitler was simply liberating the portion of Poland which was German and wished to be reunited with Germany while the Soviets had no such reason for their Polish invasion.

From previous text you learned that the Jewish diaspora world headquarters was located in London. You also learned that the entire Russian Revolution was a Jewish event; that should answer the previous question!

———————————————

There is a very relevant event that has for years been hidden from public discussion because it would reveal the true depraved nature of the allied leaders involved. On May 10, 1941 Deputy Führer Rudolf Hess flew to England in a Messerschmitt 110 at the invitation of English Duke Hamilton to open discussions with the British government about a peace proposal from Hitler to America and England. Hess crashed his aircraft having run out of fuel and parachuted to the ground. The basic offer by Hitler presented to the British and American governments was: 1) Cessation of the war in the West. Germany would evacuate all of France except Alsace, which would, as before the Thirty Years War remain German. 2) Holland, Belgium, and Luxemburg would be evacuated. Denmark and Norway would be evacuated. 3) In return for this England would maintain neutrality toward Germany. 4) Germany would withdraw from Greece and Eastern Europe. 5) Hitler would negotiate a truce withdrawal of Italy from North Africa. 6) Germany would promise to keep industries in France and England, whose economies were failing, occupied with orders of goods. 7) Germany would then take on the communist menace of the Soviet Union and dispose of Stalin. Why this did not happen and why Hess was locked up in Spandau Prison until a black American guard murdered him is the rest of the story.

The American president in 1941 was Franklin Delano Roosevelt (FDR), a consummate politician who would do anything to stay in power. As a leftist and open admirer of "Uncle Joe" Stalin he was unable to bring America out of the depression without war and was responsible for manipulating America into WWII, which kept him in power longer than any other American president in history. Winston Churchill, a politician who was deeply in debt to Jewish financers, who due to his monumental gambling debts were able to control him. Stalin feared the Germans more than anything else and obviously would be the loser in a deal between America, England, and Germany. Instead of saving a million American and British lives, FDR and Churchill ignored Hitler's offer and continued the war to its eventual conclusion three years later. On May 7th 1945 General Alfred Jodl signed the demanded unconditional surrender of all German forces in Reims, France. From May 10, 1941 to May 7th, 1945 was three years. At least 742,000 British, Australian, Canadian, South African, and American solders lost their lives to keep three profoundly evil politicians (Roosevelt, Churchill, and Stalin) in power. Of course an approximately equal number of civilian lives were also lost in those years.

Inevitably we must address the six million question. It has been the primary zionist assertion that the Nazis killed six million Jews. Let's, for the sake of argument look at the World Almanac for 1933 and 1948. More specifically let's examine population worldwide by religious beliefs.

World Almanac 1933
Population worldwide by religious beliefs: Jews

North America	South America	Europe	Asia	Africa	Oceania
4,383,643	293,474	9,494,363	882,609	630,800	30,401

World Almanac 1948

4,971,985	228,958	9,372,665	572,930	542,869	26,954

Note: The ultimate authority on WWII deaths is the International Red Cross located in Geneva. According to the Red Cross, the combined deaths in Nazi concentration camps in WWII was about

200,000 Jews and 90,000 others. The major cause of death was Typhoid fever. This equates to less than 5% of the zionist claimed deaths. Considering German population by comparison 1938, 78 million 1945, 66 million a loss of 12 million, does a Jew loss of 6 million make any sense? (Pop. Stat. Euro German) Also note that the variance between 1933 and 1945 of Jewish population coincides with that Red Cross report.

An examination of the numbers indicates no large increase of Jews in any other region of the world outside of Europe. The Jewish population in Europe fell by 221,698—wildly different from the 6 million claim! We are not denying that the Nazis were hard on Jews as they were with gypsies, homosexuals, criminals, and communists, or that this did not result in deaths, however the entire zionist construct about mass executions, furnaces, lamp shades, crematoria, soap, and all the rest is nothing but a massive socio-political extortion effort supported by Soviet Jews of the 40's. In the very first place the Nazis were after communists not Jews, the fact that the entire communist leadership of the world from 1930 to 1945 was Jewish certainly has some degree of bearing on the subject.

The entire victimhood program of the zionists in the 20th century is based on persecution of Jews in WWII. Members of the Allied nations and neutrals are by action and fact not responsible for any of the mayhem, and efforts by zionists to obtain treasure from them is despicable. Furthermore over 70 years have past since the end of the war, the time is at hand to stop these extortion efforts.

The fact that Jews (mostly communist Jews) account for just less than half of those that the Nazis singled out and that no other groups of people have made any demands for compensation demonstrates the attempt of zionists to get something for nothing.

As in all wars, the victors write the history. WWII was no exception, and as in all such cases they have taken care not to expose their own mistakes and crimes. It is factually true that the only history that is honest comes from revisionist historians who are not only shunned but also hated by academic historians who follow the crowd and make no waves. The best revisionist on WWII history is an Englishman named David Irving a bi-lingual author who has over 30 published books on WWII history. He as all revisionists do, works only from original documents and interviews with participants involved in the events, not the hearsay of fellow authors and academics.

After WWII, approximately one million German POWs were murdered (mostly by starvation) at the **direct order** of General Dwight Eisenhower. The details are found in the extensively documented book, *Other Losses,* by James Bacque. The foreword to the book was written by Col Ernest Fisher, PhD, former Lieutenant, 101st Airborne Division who was the Senior Historian of the United States Army.

CFR

CFR

✳

The commander of the Allies <<Dwight David Eisenhower>>, exposed his bias in a letter to his wife in September 1944, "God I hate the Germans…"<< Eisenhower>>. After the war, on his command, Eisenhower had over 200 German POW camps built, they had no sanitation, no housing, no amenities, and the Red Cross was not allowed to visit. One million, seven hundred thousand German soldiers were starved and frozen to death in those POW camps. The camps were simply high fences with concertina barbed wire on top in open fields in winter. Guards were warned that to give food or any comfort to the POW's would be a criminal offence. The Geneva Convention be dammed, he <<Eisenhower>> had won; now he would exterminate. The dead soldiers were stripped naked, any remaining clothing and identifying dog tags destroyed, bodies covered with chemicals for rapid decomposition, and thrown into ditches to be covered with dirt by bulldozers. In written orders in the winter of 1945 Eisenhower wrote, "Prison enclosures are to provide no shelter or comforts." Eisenhower's biographer Stephen Ambrose, who had access to all of <<Eisenhower's>> letters and orders, clearly stated that he [<<Eisenhower>>] proposed to exterminate the entire German General Staff and to liquidate as many German soldiers as possible. The details can be found in the extensively documented book, *Other Losses,* by James Bacque. The foreword to the book was written by Col Ernest Fisher, PhD, former Lieutenant, 101st Airborne Division, who was the Senior Historian of the United States Army.

This is the man who, running for president in 1952 had the slogan, "I like Ike." Eisenhower, whose father was a Jew, was promoted to five star general from colonel over the heads of 30 more senior officers,[104] including George Patton who was eminently more qualified. <<Eisenhower>> had never commanded any military unit in the field, four star general and American hero, McArthur said of <<Eisenhower>>, "The best clerk I ever had." Could FDR's pro-Jewish bias

✳ *The Politician by Robert Welch.*

have had anything to do with that? The Roosevelt's came from Holland and Roosevelt had been governor of NY, from the time the leftist Roosevelt came to be governor to the end of his life he completely surrounded himself with socialists and communists, many of whom were Jews. During FDR's tenure as a politician he appointed not counting <<Eisenhower>>, 73 Jews and communist including his first VP Henry Wallace, a communist, who had to be replaced because he was much too cozy with Stalin.

As allied historians began their massive zionist, anti-German campaign long before the beginning of the war in the 1930's, misinformation published was picked up by others and recirculated to the point where many good people became convinced of official lies and propaganda. Zionists were at the forefront of this endeavor to establish a case for the effort to come after the war of financing the establishment of Israel and evicting the indigenous Palestinians. The fact that Jews owned and controlled most of the mainstream media, including book publishing, films, periodicals, newspapers, Hollywood, radio, and TV was certainly helpful in their effort. (Today six Jewish-controlled media companies control 90% of American media.)

There exists, to the best of our knowledge, not one single document discovered in which the Nazis or Hitler ever stated a policy of racial or religious extermination of any group of people. They strongly believed that homosexuals, prostitutes, Jehovah Witness, Freemasons, alcoholics, pacifists, beggars, people with hereditary diseases,[105] the genetically disabled,[105] criminals, and others considered anti-social to be placed in KZ (concentration camps).[106] The other cause for KZ was anyone opposed to *"Gleichschaltung"*.[107] This would indicate that societal opposers to the Nazis such as Freemasons, trade unionists, and religious activists could if they actively opposed the Nazis wind up in KZ. The origin of KZ goes back to the Weimar Republic.[108] The Weimar Republic failed because of the Jewish imposed armistice terms of WWI.[109] Now 96 years after the Great War, even mainstream historians agree that WWII was caused by the Jew implemented terms of armistice of WWI.

Historically, it is important for the reader to understand the existing situation in Germany, after WWI, during the Weimar Republic. The Republic was doomed to failure long before it became a government. The terms of armistice dictated by the Jews who controlled the end of war negotiations were so economically severe on

* *Roosevelt Red Record and It's Background; Elizabeth Dilling.*

Germany that no established state could possibly have survived. It resulted in the repeated devaluation of currency, massive inflation, a depression worse than the one in America,[110] unemployment at 27% by 1933, and the highest per capita suicide rate in the developed world, which made recovery impossible. Stalin had infiltrated communist shills into the leadership of all German trade unions especially public service unions. They interrupted public transportation, sanitation, water supplies, and food delivery causing economic mayhem, in Germany and Austria. Hitler was elected in 1933; he immediately instituted dramatic changes in government. He began to plan and build Volkswagen (the peoples car), he began to build autobahns (freeways), and most importantly as before mentioned he ended Germany's dependence on the <<Rothschild>> international banking cartel. He financed the Reich's Mark (RM)[111] without borrowing from the bankers.

The Anschluss whereby Austria joined with Germany in March of 1938 was not as O'Rielly dishonestly claimed on his TV show an invasion, Austrians voted to join Germany by a 99.73% majority with 99.71% voter participation.

---

98. Clause 231 was important to the French and English because it allowed them to steal German colonies, goods, and land.
99. War Reparations in present day US dollars would be $455,640,000,000. Or $455.6 billion dollars.
100. Copies can be downloaded from the Internet (search Judea declare war on German) Also on July 4th 2016 *The Last Independence Day* (Hallberg Pub. A. H. Krieg)
101. London Times October 11 & 12 and November 13, 1940
102. Paraphrased to shorten intent was clear. [He was hinting at the central bankers cheating in not allowing audits of their holdings or of hard assets (gold and silver)] that they claimed to have in support of monitory value.
103. Deutsche Sozialkistische Arbeiter Partei and Union of Soviet Socialist Republics.
104. In his entire military career <<Eisenhower>> never once led soldiers in combat, was never shot at, and had no field experience.
105. Were usually identified at birth and killed.
106. Konzentrationslager Lager (Concentration Camps).
107. There is no equivalent word in the English language it means compliance or agreement with the majority of the population.
108. The German government before Hitler's election in 1933. They were intended to rehabilitate offenders who were usually released after working in the KZ for a specified term of incarceration.
109. Armistice means the cessation of hostilities it is not a surrender. The Armistice was signed in a RR car in Compiegne, France.
110. Great Depression of 1929
111. Reich's Mark

Auschwitz Concentration Camp
Six million is a fable of zionism.

If there is one thing that the SS[112] was accurate in, it was record keeping. Unfortunately Auschwitz after the war was, as were most concentration Camps, under Soviet control. In fact every concentration camp where mass murder supposedly took place was in Soviet controlled territory, and they refused to give up pertinent information on the issue. Russia refused to release information that they had on Auschwitz and other camps because release of such information would allow proof that the Russians and the Polish guards at these camps, killed more inmates than the Germans. The Russian and Polish troops hated Jews even more than did the Germans. Before Stalin came to oppose Jews[113] every Russian company had a political officer, usually a Jew (Bolshevik) who shared command decisions with the military leader. These men were so hated by the Russian soldiers that when they came upon German Sonderkommandos[114] Russian soldiers would point them out. The Poles (especially those who worked for the SS) hatred of Jews goes all the way back in history, many resented the Jewish invasion that had converted Roman Catholic Poland into a one-third Jewish state. When the Russians invaded Poland in 1920[115] the great fear of Poles was that the 500,000 Jewish residents of Warsaw's Nalevski district would rise up and support the Bolshevik Russian invasion. When the Russian invasion failed many Jews immigrated to other nations, and great numbers of those remaining were mascaraed by Poles in 1933 when the provisional government collapsed. Many KZ internes were too weak to travel due to lack of food.[116] The SS who ran the camps that were in fact factories for items used by the Wehrmacht[117] ("Arbeit Macht Frei")[118] had Polish Militia as military control personnel for the inmates. There are numerous messages from Berlin to the camp commanders expressing outrage at the high death rates in the camps. These were after all the factories that produced war materials, uniforms, tools, and small arms for the Wehrmacht. High death rates would mean lower production output.

The high death toll at Auschwitz is in large part due to a typhoid epidemic that was brought in by Russian POW's in the 1940's. There was until the end of WWII no known cure for typhoid in Europe, people who were weak due to poor food often died from it. Many inmates that appear unaccounted for were in fact transferred to other camps. 21,512 Hungarian Jews, from May to October 1944 so 410 must have died. More detailed Russian released records of the 1990's indicate the following all from SS archives:

Total Hungarian Jews entering Auschwitz		
	May to Oct.1944	23,117
Total above transferred	May to Oct 1944	21,527
Total above remaining	Oct 1944	1,590[119]

Summation July 1941 to October 1944
(No records provided for 1945)

Total number of Jewish prisoners Auschwitz camp	173,000
Total deaths from typhus	58,240
Total deaths due to natural causes	2,064
Total number of Jewish transfers	100,743
Total number of Jews executed	117
Total number of Jews in Camp after SS evacuation	11,839[120]

While this only lists Hungarian Jews it certainly disputes numbers claims made by zionists.

There is one other issue that seems to be missing; if the claim of six million were legitimate it would in fact be easy using modern computers to compile a list of names of the deceased. Such a list would provide actual evidence of claims. Not unlike the zionist claims against Swiss insurance carriers no such lists have ever surfaced.

Especially notable is the constantly diminishing numbers on the plaque at the entrance at Auschwitz, it began with 4 million killed and is now down to 1.5 million. At the Nürnberg trials, the Russians who had made the claims about crematoria presented no evidence of their findings, because they had not yet been built.[121] The verdict of the trial given on September 30, 1946 was 90-pages in length, only in the last six pages are Jews even mentioned. Only two items were introduced in the evidence relating to Auschwitz extermina-tions, first was a confession from Rudolf Hess who had been in British isolated detention since 1941, which was beaten out of him by his British jailors. Considering that Auschwitz was opened in May of 1942, what could Hess possibly have known about the camp that was opened when he had already been in solitary confinement in England for an entire year? The words "Final Solution" were not the product of the Nazis; it was made by one of the judges at the Trial. Wilhelm Höttl commandant of Auschwitz gave the second evidence that testified that 2.5 million were exterminated and 500,000 others died of illness, then he stated that A. Eichmann had told him in 1944 that 6 million Jews had been exterminated.[122] On August 6th the Soviet Prosecutor said; "The deposition and testimony of W. Höttl establishes that the Gestapo exterminated close to 6 million Jews."

In testimony of the deportation of Ernst Zündel, from Canada to the United States and then back to Germany, Fred Leuchter, America's leading expert on gas chamber design and operation, testified at the trial that based on evidence provided, the Nazis would have had to kill 1,693 Jews per week based on the size of the facility at Auschwitz, thus to kill 6 million would have taken 68 years. He further testified that none of the facilities he examined, and there were many, supported the ability to sustain multiple executions using hydrogen cyanide, carbon monoxide, or any other lethal gas. He concluded with the statement that claiming that these facilities were used for mass execution or even singular executions was ludicrous and an insult to every living person. In 1992 Robert Faurisson introduced a program related to holocaust revisionism. He proposed the following challenge to the Swedish media: "Provide me with a photograph of a Nazi gas chamber and factual evidence of its use as an execution device." No one has successfully provided that evidence. Zyclon B is a gas used for flea and rodent extermination; it is in fact a pesticide. The technical name is HCN (hydrocyanic acid, or prussic acid), it was in common use including the United States since 1919.[123] There are hundreds of better gases to kill people, why would the Nazis, who were very efficient, use Zyclon B? There is the misconception that these facilities were set up to kill people, this is simply not the case. The camps were set up to remove criminals from local prisons, to remove homosexuals from society, to, by Gleichschaltung, eliminate people opposed to Nazi beliefs (such as violent communist revolutionaries), to hold away from society any who actively opposed Nazi rule, and finally as industrial labor, replacing those fighting the communists on the Eastern Front. This included communists, which in large part were Jews. Eventually many Jews who were not communists were rounded up because of the part of the Jewish society that was very actively communist. Inmates were paid in coupons redeemable for goods, cigarettes, and beer at the commissary. There was a full orchestra, a theater, movie house, kindergarten, library, inmates could write home twice a week, they even had soccer teams. What happened in the ending years of the war was unfortunate but was a direct result of <<Eisenhower's>> relentless illegal bombing attacks against civilians, cities, infrastructure, and transportation facilities which produced severe food shortages for everyone, including the inmates and the camp staff.

ı As mentioned previously, the history of war is written by the vic-
✳ tors, no matter how depraved and biased they might be. In WWII the person most responsible for initiating the war and engineering America's entrance into the war was Winston Churchill (with the willing cooperation of FDR). The person most responsible for the
CFR prosecution of military affairs was Dwight Eisenhower. Churchill and Eisenhower both had total access to all information collected during and after the war. Both wrote and published exhaustive histories of the war: Churchill's 6 volume *The Second World War and Eisenhower's Crusade in Europe*. There was no mention of any "Holocaust" in their writings, even though if it had existed, its inclusion would have been a tremendous boost in justifying the massive destruction they had caused.

The real purpose of the war as hinted by the leftist/Stalinist leanings of both Roosevelt and Churchill, and verified by the actual outcome of the war was to make the world safe for communism.

---

112. Schüzstaffel
113. Stalin was married to a Jewess
114. Special troops to deal with political issues. (Usually killed Bolsheviks)
115. Polish Russian War Feb 1919 to March 1921
116. Food became difficult to get for Germans and even the German military because Eisenhower destroyed all German infrastructure especially rail which transported most foodstuffs.
117. German Army
118. Work Makes You Free
119. CSA No: 187603: Roll 285-1943-44 Frames 019-852 Roll 286-1945 Frames 001-329
120. CSA No: 187603 Roll 281-1940: Frames 107-869-Roll 282-1940-41: Fames 001-875-Roll 283-1941-42 Frames 001-872-Roll 284-1942-43: Frames 003-862-Roll 285-1943-44: Frames 019-852-Roll 286-1945; Frames 001-329.
121. 1 May 1940 to Dec. 1943
122. "Hearsay evidence" would not be allowed in any court of the world. The accusation from various sources is that the Russians actually built the crematoria in order to hide the murders of inmates by them.
123. References: The Leuchter Report: (Focal point Publications) The Second Leuchter Report: Dachau, Mauthausen, Harheim. The Third Leuchter Report: A technical report on the Execution Gas Chambers—Mississippi State Penitentiary.

WWII & the Bolshevik Revolution in Russia

Bolshevik's were over 90% Ashkenazim.

It is historically more correct to call the Russian Revolution an invasion rather than a revolution because the majority of the eventually formed Soviet government was not made up of Russians but of non-Russian Ashkenazi.[124] The Bolsheviks became a prominent issue from the end of the Russian Revolution forward. In 1919, 25 out of 32 commissars of Russia were Ashkenazi Jews. In Russia out of 384 commissars 300 were Jews. In the Quasi cabinet of the forming Soviet government in 1917, 24 out of 24 were Jews. By 1935 the entire Soviet Central Committee with 56 members, all but three were Jews and they were all married to Jewish women. In America out of 700 members of Bolsheviks 625 were Jews. The communist parties of Austria (<<Victor Adler>>), Bavaria (<<Kurt Eisner>>) and (<<Herbert Aptecker>>), in America <<Béla Kun>>, and in Hungary (<<Rosa Luxemburg>>), all were Jews. In the 20th century the prime American head of the communist party was <<Gus Hall>>,[125] a Jew.

The Katyn massacre was the murder of the entire Christian Polish officer corps by the Soviet NKVD (The People's Commissariat for Internal Affairs), most of the NKVD in 1940 were Jews. The Soviets

German soldiers unearthed numerous mass graves of many thousands of Polish officers who had been massacred in the Katyn Forest near Smolensk.

Gus Hall - avo Kuataa Hallberg (Index, pg 208)

tried to blame the Germans for this atrocity from the day the bodies were discovered until the real truth came out. It was the largest mass execution of WWII, except for the murder of 1.7 million German POW's by <<Eisenhower>> after the war. Twenty two thousand were Polish Christian Roman Catholic officers plus another 6,000 police and intelligence officers, were systematically shot in the head by the NKVD and dumped into ditches. The Polish officers and others were captured in the Soviet invasion of Poland in 1939. A huge investigation by the Russian prosecutor's office in 1990 confirmed that the NKVD carried out the executions. Not one single person has ever been prosecuted or even arrested for this heinous crime.

Remember in previous chapters that the world HQ of the diaspora was located in London and that Ribbentrop (Germany) and Molotov (Russia) had reached an agreement to partition Poland and several other nations between themselves in 1939. So, Germany invaded first then a few days later it was Russia's turn. The subsequent declaration of war against Germany and the alliance with Russia against Germany makes absolutely no sense in social or political terms. But when you factor in the Jews located in London and Moscow and the Katyn Forest massacre it all comes together.

*   Any worthwhile examination of the Russian Revolution will demonstrate that it was not a revolution but an invasion. <<Lenin>> and his trainload of gold and arms paid for by <<Schiff>>, to St. Petersburg certainly confirm this, as does the fact that the quasi-cabinet as well as the Supreme Soviet had no Russian members at all. In fact 86% of all members of the Soviet government from 1920 to 1945 were foreigners. In 1920 Sir Winston Churchill penned an article for the Sunday Herald, the largest circulation Sunday paper of England at that time. The article was titled "Zionism vs. Bolshevism." In that article Churchill admonishes all Jews to support their own nations (Israel was yet to be established in 1948) in which they lived and to actively combat the opposing Jews. He strongly argued against the "international Jew".[126] He argued correctly that the Russian Revolution was internationalist and that zionism and internationalism are one and the same thing.

It is at this point prudent to look at the invention of communism, what made it, and how it was originally developed. <<Adam Weisshaupt>>

Adam Weisshaupt
1748

the founder of illuminism was the original author of the Communist Manifesto.[127] It was published in England, written in German Script that had to be especially imported from the continent. The popularly assumed author, in fact a plagiarist, was <<Karl Marx>> with forward by <<Frederick Engels>>. We can only prove this with circumstantial evidence, which is; 1) <<Karl Marx>> was not a good student and might by any reasonable terms be considered a failure. 2) He was a failure in journalism. 3) His English was not good

Karl Marx *1875*

and in 1848, he was only 30, was exiled to England from Germany. 4) As a Jew he was banned from society of the 19th century as was his Jewish friend <<Engels>>. 5) The communist theory of economics makes absolutely no sense in the 19th century. The industrial revolution began in England in 1790; by 1848 it was fully developed. The communist theory has application to <<Weisshaupt's>> time[128] when physical labor was the means of production. After industrialization, communism made no sense. In 1867 <<Marx>> went on to publish Das Kapital, in which he theorizes that the motivating force of capitalism is the exploitation of labor, whose unpaid workers are the source of surplus value resulting in profit for the employer. This theory is wrong on many counts; first, the reason for capitalism is the production of goods to allow the producer profit. Second, labor by 1867 was already organized and industrialization was beginning to allow, through mechanization, increased wages. Third, since labor could and can seek employment from other places and for other jobs, exploitation of labor is strictly theoretical. Fifth, is in manufacturing to which this theory relates. Labor is less than one-third of the cost of production, raw materials, machinery, power use, taxes, fees, and licenses make up the other two-thirds. <<Marx>> is the typical Jew pseudo academic who has never been employed in any gainful productive occupation and has no concept of manufacturing, production, distribution, or employment.

The principal tenants of communism are identical to those espoused by zionism. In fact they are internationalism, open borders (Mexican border), state centralization (in Washington today), punishment for exceptionalism (punishment through higher taxes for accomplishment), graduated income taxes (IRS), centralized government education (Department of Education), abolition of inheritance (IRS), centralization of credit (FRS)[129], centralization of communication (FCC)[130], and equality in labor (USDL)[131] are the mainstays of both zionism and communism. It is interesting that all those issues also appear in both the Protocols as well as the Communist Manifesto. This is a clear and present danger that exposes zionism for what it really is. For those who disagree consider the zionist theocratic state of Israel. Israel is a socialist theocracy a fact that is absolutely indisputable. Electric power, water, sewerage, transportation, defense, manufacturing, all Kibbutzim, and most land[132] are community owned not privately owned. It is theocratic because non-Jews pay higher taxes, have differing labor laws and benefits, are prohibited from owning land, get different license plates for cars, get passports and ID cards indicating that they are not Jews, have religious prohibition to marry non-Jews, have restrictions on holding public office, are not allowed to be officers in the IDF, and many other issues.

One hundred years after <<Adam Weisshaupt>> invented the communist theory of economics and government, <<Karl Marx>> plagiarized it; his command of English was then marginal so he simply had the Manifest published in London but in German text. He lacked the ability to translate the Manifest. <<Weisshaupt>> was an Ashkenazim who converted to Catholicism when the Jesuits adopted him[133] in Bavaria. <<Weisshaupt>> was an exceptional student and graduated in a few years from the University of Ingolstadt in Canon Law.[134] When in 1773 Pope Clement XIV, on July 21st issued a Papal Bull[135] for the suppression of the Society of Jesus (the Jesuits), Weisshaupt who was not an order member but a brilliant student of Canon Law, was given the chair of Canon Law at the University of Ingolstadt, a very prestigious position for someone of his age, only 25 years old. <<Weisshaupt>> went on to form the illuminist[136] movement and his Illuminati name was <<Spartacus>>. The American domicile of illuminism is Bones (also called Skull and Bones, (322) The Order, and The Order of Death).[137] Its Yale home is in a building called the Tombs located on the east side of the Yale, New Haven campus. Its name stems from the architecture, being a three-story house without any windows and only one visible door.

Now that we have done the groundwork we can follow the money, usually the most productive activity of any historian, but something that academic historians tend to avoid. Woodrow Wilson was the American president when all this was unfolding. Wilson was the second progressive[138] president, Theodore Roosevelt was the first. Wilson was an academic (Princeton), who had an advisor, by most referred to as Wilson's alter ego, whose name was Edward House.[139] He used the name "Colonel" House but had never been in the military, the title was honorary from the governor of Texas. Wickham Steed was a prominent historian who wrote how he tried to impress on House the Ashkenazi nature of the Russian Revolution. House as the agent of <<Rothschild>> (European banksters) who he knew was president of the World Zionist Congress was totally disinterested in Steed's overtures. In March of 1919 at the heart of the Revolution, Steed called on House and found him greatly disturbed by Steed's opposition to the Revolution and America's recognition of the Bolsheviks.[140] Wilson did not move without the advice of House.[141] To get insight into House's thinking you should read "Philip Dru: Administrator" by Edward Mandell House. Unknown to Wilson but certainly well known by House was that the entire Russian Revolution was nothing less than the takeover of a sovereign nation by atheists Ashkenazi, and that the prime financiers were all Jews, <<Jacob Schiff>>, and <<Paul Wartburg>>[142] among them. According to Steed, House argued for the immediate recognition of the Soviets and the establishment of economic relations with the Bolsheviks who were orchestrating the Revolution.

The greatest administration input for this comes from the U.S. State Department[143] whose central theme is titled "Bolshevism and Judaism". The text of that document states that the Russian Revolution was established in February 1918 and that the following individuals and corporations were the primary financiers of the Revolution: <<Jacob Schiff, of Kuhn, Loeb & Co., Felix Warburg, Otto H. Kahn, Mortimer Schiff, Jerome J. Hauser, Guggenheim, Max Breitlung, and Isaac Seligman>>, all of whom were Ashkenazim.

Without doubt the greatest supporter of <<Lenin>> and the Bolsheviks was <<Jacob Schiff>>, who was instrumental in obtaining permission from Germany to allow <<Lenin>> and a sealed train, passage to St. Petersburg. The Germans allowed a sealed train to be loaded with over a ton of gold, munitions, small arms, grenades, and many non-Russian Bolsheviks straight through to St. Petersburg. He arranged for <<Lenin>> to be allowed into Germany from Switzerland straight from Zürich to Berlin. He convinced European zionists that this would be good for them, that Lenin would create the world's first zionist state. As it eventually turned out when Stalin came to power things did not work in accordance with <<Schiff's>> plans.

Another arm of the zionist financial operation was the financing of <<Leon Trotsky>>, another Jew communist, who was eventually assassinated by order of Stalin in Mexico where he was hiding out. <<Trotsky>> was financially supported by <<Olof Aschenberg>>, a Swedish Jew banker[144] so we see that the entire Revolution, from one political end to the other was financed by Jew bankers who developed the entire communist international system (The Comiterm) from 1900 to the 1930s.

The revolution, or more correctly its impact, was universal with the exception of China; the entire well-oiled with mammon communist machine, had Jewish fingerprints all over it. They even went as far as the <<Rosenberg's>>,[145] <<David Greenglass>>, and <<Harry Gold>> all of whom were members of the same communist cell. In America the original communist party of America was located on Rivington Street in downtown NYC, in the largest Jewish community in America (self-created ghetto). The party claims foundation in 1876; a bogus claim; the party had no offices until 1919.[146] In 1919 Lenin asked the American communist party to join the Comintern which later, when the Soviet state was established became the Soviet Union. The first American Executive Secretary was <<Alfred Wagenknecht>>. By 1924 it was <<C. E. Ruthenberg>>, in 1935 <<Earl Browder>>. Eventually <<Avo Kuataa Hallberg>> who went under the alias <<Gus Hall>>. All of them were Jews. The party roster from 1900 to today reads more like the booking record of the NYC police, or perhaps the membership roster of Congregation Emanu-El.[147] <<Hall>> was eventually arrested and convicted of attempting the violent overthrow of America was sent to Leavenworth Kansas.[148]

Regarding the Wilson administration which was very actively courting the Jewish vote and more importantly for them Jewish money, they established the continued suppression of information relating to the financing and Jewish support for the Russian Revolution. Information relating to the Communist Manifesto's 10 points, which had by the 16th & 17th amendments been vastly expanded, was suppressed, as were all matters of similarity between zionism and communism. Confidential diplomatic transmissions from our Russian ambassador[149] were all buried by Secretary of State Robert

Lansing, under direction from Colonel House.[150] House said, "We agreed to suppress this material and files. I think I have it all in cold storage" [With whom the agreement was made was never clarified... probably <<Rothschild>>.

Another transmission from Moscow was a review of the *Protocols of the Learned Elders of Zion,* a letter was sent to Washington enclosing a memorandum from David Francis with regard to "certain information from the American military Attaché to the effect that the British authorities had letters intercepted from various groups of international Jews [Diaspora in London] of a scheme for world domination. "Copies of this information will be very useful to us." House also had that information squashed. The men listed in the memorandum were all the same people who had financed the Revolution, and who in fact held one-third of the entire world's wealth.

House was the paid political agent of the <<Rothschild's>> the European bankers closely related to <<Schiff, Kuhn, Lob>>, and the <<Warburg's>> both in America and Holland. <<Warburg was Rothschild's>> American bank correspondent.

---

124. <<Central Committee of the Supreme Soviet 1935: (15 years after foundation of the state) All listed were Jews: V.V. Balitsky, K.J. Baumann, I.M. Vareikis, J.R. Gamarmik, I.I. Egoff, L.M. Kaganowitz, V.G. Knorin, M.M. Livinoff, I.E. Liobimow, D.Z. Manouilisky, I.A. Zelensky, I.D. Kabakoff, L.M. Kaganowitz, V.G. Koorin, I.P. Mossow, J.L. Piatakow, I.O. Piatinsky, M.O. Aazoumow, M.K. Ruchimovit, K.V. Rindin, M.M. Houtavitch, M.S. Tchuodow, A.M. Schvernik, R.I. Eice, G.G. Lagoda, I. E. Lakir, I.A.Lakoview, F.P. Griadinsky, G.N. Kaminsky, I.S. Unschicht, A.S. Boulin, M.I. Kkalamanowitz, D.S. Beika, and so forth 56 men in all>>. Three were atheists the rest were Jews, the atheists were all married to Jews, L.V. Stalin, (a) S.S. Lobow, and V.V. Ossinsky.
   (a) Stalin, affectionately called "Uncle Joe" by the Grey Lady (NY Times) close friend of Henry Wallace FDR's second VP. *Stalin, married to a Jewess.*
125. <<Gus Hall>> was an alias, his name was Arvo Kustaa Halberg he was an ex-con.
126. Internationalism has always, from the first day of zionism and communism, been one of the primary causes they pursued. *Open borders. Pres. Joe Biden!*
127. Manifest Der Kommunistischer Partei, Feröffentlicht in Februar 1848. Published by Burghard 46 Liverpool St. Bishopsgate.
128. <<Adam Weisshaupt>> Feb 6, 1748 to November 18 1830.
129. The Federal Reserve System (FRS) is a 1914 privately owned and government granted banking monopoly.
130. Federal Communications Commission
131. United States Department of Labor
132. A Kibbutz is a communist village in which the residents share all property jointly. Outside the clothes on their backs they own nothing, Most Kibbutzim are built on stolen Palestinian land in the West Bank and are fortified. All are by international law illegal.
133. The Roman Catholic military order of the "Society of Jesus" whose leader is called the Commander General and is often referred to as the "Black Pope".

134. Canon Law is the law of the Church. In his time the church had jurisdiction on many civil matters and was very powerful politically and socially.
135. A "Papal Bull" is a legal document (letter, charter, or patent), issued by a Pope relating to some issue, it is binding on all Catholics worldwide its name is related to the "bulla" (IT) (Seal of the Pope that adorns it)
136. Illuminism is a social and political philosophy based on Illuminism through (enlightenment). The order was started by <<Weisshaupt>> in Bavaria. Weishaupt attempted to spread it through the Rosicrucian Order (a) but that failed. He then joined the Masonic order and succeeded in infiltrating the Bavarian Masons. Through the efforts of many intellectual and upper class followers, the Illuminists were able to take over most Masonic lodges in Germany, France, and Italy, (b) they never penetrated the English, Irish. or Scottish lodges. (American masonic lodges are chartered by the Grand Lodge of England) As a side note; the reason that Gilbert du Motier, the (Marquis de Lafayette) came to America was to warn Washington and Dr. Franklin who was also a member of Les Neuf Soeurs (the Lodge of Seven Sisters in Paris) of the illuminist takeover of Masonry in France.
   (a) AMRC Ancient Mystical Order Rose Crucis (Dr. Franklin was a member.)
   (b) The Nazis closed all German lodges and sent their members to KZ. The French and Dutch lodges were successful in purging the illuminists in the early 1800's. The Italian lodges are still controlled by illuminists.
137. Yale senior society which has many prominent members, Bush, Kerry, Taft, Emerson, Kellogg, Rockefeller, Buckley, Bundy, Gillman, Harrison, Heinz, Lord, Luce, Coffin, TR, etc.
138. Progressives are in fact socialists. The socialist movement has always tried to hide their affiliation. TR was the first progressive, Wilson the second, thereafter: Roosevelt, LBJ, Carter, Clinton, and Obama.
139. Colonel Edward House was the American political agent of the House of <<Rothschild>> in Washington.
140. Through 30 years 1892-1922 Vil II PP 302
141. The Intimate Papers of Colonel House: Behind the political curtain (Seymore 1926)
142. <<Paul Wartburg>> was the author of the Federal Reserve Act and a participant in the Jekyll Island meeting in 1910 in which the bankers set up the 16th & 17th amendments to the Constitution, forever changing America from a Republic to a Democracy. Schiff was the major supplier of gold to <<Lenin>> when he went from Zürich to Berlin and then to St Petersburg.
143. USSD Decimal File 861.00/5339 [November 1918]
144. Nya Banken of Sweden
145. <<Julius and Ethel Rosenberg>> were both executed as spies they gave Stalin and the Soviets the atomic bomb.
146. NYC Public Library records (Midtown branch)
147. Largest synagogue in NYC
148. AP Oct 17, 2000
149. David R. Francis was the Charge d'Affairs in Sept. 1919
150. Rc-h 5399/pro 5399/ &3253 (State Department Documents)

Special footnote: Dr. Benjamin Franklin and the Marquis de Lafayette were both members of the Masonic Seven sister Lodge of Paris. Lafayette came to America to warn Franklin, Washington, Hancock, Randolph, Adams, and Revere, all of whom were freemasons, of the Illuminist takeover of the French Masonic order.

1948 & the Foundation of Israel* in the Levant

Better old history than new lies.
A. H. Krieg

The foundation of Israel in 1948 was preceded by a tumultuous few- decades of zionist terrorism against Palestinian Christians and Muslims. There were numerous zionist terrorist organizations marching under the blue and white banner of the Star of David.[151] The Irgun, a right-wing zionist organization founded in 1931, from March 1937 to April 1948 committed 67 terrorist attacks against the indigenous Palestinians and the British.[152] The death toll of these atrocities was 697 confirmed. Additional zionist terrorist groups were Lehi, Haganah, The Stern Gang, and Palmach. The <<Theodor Herzel>> created zionist state would grow to be one of the most violent anti-social governments of world history. Since its foundation in 1948 Israel has produced 4.25 million refugees. 950,000 Palestinians were displaced when the terrorists forced them from their homes, farms, and businesses in the 1940s. The Palestinian Christians and Muslims forced off their own land and nation were not allowed to return and were paid nothing for the property stolen from them. There were 337,000 butchered outright in Israel's war of colonization of 1948. Nothing has changed, the genocide continues, from January to July 2014, 786 Palestinians were killed by the zionist IDF in operation "Protective Edge" on June 8, 2014 there were 31 dead Palestinians and 4 dead Israelis, it was the claimed reason for "Operation Protective Edge" as retribution for 4 dead Israelis after they had killed 31 Palestinians.

The victimhood card was played on American media as a relentless lament about those poor four Israelis three of which had crossed borders for obviously nefarious reasons. The 31 dead Palestinians were never mentioned in any American media outlet. No wonder they are called the Lamestream. Arabs in general seemed unhappy with America, the reasons are blatantly obvious to any observer. American Jews who in general terms are among the wealthiest Americans control banking, media, and substantial parts of the government. Their slavish support of Likud in the Knesset which actually is less than half of the Israeli population, have the blood of thousands of Christian and Muslim Arabs on their hands, by supporting the zionist theocracy regardless of their actions, right or wrong. The zionist control in government is no more typified than the 2014 congressional summer break when 81 congressmen went on a political junket to Israel, paid for by American taxpayers as foreign aid to Israel. Let's all understand that the Israelis know how best to spend their ill-gained American foreign aid.

As a matter of historic record, <<Ze'ev Vladimir Jabotinsky>> as the first commander of the Haganah is without question the father of zionist terrorism. Haganah was founded in 1919, just as the Russian Revolution came to a head. By 1923 he founded another terrorist cell named Betar.[153]

Ze'ev Jabotinsky

<<Jabotinsky>> was so brazen that he called himself the Messiah. Movements that grew out of this were Irgun, Zvai, Leumi, Lohamei, Herut, Yisrael, FFI and Avraham, Stern also called the Stern Gang or Stern Group. <<Jabotinsky>> died in NYC, the place that funded his terrorism. <<Stern>> was captured by the British and immediately executed. The Leader of Irgun was (the weasel) <<Menachem Begin>> probably the most violent of the lot. He was Prime Minister of Israel from 1977 to 1983. Another zionist terrorist was <<Ariel Sharon>> [Scheinemann] he only stayed out of Israeli jail because he was hospitalized and in a coma. Arabs called him (the Butcher of Beirut)[154] he was in a coma in 2006 after suffering

Menachem Begin

Ariel Sharon

stoke for eight years and died in 2014. Israeli politics are among the most brutal and corrupt in the world.

Recent actions in 2014 in Gaza by the IDF are abhorrent. Gaza, where almost 2,000,000 Palestinian refugees from their homeland in Israel are squeezed into a tiny 12 x 12 mile sized plot of arid land that is completely controlled by the Israeli military, is the largest concentration camp in world history. (The UN officially classifies Gaza as an "Occupied Territory".) Gaza is an Israeli closed area by treaty with Egypt whose border to Gaza is sealed. The Palestinians in Gaza are prevented by the zionists from having a seaport, airport, or even an organized bus terminal. All border crossings are controlled by

Palestinians sit in a tent outside their apartments, which witnesses said were destroyed in an Israeli offensive, during a 72-hour truce in Beit Lahiya town in the northern Gaza Strip August 11, 2014. (SUHAIB SALEM/REUTERS)

the IDF with arbitrary rules that change daily. The Israeli navy blocks the coast even to fishing except within one mile of the coast. Israel controls water, food, banking, and is the largest destroyer of housing in Gaza. Military incursions into Gaza beginning on the 8th of June 2014 had by the 21st of July resulted in the deaths of 76% of the civilians over 513 of which were children. 17,200 Palestine homes were destroyed, 8,000 fled to other places, 2,310 civilians were killed, 11,000 were injured, 216 Israelis were injured, 66 IDF soldiers were killed and 36,700 homes were damaged.[155] Israeli deaths due to Palestinian reaction produced less than 7% Israeli civilian casualties. As a result world media again reported that Hamas were terrorists and had attacked Israel who had simply countered the attacks. Jews who were the aggressors immediately became the victims as they do every time. The zionists have stolen land, farms, businesses, homes, and schools. Residents of Gaza have the world's highest unemployment, young people have no future, no possible employment, and no access to education. If you were in that situation and a Hamas recruiter came to your shack and asked if you would like to join them and kill a few zionist what would you say?

Looking at this from a different perspective assume that you are a Palestinian Christian living in Gaza. Your father was killed in the first intifada, your farm was stolen because the apartheid wall the zionists were building ran through your property, the family was not compensated for the stolen property, and your sister and mother were killed in an IDF bombing attack by Israel's American supplied aircraft. The olive farm your family had run for four generations is gone. You could not go to college because there are none available and schools are usually closed to males under 40. Hamas has provided you some help, food, and some books, no one else gives a damn about you. There are no jobs because there is no raw material, transportation, access to markets, or manufacturing. What exactly would you do?

The conflict in Gaza and the West Bank is not founded on religion even though zionists try to make it so. The Palestinian conflict on all fronts, West Bank and Gaza, is about land and water. In 1968 the basic borders of Israel were established through the UN. Gaza is situated on the Mediterranean Sea, and is surrounded by Israel except Egypt on desert in the south. The West Bank is bordered by Israel on one side and the Hashemite Kingdom of Jordan, the Dead Sea, on the other side. The portion of the West Bank that previously bordered Syria is now under Israeli control. The systematic theft of Palestinian land and heritage is obvious.[156] Simply look at an older atlas of the Middle East; Gaza and the West Bank do not exist, the entire region Is simply Palestine. British treacherously betrayed the Palestinian people who had fought alongside them against the Ottoman Turks and been promised autonomy in Palestine. Then England showed its "gratitude" by issuing the Belfour Declaration to <<Rothschild>> as president of the World Zionist Congress and voting in 1948 in support of an Israeli state to be established on the lands of the Palestinians who had lived in it for over 50 generations. The conflict is about territory, not religion, since all non-Jews: Christians, Muslims, Druze, and Baha'i, are equally discriminated against by the new zionist inhabitants.[157]

---

151. The Hexagram of the Star of David is not an ancient symbol of the Hebrews. The star did not appear until the early 19th century. Israeli professor <<Scholem>> claims that the star is based on Kabala magic. It's a direct comparison with the satanic hexagrams of magical Satanism, which certainly gives cause to pause. Its first use was in 1897 at the Basel World Zionist Congress.

152. Trans-Jordan as it was then called (The Levant) was after WWI a British Mandate issued by the League of Nations (a) from the end of the Ottoman Empire to 1948.
   (a) Predecessor of the UN

153. Was a Revisionist zionist youth movement that was founded by <<Ze'ev Jabotinsky>> in 1923 in Latvia it soon became international and remained active through WWII?

154. Shamir PM 1983-84 & 1986-82 he was in the Lehi party. (Died in 2012)
   a. <<Sharon>> as a general in the IDF was responsible for the killing of at least ten thousand Christian and Muslim Arabs in his long military career.

155. UN/ Human rights Watch/ Gaza Health ministry/

156. Palestine has since 1897 lost all its lands. Israel gradually displaced Palestine by 1947 60% of Palestine had become Israel, by 1948 it was 75% by 1956 it was 80% today its 90%.

157. Statistical Abstract of Israel, 2006 (No. 57)

Syria

Poor Syria, poor Christians, Alawites, Shias, Druze, and everyone else not a Wahhabi Sunni Muslim.

The Alawite Islam sect of whom the Assad family is a member has run Syria for many decades. The present leader of Syria is Bashar al Assad; a British educated Dr. of ophthalmology who is married to a British lady. Bashar came to power after the death of his father in 1971. The family's involvement in politics goes back to 1927. They have always run Syria as a secular nation in which religious freedom was granted to all citizens. Sunni as well as Shia Muslims, Roman and Druze Christians, Alawites and Fatimaists were all protected and lived together in reasonable harmony. Unfortunately Syria borders Israel, which has since 1948 wanted to expand into that nation. The Golan Heights which are part of Syria have been in Israeli hands since 1967 and have been under IDF military rule ever since.

Bashar al-Assad, president of Syria and his wife Asma al-Assad

Israeli agents who follow the policies of destabilization as listed in previous chapters in fact instigated the present civil war with Israeli paid mercenaries. The saddest part of this war has been the over one million Christian refugees created by the Caliphate, whose intolerant Wahhabi Sunni religious extremists in Saudi Arabia are the largest financial supporters of the Caliphate. Bashar like his father before him is decidedly pro-Western, and as such has been sadly mistreated by the West. Everyone except Sunni religious fanatics is on the losing side of the conflict, which is being

Hafez al-Assad served as president of Syria from 1971 until his death in 2000. He is widely criticized for his brutal tactics but also praised for stabilizing the country.

directed from Jerusalem. It is part of the Israeli strategy of splitting neighboring nations into smaller and more vulnerable morsels for the Israeli Hegemony to gobble up. The end game never changes, it remains today what it was in 1948 Eretz Yisrael. The Syrian conflict that has been ongoing since 2011 and cost hundreds of thousands of lives, and close to 2 million refugees, was started by Israeli paid mercenaries and militias, which in fact used poison gas[158] against pro-Assad supporting civilians in Hama and Ibiid provinces.[159] American news systems run by zionists then claimed that the Assad military were responsible based on Israeli intelligence. The very idea that the Mossad (one of the main entities in the Israeli Intelligence Community) is in any way or manner trustworthy is ludicrous. Proof of the claim is that simple rockets whose launchers were all in rebel-controlled areas delivered the gas. Incidentally the very same rebels that sold hostages to ISIL (The Caliphate) for $50,000 that later beheaded them for publicity and who signed a non-aggression treaty with the Caliphate in fact did this while the US military was training them in modern warfare to fight against the Assad government. Some months later after the state department (Hillary's Arab Spring fiasco) delivered several hundred Toyota all-wheel drive pickup trucks[160] with Russian machine guns mounted in the beds, and Secretary of State Hillary Clinton gave them $500 million, they became allies of the Caliphate. The U.S. State Department did not even provide American trucks, purchasing Toyotas instead.[161] In September of 2014 with much pressure from ultra-stupid Senator McCain, Congress had voted to train ISIL fighters.

CFR

Israeli policy can be better understood through the prism of Iraq. Iraq, like Syria, was a secular state. There was little religious turmoil. There was peace, and any Iraqi you ask today will tell you bluntly that things were far better under the Hussein government than they are now. Exactly the same result has been achieved in Syria. In accordance with Israeli published plans, Iraq will break up into three separate nations all much smaller, then the Israelis can play them against each other, and eventually conquer them as is outlined in the Oded Yinon Plan.

158. Chlorine gas fired into residential neighborhoods using rockets, verified by UN inspectors as fired from rebel held territory.
159. Chlorine gas used by al Qaida (CNN Report)
160. You must have seen TV images of the long lines of white Toyotas in Syria and Iraq which were delivered by the US Department of State.
161. This is what the Benghazi incident was all about. Ambassador J. Christopher Stevens was sent to negotiate with al Qaida in Libya out of the Gadhafi small arms stockpile to be delivered to Syria & ISIL via Turkey.

Travel in Israel in the 21st Century

Is virtually impossible for Palestinians, Christian, and Muslims.

There are hundreds of old roads and highways in the Israeli occupied areas of the Levant, many built long before 1948; most of these have been rendered impassable by the IDF with either mounds of dirt or ditches. There is an extensive Israeli highway system in the West Bank; Palestinians are not allowed to use it except in special small sections. All Palestinian cars are issued special different color license plates, Palestinian plates are green and white, Jewish plates are yellow, so that Israeli Police and the IDF can immediately spot non-Jews and prevent them from using roads built on their own land. There are scores of checkpoints in the West Bank some on borders, other at arbitrary locations within Palestinian territory. Checkpoints always stop and search all Palestinian registered cars. It can thus take a Palestinian Christian or Muslim up to 6 hours to travel from Jerusalem to Nabulus a distance of only 46 Km or 27 miles. Checkpoints are used to stop all vehicular as well as pedestrian traffic. In many cases delivery trucks must be unloaded and all contents

Palestinians wait in traffic to enter Jerusalem at Qalandia checkpoint between the West Bank city of Ramallah and Jerusalem. (AP PHOTO/MAJDI MOHAMMED)

transferred to a vehicle on the other side of the checkpoint because it is not allowed to cross the checkpoint. It is important to understand that these are not peripheral border checkpoints they are located all over the inside of the West Bank. The Israeli (zionist) plan is to prevent Palestinians from gaining employment due to inability to get to work, likewise to prevent higher education by preventing the student from going to school or university. Rules on checkpoint crossing are arbitrary and capricious. Rules are changed daily and are never advertised beforehand. As an example, you are a 30-year old man and want to go to the hospital to see your sick mother. You get to the checkpoint and are informed that all Palestinian males under age 40 are restricted from travel that day. Exceptions are never made; pregnant women have lost children because they were prohibited to travel to the hospital. People have died right there at the checkpoint because they were not allowed to go to the hospital. Other checkpoints will only be open for certain hours, which are never posted. You might have walked and hitch hiked all morning only to find the checkpoint locked up and IDF guards just looking down the barrel of a machine gun as you approach. If you are returning from a trip and the checkpoint is closed you will have to sleep on the ground and hope they will open the next morning for your age and gender. You would think that Palestinians would simply use their own roads, but the zionist thought of that also and have made those roads impassable with various types of obstructions. None of this has anything to do with the safety and security of Israeli citizens, it is simply harassment in an attempt to force Palestinians to become refugees somewhere else. This colonialization of the Levant will not end until America stops foreign aid and Germany demands, and receives, reparations for the damage by Jews leading up to WWII. The latest effort has been the construction of the apartheid wall, which likewise has nothing whatever to do with safety. Every inch of that wall has been built in the West Bank, not one inch sits in Israel. In many places the wall is up to six miles inside the West Bank. The wall's construction in fact eliminated over 100 Palestinian villages. The dream of the wall was that of the "Butcher of Beirut", <<Ariel Sharon>>. The wall is an absurdity! As are all those checkpoints and other harassments. They do not produce safety they produce anger and Palestinian hatred. They produce the very thing they are supposed to stop.

Palestinian Zionist Settlements

A Kibbutz is a communist co-operative.

"Settlements" in the West Bank are zionist communities constructed on confiscated Palestinian land. Palestinians are not allowed by zionist edicts to live in these communities even though they are built on Palestinian land. They are called Kibbutz, a form of community that is communist, most are fortified. Since Palestinians are not allowed to have guns, or any weapons for that matter, the squatters living in these communities often threaten and intimidate the local population with their guns trying to force them to move away from the proximity of the Kibbutz. This is not a new issue. The first Kibbutz, Degania was built in 1909. By 2010 there were 121 authorized ones and 102 unauthorized ones, no Palestinian has been paid one Shekel for the land. Israelis and zionists will avoid informing on the social and political structure of these villages because they do not want the fact that they are communists publicized. A Kibbutz is a commune in which all property is jointly owned

The illegal Israeli settlement of Ariel in the West Bank.
PHOTO FROM WIKIPEDIA

Israeli bulldozers flattened a village inhabited by the ancient Palestinian Bedouins, a tribe that has lived on the land for thousands of years. Israeli authorities have systematically run the indigenous Bedouins off of their land to pave the way for Jewish-only settlements. (AP/SEBASTIAN SCHEINER)

except the clothing worn by its inhabitants. Many of these communities are not only communist but are run by religious fanatics that zionists call zealots[162] who are openly very hostile to Arabs and often shoot them. This is a concerted effort at colonialization far worse than anything ever done by Europeans in Africa. In South Africa for example the standard of living of the natives was greatly improved during "White Rule". The process is in fact prohibited by International law.[163] The Israeli government does not only support the policy of constructing these fortified villages they grant any Jew who will move into one the amount of $20,000 cash,[164] additionally their mortgages are subsidized. The largest percentage of new settlers is Russian Jews and other East European Ashkenazim, none of whose ancestor's ever lived in the Middle East. The total illegal population of zionists in the West Bank is now 534,223 of which 314,132 live in Kibbutzim. The rest are in Jerusalem where Palestinian property is being stolen on a daily basis. Growth proves a continuous colonialization 1948 [2,810], 1972 [10,608], 1993 [106,595], 2004 [411,156], and 2010 [534,233]. You can see by these numbers the exponential growth of colonialization primarily with recent Russian Ashkenazi immigrants.

---

162. Radical Zionists most of which are communists.
163. Fourth Geneva Convention Article 49
164. Provided by American foreign aid for resettlement (100,000 Shekels)

The Historic Implications of the Balfour Declaration

The Source of Middle East Terrorism

The Balfour Declaration was the dirtiest piece of political treason ever committed in world history. As previously stated General Allenby granted the entire Levant to the Palestinians in perpetuity if the Palestinians would ally themselves with the Crown and defeat the Ottoman Turks in WWI. London was very aware of this. Allenby had asked permission to make the deal with the Grand Mufti. The British Expeditionary force was led by Archibald Murray and had resulted in a stalemate before Cairo. Allenby the new commander saw himself greatly outnumbered and outgunned by the Turks and due to his inability to get more troops from England because of WWI commitments in France, he made the deal with the Grand Mufti securing Palestine forces as a British ally. The written agreement was that if the Palestinians helped the British defeat the Ottoman Empire in Egypt that the Palestinians would be granted autonomy in their Palestinian homeland in perpetuity, which would be guaranteed by the Crown.[165] No thought was given in London to the fact that in 1917 the entire Palestinian state had been given to the zionists. The Balfour Declaration was named after its author Lord Arthur James Balfour.[166]

Lord Arthur James Balfour

The declaration is a manifest of political lies. First, the Crown in full knowledge of this declaration made a subsequent agreement with the Palestinians to grant them autonomy in the same region in 1917. Second, Palestine had been under Ottoman rule for 366 years, and before that had been part of the Byzantine Empire for 1,077 years, and was under Constantinople Christian rule for over 1,000 years before that. The Crown had absolutely no right to give this land to anyone. In fact Palestine as part of the Levant had not been autonomous in over 3,000 years. Third, the Crown was fully aware by 1919 that their grant in the Declaration, protection of religious and civil rights and freedoms, were totally impossible for them to enforce. Fourth, any fourth grader will understand that the declaration is unenforceable in its entirety by a nation that is 2,245 miles removed from the Levant.

The Jewish and zionist claim that they have rights in the Palestine portion of the Levant is based in Biblical pre-history and has no factual evidence. It is based on verbal history as passed on by the Hebrews. Furthermore it has no relevance upon Ashkenazi who were never residents of the Levant and did not become Jews until the 6th century AD. The only documentation we have is from Roman times in which the Kingdom of Judah in 50 BC consisted of a tract of land bordered on the west by the Philistine City States, on the south by the Kingdom of Edom and the tribal lands of Arubu, and on the east by the Dead Sea, and the north by the Kingdom of Israel that was bordered on the north by the Phoenician States, and the west by the Mediterranean Sea and the east by Aram-Damascus. This autonomy was a short lived one, prior to that it was part of the Babylonian empire and prior to that it had been part of the Pharaohic state of Egypt. Again the authors admonish the reader to remember that the residents of that region in 50 BC were not Jews they were Hebrews. Today's Jews are over 95% Ashkenazim and have no relationship with the Levant.

Lionel Walter Rothschild
2nd Baron Rothschild

Why the declaration was made is another fact of history unreported by the mainstream media in any of its forms. At the end of WWI the British government was bankrupt. They had two options: borrow money from America which was wealthy, or go hat in hand to Baron <<Rothschild>> the world's wealthiest man, a peer of the Realm. They went to <<Baron Rothschild>> who was at the time also president of the World Zionist Congress. Rothschild was a hard bargainer; they would have been better off with the Americans. His deal that was accepted was the Balfour Declaration and control of the Bank of England, both of which were granted. There are a couple of interesting issues with the Declaration. It was not written on official British Foreign office stationary, and Balfour signed it but not as the Foreign Secretary and missing all his titles.[167]

165. Summer 1919

166. The **Balfour Declaration:**

> Foreign Office
> November 2nd, 1917
>
> <<Dear Lord Rothschild>>,   (President of the World Zionist Congress)
>
> I have much pleasure in convening to you, on behalf of His Majesties Government, the following declaration of sympathy with the Jewish Zionist aspirations, which has been submitted to, and approved by the Cabinet.
>
> "His Majesty's Government view with favor the Establishment in Palestine of a national home for the Jewish people, and will use their best endeavors to facilitate the achievement of this objective, it being clearly understood that nothing shall be done which may prejudice the civil and religious rights of existing non-Jewish communities in Palestine, or the rights and political status enjoyed by Jews in any country."
>
> I should be grateful if you would bring this declaration to the knowledge of the Zionist Federation.
>
> Yours Sincerely,
> Arthur James Balfour (Foreign Secretary is missing)

167. Foreign Secretary, 1st Earl of Balfour, KG, OM, PC, DL.

NOTE: There were three defining treaties or agreements that established the modern Near East. These are: MacMahon-Hussein correspondence of October 1915, the Sykes-Picot Treaty of 1919, and the Balfour Declaration of Nov 1917. These three agreements of treachery have made the mess now existing in the Middle East. The MacMahon Agreement made by Allenby triggered the alliance between the Crown and Palestinians, against the Ottoman Turks in WWI. Then in a series of letters the Crown agreed to a unified Arab state after the war, subject to the exclusion of Lebanon and Syria which were French colonies. The Sykes-Picot treaty separated Arabia into British and French (Blue and Red) zones in direct opposition to the reached and verified agreement with Sheriff Hussein as leader of the Palestinians. And the Balfour Declaration was in direct conflict with all the others, promising Palestine to the Jews who had never lived there in plurality of population. Out of all this came the partitions that created the nations of the Middle East, Syria, Lebanon, Jordan, Libya, Iraq, and Israel. Then in 1920 the San Remo and the 1921 Cairo conferences put the finishing touches on the nightmare. It was the Crown's ultimate plan to get rid of the Jews in England.

A word about Judeo-Christianity
Is the invention of zionists.

Christian-zionists (Christians who are radical supporters of the state of Israel) beginning in the 18th century planted a bomb in Christian society by inventing a new hyphened word, Judeo-Christian. This new hyphenated word is akin to hot-cold, old-young, heavy-light—it makes no sense whatsoever—it is the use of two words as a conjunction that are unrelated and in fact opposite. Our very first query should be what is implied by this conjunction? Is it in fact, Ashkenazim, or zionist, or Jew, or Talmudic, or Judaism Jew, Protestant, Anglican, Catholic, or Russian or Greek Orthodox? Not unlike the actions of Ashkenazi in social discourse, they never clearly define if they are a race, religion, or a nationality; in fact they claim all these things and simply pick the most convenient for the situation at hand. To clarify, Ashkenazim are not a race they are a sub-grouping of the European Caucasian race, they are not a religion they are converts to a religion, and they can no longer be a nationality because their homeland was extinguished over 1,400 years ago. Zionism is not a religion it is a socio-political movement seeking to steal other people's lands to create a nation for themselves in the Levant. Jews in any true sense are Hebrews, and are only 3% of the total Jewish claimed population placing their total numbers at less than one million worldwide. Talmudists, would be believers in the Talmud, which would include zionists reformed, and conservative Jews of the 20th century. Judaism is a religion and nothing else. The words Judeo-Christian are not synonymous they are antonymous. They were invented for the sole purpose of obtaining Christian support for the state of Israel and for zionism, in more explicit terms to get Christians aboard in the fight against Islam, the rightful residents of the region.

The success of zionists in this endeavor is astounding. Through their almost total control of American media, especially movies, radio, and TV they have created a media system in which Protestant media preachers most of whom have become wealthy in the process, endlessly preach a zionist Judeo-Christian message.[168] Christian zionism is a religious cult. These kooks actually preach that; God will bless whoever will bless Israel, regardless of what it does, and God will curse whoever curses Israel. So according to this religious teaching it's okay for Israel to murder 2,000 civilians, 400 of which are children for the loss of three IDF infiltrators into Lebanon.

The present Judeo-Christian media blitz is the Iranian development of nuclear weapons. We know about this from <<Benjamin Netanyahu>>, John McCain, Lindsey Graham, <<Diane Feinstein>>, <<Charlie Schumer>>, and an entire troop of zionist politicians, all of whom know which side their bread is buttered on. Are they all in the Knesset? For the last 6½ years McCain and company have been saying that Iran will have a thermo-nuclear device in three months. The fact that Israel has over 400 nuclear warheads about 396 more than they could possibly need seems to be irrelevant to these twits. The fact that they have repeated this threat 36 times and been wrong every time seems also to have gone by the wayside. Come to think of it I remember the Weapons of Mass Destruction reported in the hands of Saddam Hussein in Iraq that Colin (Colon) Powell and George W. (WAR) Bush, were so adamant about, actually all based on misinformation produced by the Mossad.[169] Judeo-Christian is a total ruse, a misconception in religious terms, Christ said, "Turn the other cheek," the Old Testament said "An eye for an eye," the Tallmlud says, "Even the best Cuthean's should be killed," the three could not be further apart. Reading the Koran and the New Testament clearly demonstrates that Christianity has much more in common with Islam than it does with Judaism. With the enactment of the American Communications Act by Hillary Clinton, her husband was able to pass the law through congress, thereafter the zionists were able to consolidate their control of American air and print media.[170]

---

168. Paul Crouch, John Hagee, Hal Lindsey, James Dobson, Jerry Falwell, Joyce Meyer, and Pat Robertson.
169. Yellow Cake from Niger—it was forged papers by the Mossad to the Italian (SIM) Sevizio Informazioni Militari who sent it to MI5 who sent it to the CIA.
170. <<Newhouse, Clear Channel, (Radio) A7E, Abbe Raven, Comcast, Brian Roberts, CWTV, Dawn Tarnofsky-Ostoff, Discovery David M. Zaslav, Disney, Anne Sweeney, (Philip Miller) ABC. Paul Lee, Hears Entertainment, Scott M. Sassa, Home Box Office, Eric Kessler. ION TV Brandon Burgess, FOX Rupert Murdoch, MGM, Mayor Bruce Tuchman, NBC, Robert Greenblatt, PBS Paula Keger, Rainbow Media, Joshua Sapan, IFC, Jordan Sering, Showtime, Mathew C. Blank, Sonny Pictures, Steve Mosko, Turner Broadcasting, Philip I. Kent, Warner Bros. TV Bruce Rosenblum>>. Of the 67 positions in management in entertainment Jews hold industries 57. That can be converted into Jews are just under 3% of the population but are 87% of the media management.
The largest US Media corporations are controlled by: AOL, Time Warner, <<Gerald Levine, Universal Studios, Edgar Bronfman, Viacom, Summer Redstone, GE, Dennis Dammerman, News Corp Ltd., Peter Chernin, Walt Disney Co., Robert A. Iger>>, and that's 90% of American airwave and cinema media.

Anti-Semitism

Is an oxymoron.

It is absolutely disgraceful to hear members of the clergy fall into the anti-Semitism trap. This one is even worse than Judeo-Christian. The Semitic Caucasian race has two branches, Hebrews and Arabs. Therefore any person that is accused of anti-Semitism is opposed to Arabs and Hebrews. Since the percentage of Hebrews as part of Judaism is about 3% in the entire Diaspora including Israel, the word in application to modern Jews is an oxymoron, as it in fact only would apply to Hebrews and Arabs, not to Ashkenazi of the 21st century that comprise 97% of all Jews today.

Jewish and Arab residents of Jaffa in 1949.
PHOTO BY KLUGER ZOLTAN/GPO

Interior of Historic Main Entrance to the Karaite Synagogue Compound in Istanbul

The Reality of Zionism

Zionism is a nationalistic, socialistic, and theocratic political movement.

In the beginning the only Hebrew religious text was the Torah, the first five books of the Old Testament. Over time and more exactly during the Babylonian Captivity, this ceased to be and new writings no longer by priests of the Hebrews but by rabbi's interpretation of the Old Testament became prominent. This new writing was called the Talmud. It was no longer the word of God it was man's interpretation of what rabbis thought God said. There also began to appear Qabbalist text dealing with numerology. Soon the Babylonian and Jerusalem Talmuds became the prime religious texts of Judaism. Explanations and elucidations soon followed. It is factual to say that modern Judaism does not even share a similarity with the old Hebrew religion of the Old Testament, nor do modern Jews keep any of the old covenants that were reportedly made between God and the Hebrews. Thus we must examine why and how this occurred so as to gain understanding of our modern world in religious as well as social circumstances. It behooves us to keep our eyes on the ball to see what these zionists have planned for us.

In the Babylonian Captivity[171] a simple nomadic society was transported to the capital of the Babylonian Empire, Babylon. The impact on those Hebrews must have been a redefining experience. Babylon was the most advanced Caucasian civilization of that time. The Hanging Gardens of Babylon,[172] libraries, water delivery systems, sewerage, paved roadways, streetlights, an established bureaucracy managing the government, and a developed banking system. Think of this; these Hebrews were not even farmers they did not grow crops, they had no industry save weaving, they were nomads, they were illiterate, their entire religious texts were memorized and verbally transmitted. The first change was the elimination of the hereditary priesthood. The Babylonians had no use for Hebrew priests, and the memorization of the Torah was considered a waste of time. They replaced the priests with rabbis (lawyers) who went on to write the Talmud. The captivity lasted 70 years. In 505 BC the average lifespan was no more than 35 to 40 years. Only about a third of the Hebrews returned to the Levant after the captivity was over. It would be reasonable to assume that almost none of those returning had been born in the Levant.

At about the time of the return from the Babylonian Captivity[173] the Sanhedrin[174] of the Jews rejected God and turned their entire three-millennium old religion around. Corresponding to this change in the status of their religion a new and very different Jewish nation came into being. It was this change that Jesus Christ was opposed to. The founding patriarch of the new state, which developed after the crucifixion, was Pharisee[175] <<Rabban Johan ben Zakkai>>.[176] It was <<Zakkai>>, who set into motion the design for the Jewish people to adopt the Talmud and away from the Torah. This is assumed to have been for the world rule that the Sanhedrin felt Christ had cheated them out of. Demonstrating the impact of Zakkai, even today he is venerated with monuments in Israel, (during the siege of Jerusalem by the Romans <<ben Zakkai>>) double-crossed the Jews of Jerusalem and went over to the Romans. The Romans after taking Jerusalem made him "Patriarch of the Jews" the sole representative before the Roman state, senate, and Emperor of the Jews, and head tax collector of all taxes from the Diaspora for the benefit of Rome. Thereafter, the singular and underlying objective of the Jewish community became the undermining and destruction of Christianity, and it has remained so ever since.

In consolidating his power with aid from the Romans <<Zakkai>> created the Beth-din, a court of laws that superseded the Sanhedrin. And thus began the change of the Jews from a society ruled over by the laws of God as written in the Torah, to the rule over Jews by men by the Talmud, interpreted by lawyers.[177] Although the new body was also called the Sanhedrin it had no commonality with any biblical concept of Sanhedrin. With the destruction of the Temple, Rabban[178] founded the Jabneh Academy with the duty to write and compose new prayers, liturgy, and practices in accordance not with the laws of God but the laws of man—The Talmud. The Babylonian Talmud was already a fact of life as produced in Babylon. In the new laws the Talmud has precedence over all other Jewish writing.

Thus the new Jewish existence was very different from what <<Moses>> gave them. The rabbis as heirs of the Sanhedrin wrote text based on their personal opinions, individual bias, and an incredible hate of Christians—and later Islam. These rabbis compiled the Talmud, which is today's Jewish law. They were the sole arbiters of what is right or wrong, and how law applied in every instance over social, religious, moral, dietary, and all legal matters relating to Jews, their disposition, and their relationships with other cultures and religions. First it was expressed as tradition but in time it was written into the Talmud. Laws adapted and changed and thus with time Jewish law became an end unto itself, and the means by which the new class of rabbinical scholars (lawyers) were able to manipulate and control the society and thus the entire diaspora.

This new Jewry had no ties with the old Torah or practicing traditional Hebrew religion. They no longer practice the laws as set forth in the Old Testament, their religious leaders are not priests but rabbis (lawyers) readers and doctors of the law that they themselves wrote, interpreters of the Talmud. Without the traditions as set forth by the now departed priests of the temple and without their organized practices true Jewish tradition disappeared from the scene. There are only two remaining practitioners of the old Jewish religion. Both are severely persecuted by Rabbis; the Ethiopian Jews who were never exposed to the Talmud due to their isolation in Ethiopia, and whose priests are prohibited from religious practice in modern Israel (you will learn more of them later), and the Karaite Jews[179] who made an attempt to free themselves from the rabbinical dictatorship[180] in the 8th century AD. They accomplished this by denial of the Talmudic concepts as propagated by rabbis. They advocated a return to the old system of worship and the Torah as the prime religious text. The Karaite were relentlessly persecuted, and when the head of the Diaspora was transferred to Cordova Spain in the 10th century, rabbis finally succeeded in obliterating the entire sect. It is important to recall that when Spain was under Muslim rule before the Inquisition it was the most advanced nation in Europe. When the Inquisition came[181] and the Muslims were expelled, after they lost the war many Jews were also expelled. Those remaining in Spain as well as the rest of Europe and the Ashkenazi were now all subject to rabbinical tyranny. In order to maintain control of their flocks the rabbis demanded and the Christian church was more than pleased that Jews should live in ghettos.[182] While there is much bias against Jews by Christians as well as Muslims, it is certainly not a one-way street, with much animosity by Jews against non-Jews. In the end the story of victimhood does not play. Jews have been thrown out of over 100 places because of their hostile interactions with the indigenous populations.[183] If you have been forcefully removed from one after another locations in some instances three times, then you should look to yourself not at others.

Another important issue is the long list of UN resolutions since 1948, against Israel.[184] Almost all have been stymied by American UN vetoes. This of course makes America a pariah in the Middle East and to some extent the rest of the world. Americans should always remember that before Harry Truman accepted a $50,000 contribution for the DNC whereupon America became the first nation to recognize Israel, we had no enemies in the Middle East. Our basic choice is between 1.5 billion Muslims or 6 million Jews. America's obnoxious behavior in UN vetoes has time and again sided with the wrong people. We don't recall a single Arab spy against America but can name many Jews who acted not alone but with the active collusion of the Israeli government.[185] The continuously replayed scenario of, "Israel our closest and best ally in the world" is ludicrous. The top 30 most egregious spy cases in our history did not come from China, not from Russia, not even North Korea, and certainly not from Arab sources, every one of them was by a Jew. But it gets worse. <<Jonathan Pollard>> stole over 500,000 pages of intelligence related to American self-defense for the Israeli Mossad who paid him. This was not offensive technology it was defensive technology. He had been employed as a Naval analyst. After his arrest and conviction he was sent to prison. Israel has tried to get him released ever since and finally succeeded in the 21st century. After the Mossad got the information they sanitized it so sources could not be traced and sold it to the Russians, at the time America's most dangerous foe. On that line there is one other issue. Our newest jet fighter is the Lockheed F-35. The Department of Defense had issued two design contracts, one to Boeing the other to Lockheed. DOD purchased the Lockheed unit. Israel asked for and was provided the losers bid specification with the stipulation that they be held secret. Israel promptly sold the plans to the PRC (Communist Chinese) who promptly used the plans to build their own copy of America's F-35. These are not the actions of friends, but implacable enemies—never to be trusted—acting in the knowledge that their paid-off members of the US congress and other high US officials will protect them no matter what they do. *Deep State !*

This then brings us to the basic conceptual differences between Judaism and other monotheistic religions. We address this paragraph primarily to Jews reading this book. C. S. Lewis was an

Anglican Catholic convert from atheism. In the late 40s he hosted a radio program on the BBC. His program was, understanding right from wrong, ethics, and morals. Lewis was especially adroit at explaining Christian concepts. His many books and stories certainly attest to that. Lewis, speaking of moral law, claims it to be universal to everyone. The way he explains this is as a consideration made by man when faced with a difficult decision. "As you walk down a street you hear shouts for help, a man is drowning in a lake by the roadside. You are faced with a dilemma of three possible options:

1) You hear the shouts for help, assess the situation, and are now faced with:
    a) Self-preservation, which is your first consideration
    b) The desire to help another human being in trouble
    c) An inner voice, which tells you; you must suppress your self-preservation instinct and do what you can to save the drowning man."

The Talmud is emphatic in addressing this dilemma. If it is a Jew save him; if it is a non-Jew let him drown, he is an animal without a soul. This is one of the conceptual differences between Christianity and Judaism; it is in fact what Christianity boils down to. i.e. doing the right thing by your fellow man, even in cases of considerable personal danger. Not only is this missing in the Talmud, but also is in fact rigorously opposed by it. What Lewis brings to bear is that life presents moral choices between right and wrong. The fact that the Talmud comes down on the wrong side should be made very clear to all non-Jews.

In this our 21st century we can clearly see that our youth lack the ability to differentiate between right and wrong. This is based in a lack of religious education, the materialistic society requiring both parents to work in order to have the same amount of stuff as the previous generation, and the total lack of parental guidance due to so many single parent families. This is most pronounced in our Black communities where over three-quarters of children are brought up in single mother homes. No father often results in bad kids, especially boys. The state run education system, which is more akin to leftist brainwashing daycare than education, paints all issues in various colors of grey. Most teachers are female, and the AFT/NEA[186] has the single largest lesbian participation of all labor unions. Cultural Marxism (PC) one of the most rigorously enforced practices of American education also has a big stake in this abhorrence.

Chicago recently learned that most of their applicants for teaching positions couldn't pass standardized 8th grade reading tests—so what did Chicago do…they dropped that requirement!

The Talmud as you should be aware by this time is the absolute Jewish law under which all practicing Jews must live. It is also an instrument of segregation, gender separation, and Jewish hegemony, which has been attempted by all Jews for millennia. There are many restraints in the Talmud, which makes it impractical for Jews to integrate into Christian or Muslim societies. Having lived among Jews you begin to understand some of these issues. Your neighbor will not allow you into his house because as a Goim you will pollute it. If a Jewish woman takes a bath she must take care that her first encounter be with a Jew for if it is a Goim she must bathe again because she will have been exposed to someone unclean.[187]

In general terms Jewish rabbis who want to control their "flocks" foster the construct of ghettos. Ways to accomplish this is to denigrate Christ and Muhammad at every turn, to continuously insist on religious segregation, to build Jewish centers with sports, libraries, swimming pools, and other amenities, preach globalism, internationalism, open borders, so that the "flock" will not be exposed to Christians or Muslims and non-Jewish society will be excluded. No one can oppose these facts because the Talmud does an exemplary job of instructing Jews about it. In fact Mary is called a whore, and every Christian and Islamic saint is slandered and denigrated on page after page.

<<Bernard Lazard>> was a prominent banker; he outlined exactly what Jews think of themselves—*"[we are] energetic, vivacious, infinitely proud, and consider ourselves superior to all others. The Jews want power. We have an inbred taste for domination. Since our religion names us as 'the chosen of God's race' a fact we have always attributed to ourselves. We do believe ourselves to be above all others."* Talk about a massive superiority complex! (By the way, that is exactly what primitive African tribes think about their tribe!) There are several mistakes in his statement. To call the ugliest of the Caucasian sub groups vivacious is a real stretch. Proud of what? Superior as gonif's.[188] Not chosen by anyone but themselves. It is this superiority complex that is at the root of the "Jewish Problem". As has been demonstrated time and again, Jews are the problem and they and no one but themselves have created their Jewish problem. Jews encounter opposition by the fact that they, by their

actions have alienated themselves from the communities in which they live. Their desire for a "homeland" is simply the result of their inability to get along with the rest of the world who don't consider them to be "God's chosen people."

Had Western nations followed the model set forth by the Eastern Empire[189] and chosen to follow biblical law regarding usury based on biblical and Quran law and not allowed the Jews to control Western banking things would have turned out differently. They chose instead[190] to engage moneylenders, Jewish advisors, and Jewish bankers, as the course of financial expansion. With the then adopted fractional reserve banking, the Jews came to control the entire financial structure and through that the entire society. Once their trap was sprung the prey was lost in a never-ending cacophony of borrow, pay, loan, interest, principle, inflation, deflation, principal expansion and so forth. By the end of the 18th century they owned everything of worth. They started wars for profit financing both sides as they have ever since they entered the arena of banking, after the Babylonian Captivity, and that was over 3,500 years ago.

Loan capitalism is the very system we still have, as the Jewish control apparatus of all Western economies. It was the product that came out of the Babylonian Captivity and is the instrument used today to control societies. <<Baron Rothschild>> put it best, "If I can issue and control the money of a nation, I care not who makes the laws." Loan capitalism is a system in which wealth is measured in terms of debt, or more exactly, in which the currency (Fiat money) of the community is basically created out of the interest charged for bonds sold for future interest returns. This was the system used throughout most of the 20th century that was eventually replaced with the "Petrodollar".[191] The petrodollar system along with the previous one failed when interest rates dropped to under one percent as the W. Bush and then the Obama administrations tried to grapple with the depression that began in 2006. Issued government bonds could no longer be sold, there were no buyers. The Keynesian monitory system that had been instituted at the Breton Woods Conference in July 1944 was the crown of Jewish banking.[192] It resulted in the Breton Woods System, the crux of which was that each nation would adopt a monitory policy that maintained an exchange rate to the dollar, which would then be the international reserve currency. The IMF[193] would then be able to bridge any temporary imbalances. Fiat species no longer had to be backed by hard asset, so everyone

* Pg 79-80, Financial Terrorism by John F. McManus.

could just print money to their hearts content. This worked until the late 20th century when a worldwide economic collapse became imminent. The ECB[194] and the FRS continuously dropped interest rates until they were at 0.25% and could not be reduced any more. Absolutely no one would purchase a government bond that paid only 0.25% interest, with a 7.5% inflation rate. The Bankers then went to "Quantitative Easing," a ridiculous term for lack of another, which was for the FED to purchase its own loan papers. Sort of taking money out of your left pocket and putting it in the right and charging yourself 0.25% for the movement of the paper. The system began to totter. *Bernanke, Fed Chairman.*

This system is the massive fraud perpetrated by the Jewish banking consortium against the citizens of the world. It is usury on a scale beyond even what the Babylonians contemplated.[195] For many generations they have worked this system, to bring down one nation after another and one man after another, until now they jointly have 80% of the world's wealth. All the world's great empires fell to moneylenders. Constantinople, Rome, Spain, Holland, England several times, The Holy Roman Empire, all fell to the bankers. From 2,000 years ago to today they financed both sides of every conflict—Napoleon, WWI, and WWII included. In fact the Napoleonic war and its end at Waterloo proved to be the second largest windfall for the <<Rothschild's>>.[196] A unique feature of the Jewish money game was that they were not allowed to place pictures of men on coinage, (graven images) thus they used the Babylonian invention of credit instruments. (Fiat) This was only possible because the Kahal[197] demanded that all Jews stand behind the credit fiat issued by any Jew of the Kahal. Thus if a Jew banker in England issued a credit instrument to any individual that instrument could be cashed anyplace in the world by any Jewish banker. This is in fact exactly what the Knights Templar did before they were extinguished, minus the usury interest. The Jew bankers created a guaranteed paper document for payment of any debt. Naturally this served just like loans to governments, Popes, and emperors charged interest for the service, usually as today, based on an elapsed time formula. They then would discount the loan documents based on time schedules. Transactions functioned in the following manner. Should any Jew be unable to meet the obligations of an issued document the entire community would stand to make up the difference. In fact the guarantor could simply draw on the asset of any other Kahal member, the payment would not be due until the end of the Jewish year and according to the law would not be interest bearing. Interest bearing formulation is Biblically and in the Koran forbidden because it makes money without labor or raw material. Such transactions are forbidden between Jews, but we learn in the Talmud (Mosaic Law) that all is legal in transactions dealing with the "UNCLEAN" Christians, Muslims, and other non-Jews.

---

171. About 605 BC

172. One of the wonders of the ancient world

173. Apox. 535 BC

174. The word stems from Greek meaning assembly or meeting. See Numbers 11:16. They are in tribal terms a meeting of elders the Israel court of last appeal.

175. A member of an ancient Jewish sect distinguished by strict adherence to tradition and the Talmud. Presumed by Jews to be superior in sanctity.

176. 30 to 90 AD principal starting author of the Mishnah.

177. Rabbis are the interpreters of law.

178. Secondary name for <<Zakkai>>

179. A Jewish movement strictly following the Torah, (Hebrew Scripture) characterized by the Tanak (a) as the supreme authority in religious law, as opposed by the rabbinical concepts.
   (a) The traditional Hebrew text known as the Masoretic Text. (Old Testament)

180. Iore Dea 198-48

181. The Spanish Inquisition (Santo Oficio de la Inquisicio'n) established in 1478 under Isabella of Castile and Ferdinand II of Argon

182. The origin of ghetto comes from Venice. Actually not for Jews but for glassblowers. When Venice was at its height they had many artisans and wanted to keep secret their manufacturing methods so they banned them to islands. They did the same with Jews because the rabbis did not want them exposed to Goim.

183. Historical expulsion of Jews by indigenous peoples. (location is preceded by the year)

250	Carthage	415	Alexandria	554	Dioce'se	612	Visigoth
642	Visigoth	855	Italy	876	Sens	1912	Mainz
1182	France	1182	Germany	1276	Bavaria	1290	England
1306	France	1322	France	1348	Switz.	1349	Heilbronn
1349	Saxony	1360	Hungary	1370	Belgium		
1380	Slovakia	1388	Strasbourg	1394	Germany	1394	France
1420	Lyons	1421	Austria	1424	Fribourg	1424	Zurich
1424	Cologne	1432	Savoy	1438	Mainz	1439	Augsburg
1424	Holland	1451	Holland	1446	Bavaria	1453	France
1453	Breslau	1345	Wurzburg	1502	Mainz	1483	Warsaw
1485	Vincenzo	1492	Spain	1492	Italy	1495	Lithuania
1496	Naples	1496	Portugal	1498	Nurnberg	1498	Navarre
1510	Brandenburg	1510	Prussia	1514	Strasbourg	1515	Genoa
1519	Regensburg	1533	Napoli	1541	Napoli	1542	Prague
1542	Bohemia	1550	Genoa	1551	Bavaria	1555	Pesaro
1577	Prague	1559	Austria	1561	Prague	1567	Wurzburg
1569	Papal States	1571	Brandenburg	1582	Hungary	1593	Austria
1597	Cremona	1597	Pavia	1597	Lodi	1614	Frankfort

1615 Worms	1619 Kiev	1648 Ukraine	1648 Poland
1649 Hamburg	1654 Byelorussia	1656 Lithuania	1669 Oran
1669 Vienna	1670 Vienna	1712 Sandomir	1727 Russia
1738 Wurzburg	1740 Byelorussia	1744 Prague	1744 Bohemia
1744 Slovakia	1744 Livonia	1745 Moravia	1753 Coved
1761 Bordeaux	1772 Russia	1772 Poland	1775 Warsaw
1789 Alsace	1804 Villages Russia	1815 Lbeck	1815 Bremen
1815 Swabia	1815 Franconia	1843 Russia, Austria, Prussia	
1862 All regions of the United State under Grant's command			1866 Rumania
1866 Galatz	1880 Russia	1891 Moscow	1919 Bavaria
1938-45 All of Nazi controlled Europe		1948 Arab Countries	

184. UN Resolutions against Israel:
    1955 to 1992: 106, 111, 127, 162, 171, 228, 237, 248, 250, 251, 252, 256, 259, 262, 265, 267, 270, 271, 279, 280, 285, 298, 313, 316, 317, 332, 337, 347, 425, 427, 444, 446, 450, 452, 465, 467, 468, 469, 471, 476, 478, 484, 487, 497, 498, 501, 509, 515, 517, 518, 520, 573, 587, 592, 605, 607, 608, 636, 641, 672, 673, 681, 694, 726, 799, (65 in total resolution against Israel)
    UN Resolutions against Israel Vetoed by the United States:
    1972 to May 1990
    30 in total.

185. Jewish Spies Against America:
    <<Julius Rosenberg, Ethyl Rosenberg, David Greenglass, Morton Sobell, J. Robert Oppenheimer, Leo Szilard, Bruno Pontecorvo, Morris Cohen, Lona Cohen, Robert Soblen, Jack Soble, Victor Perlo, Lee Pressman, Jacob Albam, Nathen Silvermaster, Isaac Romeine, Alexander Trachtenberg, Israel Amter, Gus Hall, Philip Barr, Philip Carl Weissberg, Harry Dexter Weiss, Alfred Sarant, Harry Goldodnisky, Theodore Hallsberg, Yakov Golos, Armand Hammer, Samuel Dickstein, Jonathan Pollard.>>
    With friends like these you don't need any enemies.

186. American Federation of Teachers & National Education Association

187. Iore Dea 198-48

188. A Gonif is a disreputable dishonest person (from Yiddish)

189. Constantine's law

190. Charlemagne (Karl der Grosse)

191. The petrodollar was produced in the Nixon administration and was the brainchild of <<Heinrich Kissinger>> who negotiated a deal with the Saudis to base the value of the dollar on oil. A return for which the American Government would in perpetuity protect the Saudi Royal family in perpetuity.

192. Breton Woods Conference (United Nations Monetary and Financial Conference) was attended by the allies of WWII 44 nations and 730 delegates,

193. International Monitory Fund

194. European Central Bank

195. Usury comes from the Bible. It is a prominent issue for all members of the Book. (Bible, New and Old Testament, and the Koran. Compound interest is usury. Mortgages in which interest and principal are unrelated and calculated on a time basis that allows the actual interest charged to be ballooned from the given rate (say5%) to an actual unpublished rate of over 40%.

196. When the battle of Waterloo ended <<Rothschild>> agents communicated to London that Wellington and von Blücher (Prussian ally of the British) had lost. The London stock Market collapsed and <<Rothschild >>agents bought everything at 0-2cents to the dollar.

197. The Kahal is the social structure of the Diaspora. It is the social religious and political organization of the Jewish community. (Also Qahal)

Fractional Reserve Banking

Banking is international, anyone suffering the delusion that large banks are national is sadly mistaken.

The means used to achieve zionist control over governments, institutions, and individuals is called fractional reserve banking. It is the most misunderstood financial issue of our time. So, before we progress we must gain an accurate understanding of this complex issue. Simplistically, fractional reserve banking is the process whereby only a fraction of the deposited money in any bank is actually on hand and available for withdrawal by the depositor. Bankers claim that this is done in order to expand economies—a lie. Fractional reserve banking is an instrument to optimize bank profits at the expense of the depositor. The real story behind this is how much money the banks must hold of your deposits. The FOMC[198] of the FRS is the regulating organization. Here are the rules for 2016. First the FRS will pay member banks interest on required reserve balances and Excess balances. Hey, what a deal they get our money, and our taxes pay them interest on any funds they don't loan out to another sucker. Deposit requirements by member banks are:

Liability	% of Liability	Date
$0 to $14.5 million	0%	1.22.15
More than 14.5 million to 103.6 m.	3%	1.22.15
More than 103.6 million	10%	1.22.15
Nonperson time deposits	0%	12.27.90
Eurocurrency Liabilities	0%	12.27.90

Looking at the worst possible scenario for the bank, they will have to have available 0% of the total deposits in their bank for amounts under $14.5 million and 3% on amounts under $103.6 million and 10% for those over 103.6 million. So, let's do the math. You have a bank and your total deposited amount is $200 million.

$200,000,000 except amount 14.5 million = balance $186,500,000
$186,500,000 at 3% = 599,995.65 = balance $186,011,111
$186,011,111 at 10% = 18,601,110 = balance $167,410,001

Based on this the banker will be paid 0.25% interest on $32.58 million and can loan out the remaining balance of $167.42 million at the prevailing interest rates say 5% and then turn the entire equation over again and over again to the diminishing return. The total amount that he will loan out on $200 million is $1 billion $330 million. That's a great deal. Now you know why so many people want to be bankers. <u>This is the way to make money out of thin air.</u>

Well, we bet you thought that was it, well, no—there's much more. Let's look at the mortgage markets, the most profitable banking enterprises and the biggest rip-off. Suppose you were about to buy a house, and had agreed on a price, for the sake of argument let's say $200,000. You will pay down 10% so that you can get a better deal from the bank. Your mortgage will be $180,000 for 30 years at 4.4%. Terms: VA, Credit excellent, day 60 locked, veteran, partial disability, no previous VA loan, with my bank, Closing charge $7,787, VA rate 3.863% monthly payment $911.19. 30 years x 12 months = 360 payments = $328,028.84. Wait, you just borrowed $180,000 for a fee of $148,028.84 but actually that's only part of the story. Bankers know that in over 50% of cases the homeowner decides to move within about 15 years. What bankers do is called front-end loading. They separate interest payments from principal payments. They invert the percentages so that for the first 15 years you pay only about a third of the principal and two thirds of the interest. By doing this they actually triple the quoted interest rate from the 4.4% quoted to 13.2% this is on money that they borrow from the FED at 0.025% making a total profit on your mortgage of 12.95%. Do you know any place you can get secured investments that pay 13%? Then there is one other question. Why are they charging you an up front fee of $7,787? For the privilege of loaning you money on which they make a profit? The banks total profit on your mortgage if terminated in 15 years will be $67,920. Plus the additional front fee of $7,787 for a total of $75,707.

<u>The big business in banking today is not mortgages, or loans or even those exorbitant car loans. The big business is borrowing money from the Fed at 0.25% and investing it in the markets via hedge funds and other such instruments and the conversion of the 0.25% loan into federal treasury notes at 3 to 4% with a guarantee of a minimum 2.75% margin profit, completely secure with absolutely no risk. The taxpayers are on the hook for all interest payments via inflation.</u>

The driving issue in banking today for the large banks, you know those we can't allow to fail, is inflation. The average person so long as inflation is below 3% takes little notice. The problem here is two-fold, first is that the inflation in the last ten years has been almost constant at about 7.5% annually. The government reports on inflation BLS[199] claims an annual rate of $100, in 1980 as $287.30, in 2014 and for the last 6 years at 1.5% that's completely false. There are three reasons why government lies about inflation. #1 All government employees have a clause in their employment contract that stipulates that their salaries must be increased by the percentage of reported inflation. #2 Banks and government taxes increase with inflation, but your money is worth less, so payments are increased automatically based on the inflation index, but your real income decreases. #3 All government contracts and many labor union contracts have a clause that requires the employer to increase the pay of the employed by the government's calculation of inflation. From 1950 computed average middle class workers' incomes have actually fallen every year when computed in constant dollars. This is the primary reason why the middle class gets poorer and the rich richer every year.

With the XVI Amendment to the Constitution and our legislative bodies, relinquishing their power over the issuance, interest rates, coinage, and tax collection of monies they turned the entire American financial system over to a private consortium (actually a monopoly). The "Federal Reserve System" (FRS) is not Federal, as the name claims, it is not a Reserve because it has no reserves, and it is certainly not a System but a corporation.[200] The FRS is a government unto itself; it issues credit, prints bonds, and issues an order to the Department of the Treasury to have the Bureau of Engraving and Printing (BEP)[201] print up whatever they say. It sets the prevailing interest rates, it through the IRS acts as the collection agency, it controls every single thing to do with Americas' finances. The real problem with this system is that every corporate entity has self-preservation as a top priority; thus such a banking system is more interested in self-preservation and its own financial gain than the general good of the nation. This has become very obvious in the last 20 years in which the FRS acted not in accordance with national priorities but rather with enhancing its own position. The second and equally bad issue is its reliance on political pressure that is all but guaranteed in a system where the FRS is always dependent upon the actions of legislative prerogative.

One lie represented by the banking system (FRS) is their claim of worth. This claim was once upon a time based on gold and silver and then later on debt. then on oil, and now on air. During the Obama administration in 2012 interest rates on T-Bills had been so severely reduced that they could no longer find customers to purchase them. When inflation is understood by everyone to be over 7% and the government tries to sell bonds for 0.25% nobody will buy them. As a result the FRS began ordering the Treasury to buy their own debt. I know it sounds ridiculous and it is. Actually beginning in March, 2012 the Treasury purchased $85 billion of government produced debt every month for 14 months and then reduced that to $55 billion a month. The total to date (2017) is estimated at $4.7 trillion (which is not reported as part of the national debt as required). Additionally, every legislative demand for an audit of Fort Knox, the NYC bank gold deposits, and an audit of the FRS books has been blocked. Considering that there is no gold left in Fort Knox, and the NYC banks are drained, that's not really surprising. As to a FRS audit. it would reveal that beginning in 2012 the 12 branches of the FRS were instructed monthly to increase their credit balances by $70.8 million every month and beginning in 2013 by 4.85 million. Could you imagine what would happen to the CEO and CFO of any corporation found padding his corporate books by $70 million or $4 million a month?

Through the encroachment on the prerogative of the individual states, by the bankers they initiated the XVI and XVII Amendments, the usurpation of states' rights was consummated. State banks were stripped of their assets they went to the FRS system. The fact that congress relinquished their mandated constitutional rights is inconsequential. In any such system as now exists in America, the inevitable outcome is a conflict between the people and the bankers, that conflict is yet to come, but is boiling in the kettle of public opinion. This conflict will eventually include "Free Trade" the ✳ "Trojan Horse" of internationalists by which they have destroyed the machine tool industry in America. The consortium and multinational traders like Walmart, Target, and others combined with the banking industry, is a bargain made in hell, between multinational corporations and international banksters to systematically destroy American manufacturing in order to up internationalists profit margins. What has been accomplished in a very subtle way is that American sovereignty has been sacrificed on the altar of Ashkenazi banksters and internationalist tycoons.

✳ USMCA To replace NAFTA. Rockefeller + Kissingers dream!

* Anyone who thinks that the FRS is not a Jewish operation should consider <<Greenspan to Bernanke to Yellen>>—that's over 40 years of Ashkenazi FRS control. The largest contributors to political campaigns are trial lawyers, banks, drug companies, and of course the illegal drug industry and pornography, all of which are dominated by Jewish interests. The amounts of money involved are simply staggering. The legal drug industry turnover 1990 to 2000 is $8,500,000,000,000, trial lawyers just in Texas contributed $7,391,000 to Texas politicians in 2002, in 2008 illicit drug industry sales internationally were $352,000,000,000, and pornography outsells GM every year. First of all, your local banks are all involved regardless of the misinformation that Homeland Security and the NSA publish. The mammoth amounts are far too large for anyone but the big banks. Somebody obviously knows something. In Mexico, a drug republic, the Salinas brothers one of whom was the president of Mexico, were caught by the Swiss government with an over $100 million laundry scheme that was channeled through two NY banks, J. P. Morgan Chase and Citibank, both are FRS prime stockholders. Is someone trying to tell us that the FRS was unaware of multiple $50,000,000 transfer payments that went through two banks that they annually audit and who own large portions of FRS stock? Now, do you honestly believe that the FRS, CIA, NSA, IRS and all the rest of the alphabet soup of government agencies are not fully aware of who and what is carrying out cash transactions in the trillions of dollars? Do you honestly believe that "The American Patriot Act" prevents money transfers by FRS member banks? Thus the people are at cross-purpose to the power elites. Then there was the Washington Post, that paragon of leftist thought, running an article[202] that, "Cash-washing on such a huge scale was inevitably done through the FRS, as was discovered by the congressional committee investigation into the matter." Then the GAO[203] advises that the worst offenders were Israel (our "greatest ally"), Russia, the Ukraine, and the soon to be North American Union's co-member Mexico. All those transactions would be through the central banks of those nations who do not deal with your local S&L. This will put to rest any belief that the Homeland Security and NSA matters have any credence relating to average citizens financial behavior.

Back in the 14th and 15th centuries the Spanish king Charles V through the Inquisition fought hard to expel Jews who had during the Moorish ascendency gained control of Spain's banking and finance business. A full third of the Jews living in Spain converted to Roman Catholicism and by that act retained their position in Spanish society. In fact numerous Jewish Spanish families had their sons become priests some even bishops, which cemented their social positions. After this period European economic history was shaped by an alliance between royals, the church, and the Jew bankers. They were interdependent from the 14th century forward.

It is simple to follow how the finances of Europe, then the British Empire, and then America gradually came under their control. It was a deal made by rabbis back in the formation of the diaspora with mammon. The deal was to turn away from God, to turn society and man into a bunch of money-grubbing materialists and elevate the Jews as the bankers of the entire enterprise, it's in the Talmud, it's in the Protocols, but if you really want to see it up close read the Protocols of the Learned Elders of Zion, which will make it all very clear.

Note: This quote is by President Woodrow Wilson after he had signed the passage of the XVI and XVII Amendments. "I am a most unhappy man. I have unwittingly ruined my country. A great industrial nation is controlled by its system of credit. Our system of credit is concentrated. The growth of the nation, therefore, and all our activities are in the hands of a few men. We have come to be one of the worst ruled, one of the most completely controlled and dominated government in the civilized world. No longer a government by conviction and the vote of the majority, but a government by the opinion and duress of a small group of dominant men."

Read: The Committee of 300 and The Tavistok Institute Of Human Relations by Dr John Coleman.

---

198. Federal Open Markets Committee
199. BLS Bureau of Labor Statistics
200. Incorporated in the State of NY. Reported in the NY Times on Sept. 23 1914.
201. Bureau of Engraving and Printing
202. Article by Even Greider
203. Government Accounting Office (arm of congressional oversight)

Lucifer's Lions

Four corners on my bed
Four angels round my Head.

Mathew, Mark, Luke, and John
Blessed the bed my head lay on.
Darwin, Marx, Einstein, Freud
Evangelists of a new die,
Show me bliss to be enjoyed,
Drained to the lees, before I die.

Darwin tells me, I'm an ape,
In only a slightly different shape:
For Freud my ego's wholly bestial,
The sexual alone is celestial:
An if Einstein's space-time heaven
I may be relatively shriven,
Marx with messianic creed
Of envy, slander, sloth, and greed
Will send me soon heel-bound top speed.

Four corners to my bed…
Mathew, Mark, Luke, and John.
Let me not be put upon,
By pseudo-science or learned lie.

Four angels round my head
From Satan's pride of lions deployed
To baffle, swindle, and enslave us.
Michael, Gabriel, Raphael save us!

Let Truth's writ run, here as on high,
And falsehood, wingless, plumb the void.

Anonymous

101

Part II

The Balance of the World

Who holds the balance of the World?
Who reign O'er congress wither royal or liberal?
Who rose the shirtless patriots of Spain?
Who kept the world, both old and new, in pain?
Or pleasure? Who makes politics run glibber all?
The shade of Bonaparte's double dealing?
Jew Rothschild and his fellow Christian bearing!

Lord Byron 1818

Controversial as this book is we have taken care to research each of the contestable facts and subjected them to multiple informational sources. The authorship of revisionist books results in two immediate responses; firstly vilification and slander against the author, and secondly the attempt by opponents to destroy the credibility of the text, that is not to mention excluding it from review in the Lamestream media. We believe that discrediting this book will prove to be challenging for any of its opponents. It is a sad comment that the release of honest information in the 21st century should be so impeded by Cultural Marxism (PC), the media, book publishing and distribution, magazines, radio & TV. Most news print is under the control and influence of a very small group of individuals, all of which walk in lockstep with the zionist Marxist drummers.

The Kulturkrieg raging in America today is resulting in the rapid disintegration of our heritage and is managed by a group of zionists whose purpose is the elimination of Christian unity. They simply feel unsafe in any society that they do not control, and for that matter even when they control it, as in Israel. Following the examples of Stalin and Mao, they are still determined to exterminate any opposing individuals—real or imaginary. This is the story of Judaism from the 5th century BC to today, they will not assimilate, they refuse to accommodate alternative views, and they are "A People Apart" or as they claim "The Chosen of God". This sort of sentiment is not an inducement for cooperation. From the Babylonian Empire to Rome, Napoleonic France, Germany, and the American War Between the

States, there is no time in history that they were able to get along in societies with which they interacted. Worse, the moment they attain a few percent of the overall population they begin to scheme for control. The sad thing in America is that a large segment of Christians,[204] characterized as Christian-zionists, misled by TV and radio evangelists, are radical supporters along with many politicians.[205] This gives them inordinate political clout in legislative matters. In the absence of any serious opposition and the support of many unknowing others, and those seeking favors from them, they have come to control much of our society just as envisioned in the Protocols. By dividing their opponents into small splinter groups they prevent unity of opposition. Through these[206] social means, our culture, and Christian cohesion, are being torn to bits, while the pathetic sophist academics and the controlled media cheer from the sidelines. The value system[207] is and has been systematically destroyed by the zionist menace. Our Western Caucasian Christian society has lost its moral compass that served us so well for 2,000 years and our society and America are being destroyed from within as you read this.

In former times we were the best, most accomplished peoples of all time. Today we are but the servants of our zionist masters. Promotion is no longer based on what you know and what you can do, no, today promotion is based on what zionist you know and how well you can kiss his behind. All this is in complete opposition to the basis of America as established by our forefathers.

These new systems imposed on us are alien to our society, and are disruptive of our republican ideals. Social and political systems do not function in a vacuum. The interrelationship between economics, politics, morality, religion, and social behavior cannot be logically separated. These Jews who today are the capitalist owners of all, are not satisfied with just ownership they want to control it all. They are plotting the destruction of our nation, the elimination of nationalism, destruction of our religion, the merging of races, societies, and nationalities, while rigorously segregating themselves. They have altered our value system to one of crass materialism, with pantheism as our religious base. Ethics and reason are thrown out the window in domestic and foreign policy, we see but one unity it is in zionism; they seek the dominance of all opposing peoples and systems of life. The republican principles of our forefathers are being crushed to create a worldwide feudalistic dictatorship by Cultural Marxist zionists.

Our schools now teach our children that they live in a "democracy," never considering that no democracy in history ever survived for more than 40 years. Once the populace understands that they, by a simple majority of one, can vote themselves free stuff, and politicians understand that by offering and giving free stuff, can ensure re-election,[208] the jig is up and the system collapses. Hillary Clinton & <<Bernie Sanders>> with 50% of our voting population on some form of government dole recently demonstrated that we are now at the breaking point. In a republic which is what America always was, actions of social and political determination are the product of rules, in our case the Constitution and the Bill of Rights not by the arbitrary opinions and norms of the populace. Citizens are thereby always fully cognizant of the intent of and application of the law, which in a democracy is not the case because law can be changed by a simple majority vote, to comply with the norms of the day. Zionists love their alternative way[209] because it allows government the possibility of manipulation and "Selective Enforcement".[210] This is what the Supreme Fools are accomplishing with their view that the Law, Constitution, and Bill of Rights are "Living Documents" open to their personal whims. As Dr. Ben Franklin so aptly put it when queried by a lady outside the Continental Congress in Philadelphia, "What have you brought forth Dr. Franklin," to, which he replied, "A Republic if you can keep it Madam." We are failing miserably!

Benjamin Franklin

The difference is huge. Zionists have from the first day they arrived on our shores exerted every effort to disrupt and or destroy our Republic for their own gain.

' This New Order, or New World Order, or as <<Heinrich Kissinger>> CFR in his new book calls World Order, has been in development by the Jews for many decades. It is, while not named, the running theme of the Protocols as well as <<Marx's>> Communist Manifesto. The theme is identical for both.

New York Times Bestseller

Henry Kissinger World Order

Henry Kissinger

105

In today's America the Kulturkrieg is in full bloom. The zionists are working hard through their control of the media to stir up inter-racial animosity and violence (especially between Blacks and Whites) by presenting fake and exaggerated news designed to inflame the more gullible individuals of both sides. These groups must realize that there is much to be gained from our mutural cooperation rather than mindless externally sponsored antagonism. Jews have supported racism from day one. A White suffragette started the NAACP with the aid of 4 other Whites.[211] The Jews especially from NY have funded and supported all Black movements, most

were started by Leftist or communist Caucasians. The simple truth is that racial strife is an advantage to Jews; it keeps people's eyes off what is really taking place. Perhaps that is why <<George Soros>> (Geörgy Schwarz) funded the riots in Fergusson with $33,000,000. Thus the orchestration of racial division is set in zionism with Black against White, Hispanic against Black, rich against poor, men against women, young against old, queer against straight—every possible

George Soros

group of citizens has been drafted into the Kulturkrieg. While all this transpires Jews endlessly portray themselves as victims, victims of oppression, victims of genocide, victims of the holocaust, victims of Whites, Blacks, Hispanics, even chickens.[212] While all this is transpiring behind the scenes Jews are ruthlessly perusing extortion from any group of people that through their hard work have become successful.[213] All this is attributable to the myth of victimhood. Through this they have inched themselves as well as the state of Israel much of it from gormless people who through self-deprivation want to make amends for mythical wrong. It is a fact that without a constant inflow of cash from Germany and America the Israeli socialist theocracy would have collapsed by 1950.[214] To place all that into perspective the founder of modern zionism <<Theodor Herzel>> in August 1902 said, "When we sink we become revolutionary proletariat, the subordinate officers of the revolutionary party; when we rise, there rises also the terrible power of the purse."

Thus the bonds that tie Americans as countrymen to their communities are being systematically weakened. All this is to the benefit of the international banking cartels and corporations. "Free Trade"

Soros is a board member of the CFR. London School of Economics!
It's happening today - 4-21- 106 *George Floyd & riots;*

another slogan of the internationalists to undermine American small business manufacturing and family farms is another tentacle of the process. Twelve million American blue-collar workers have lost their jobs, while 57,000 small manufacturing enterprises were forced out of business, all the while hundreds of family farms have been bought out by multinationals, all so that consumers could buy goods made in China for a higher price at lower quality, with bad food thrown in.

In the meantime there is an entire orchestra playing a new tune—the ridiculous notion that multiculturalism befits society. Advertising of mixed race families is relentlessly brainwashing Americans, especially in TV advertising, the constant message is that mixed race is beneficial for society. We find that odd, considering the mutts are dirt-cheap and thoroughbreds are expensive, that breeding a Chihuahua with a Grey hound will not produce a race dog, why can't mules reproduce, would you breed an Arabian race horse with a Belgian draft horse, hell no the product would be worthless. Would you breed your citizens who have average IQs of 100 with foreigners with average IQs of 70? So where is the benefit in racial mixing? That is, by the way, biblically prohibited, which is why Jews don't do it. (Adultery is not sex with another while married; it is sex with someone of a different race.) What good is the entire animal kingdom; in fact the process of natural selection if we turn it all upside down as a species, while the false theory of evolution is pressed upon us.[215] The fact that minorities commit over 85% of all crimes simply tells us a lot about multiculturalism.

Biblical early Hebrew history is a record of wanton destruction, continuous war with all different religions, and ill tolerance of others; it is a narrative of violence not seen in any other religious texts. The chronicle is highlighted by human sacrifice, idol worship, genocide, and mass murder, and war at the behest of Jewish priests who had total power over the theocracy that was Judea. As a national organization as well as individually they have practiced organized, systematic, and ideological racism against every group of people with which they came in contact. The present antagonism and hostility toward Islam and Christianity is not new, it has been happening for millennia. The moment they attained military superiority, genocide for any neighboring or weaker government or smaller states was the order of the day. Their God through priests' and later rabbis told them to do these things. Priests always had the ability to talk to GOD!

Bill Gates owns over 242,000 acres of farmland. Thats why I object to billionaires!

Ancient Egypt was a blooming civilization already 3,000 years old when a wandering tribe of nomadic Hebrews came upon them. The "Book of the Dead"[216] is where much of Hebrew mythology came from.

Karl Richard Lepsius, *first translator of a complete* Book of the Dead *manuscript.*

204. About 40 million
205. Sarah Palin, John McCain, Rosa DeLauro, Michelle Bachmann, and scores of others.
206. Used means, Homosexuality, Feminism, Pornography, Open borders, Control of Public Education, Control of banking & media, free trade and legislative action.
207. Hard work, honesty, entrepreneurship, Ethics, and morals
208. Legislative re-elections in America of incumbents are now at 88%
America now has 49.6% citizens on government dependency or about 150 million (Heritage Foundation 2013 Index)
209. Jews migrated to early America in two waves. First a very small group of Sephardic Jews in the late 1650's, New Amsterdam, Newport, Charleston, Savannah, then a large Ashkenazim group in the 1740's Not one was involved in the foundation of America or the establishment of our government.
210. Selective enforcement is when government has produced a volume of laws so large (IRS) that no person can be familiar with all the laws, that government uses those [unknown] laws to be selectively enforced to frighten the populace into compliance of even non-existent laws.
211. <<Mary White Ovington, Oswald Garrison Villard, William Wilson Walling, and Henry Moscowitz>>.
212. In the ceremony called Kapparot performed on Yom Kippur a chicken is swung over the head and the sins of the participant are transferred to the chicken.
213. Case in point: The extortion of Swiss banks and insurance carriers by unproven claims that Jews had deposited money in Swiss accounts and insurance that was never paid out. In fact Nazi law under penalty of death prohibited the transfer of funds for deposit accounts and insurance contracts out of Germany from 1938 to 1945. There were transfers from Swiss accounts that had been established before the Nazis but they were only made under the signature of the account owner. (ICE Independent Commission of Experts Switzerland and WWII)
214. In 1999 Germany provided $5 billion in reparations for slave labor. 1) The Nazis paid internees with script. 2) Less than 1/2 of KZ internees were Jews. Why are they the only ones getting German reparations—could it be the squeaky wheel scenario?
215. The theory of evolution is called a theory because it is unproven. Evolution as proposed by Darwin is dubious at best. That the genetic material we are made of changes in development is without doubt. But the concept that Homo Sapiens stemmed from monkey is stupid. There have been more hoaxes and errors made by anthropologists than any other known science. It should also be noted that anthropology like psychiatry, sociology and psychoanalysis are all Jewish soft sciences. Soft science is not based on fact but theory. Biologic evolution states that we evolved from our ancestors. Our ancestors never included monkeys.
216. "Book of the Dead," ancient Egyptian funerary text of 1550 BC origin. Probably where most of the Old Testament came from.

✱ See pg 221, My Awakening by David Duke.

The Community
The Kahal

*At the time of the war between the United States in the
late 1850's, one pound sterling was equivalent to about
11 Gulden, or 22 Franken, or 5½ Thaler. Between 1790 and
2,000 consumer prices have risen 4,600%. Thus one pound
sterling in 1790 would have a current American dollar purchasing
power of $4,600 in today's money. The largest part of these
funds have ended up in the pockets of zionist bankers.
The process is called inflation! Its how bankers make real profit.*

The Jewish community as stated above is engaged in victimhood
as a prime bargaining chip to extort funds from other societies. They
have used this process most effectively in the last 71 years or since
the end of WWII. Realty indicates that about 33 to 35% of Nazi
interns were Jews, in fact Russian POW's and criminals were more
numerous. Why is it that we don't hear complaints from Gypsies,
Free Masons, and Catholic and Anglican priests, Russian POW's, or
even homosexuals, we only hear from Jews. The entire holocaust is
a huge money making machine that has been internationally consummated. Prof. <<Finkelstein's>> Book "The Holocaust Industry"
more than proves that. That is not to say that Jews as well as other
internees were not harshly treated, but the entire six million, is a
fable for profit.[217] The total amounts extorted since WWII is well over
one trillion dollars. What about the Palestinian Holocaust?
The authors do not deny that the Nazis persecuted Jews, among
many other ethnic and gender groups, but the 6 million is a farce. The
rest of this book will verify that. It has in fact been scientifically proven
that the claimed numbers of Jews killed in KZ was totally impossible
based on the facilities available and liquidation on that scale would
have taken over 60 years based on a 24-7 operating schedule.[218]
Concentration camps by the way are a British invention of the Boer
Wars.[219] The Jewish Bolsheviks murdered far more humanity than
died in the entire second WW.[220] Could it be, that one of the reasons
for the holocaust myth, is to divert attention from what they did?
The Palestinian Holocaust is real, it has been going on for 70
years and America is sponsoring it with funds and weapons to Israel.
The hostility of all societies against Jews, when examined from a
neutral perspective clearly demonstrates that Jews are the cause of

their own created problems. As a religious group, Jews have one of the longest recorded histories. This history amply shows that they have always been unwilling to co-exist with the cultures and societies into which they moved in the last 3,000 years. Their hostile behavior becomes intolerable and results in their expulsion.

On the issue of race, anthropologists separate Homo sapiens into Caucasoid, Negroid, Mongoloid, and Australoid. Jews and Arabs are of a subgroup of the Caucasoid race called Semitic; Ashkenazim are of the Caucasoid sub grouping of Turkmen. There is no such thing as a Jewish race. It is simply another of those annoying zionist efforts to confuse and befuddle issues. Jews invariably call themselves a Race, Religion, or Nationality, whichever suites their advantage at the time of confrontation. Wishing something were so, unfortunately for them, does not make it so. With today's DNA testing we can clearly determine the racial identity of any human and place him within the corresponding racial group and sub-group. The only commonality within the entire Jew group is religion, and that has nothing to do with race or nationality.

A challenging concept of the latter 20th century was the one of racism. We believe that we can all agree that racism requires the practitioner thereof the desire to lord it over others. This concept in broad terms does not apply to the White Europeans, but most certainly to the Semitic peoples. Both Jews as well as Arabs have over history demonstrated remarkable expansionist and domination traits, Christianity in strict historic terms only did that violently during the Crusades, which was actually an attempt to return the Levant to Christendom as it had been from 330AD to 1282 AD almost 1,000 years before it was forcefully overtaken by Islam. Understanding the differences among races does not make one a "racist." The presence of religious (God's "chosen") or moral superiority over others is what makes one a racist. No one can say that Jews and Ashkenazim have not amply demonstrated those traits from prehistory right into the 21st century.

---

217. Germany from end of WWII to 2,000, $110,000,000,000 American aid to Israel $800,000,000,000, Indirect American aid in tax breaks. Resettlement funds etc. $50 billion. Then there are the Swiss banks and insurance carriers; never mind that the Swiss took in 40,000 Jews and facilitated over 1,000,000 transit papers for Jews, out of Nazi Germany.
218. Leuchter Reports
219. Boer Wars (RSA) for the killing of Afrikaner women and children.
220. Over 66 million in Russia (Kremlin release 2010) and 100 million in China. That does not even count Georgia, Poland, Belarus, German POW's, Hungary, Yugoslavia, etc.

Morals & Ethics

Any Republic without a moral and ethical anchor, that turns itself Into a democracy, will decline and will in time become totalitarian.

The Greeks, arguably the founders of Western Civilization, knew well and clearly what defined their culture. The Greeks understood that community; race, religion, and culture were closely related. Rome for its formative years[221] well into the Valentinian Dynasty[222] was also well aware of this. We have come to accept that economics is another factor not to be omitted. Today revisionist historians are universal in their understanding that civilizations collapse because the harmony of racial, religious, economic, and cultural cohesion is disrupted. This, in past history was caused by the importation of slaves; open border polices, geographic expansions and inclusions of other cultures, and trade policies that destroyed domestic production.[223] The culture was diluted, trade changed from domestically produced goods to imports, the population got lazy, and government began massive vote buying polices through the distribution of free services.[224] The current Ashkenazim supported and instituted programs of multiculturalism and the concept that all humanity is equal is scientifically nonsense—and an affront to common sense. Every group and every individual is unique not "equal." Multiculturalism is a means by which society is debased.

The proof of the differing characteristics of race lies in the fact that a forensic doctor or anthropologist can after examining a skeleton determine if it was male or female and what racial group it belonged to. PC foolishness has today reached heretofore unheard of absurdity: women in combat infantry, female firemen, within this decade we will see dwarf basketball players, and female ice hockey stars. The brotherhood of man as so often touted in academia, has been perverted to a culture with no differences, a society in which all beings are equal. Out of this concept will come a society without variance and the degeneration whereby all truth is gray, and all things are equal. A man cannot bear children, a woman is physically weaker than a man, large racial differences in IQ, violence, standard of living, etc., women have more patience than men, and sociologically men are more mathematical and mechanical and women are more verbal and caring. These are indisputable facts of science. The Ashkenazim are the instigators of all of this multicultural crap. It does not go without notice that they practice the most rigid racial and gender[225] separation on the planet. They have even built an apartheid-separating wall between themselves and their genetic cousins the Arabs. Through these actions our culture, Christianity, our Western Culture, have, and continue to be undermined so that Ashkenazim can rule us. That is the ultimate goal as presented in the Protocols, Communist Manifesto, and the Talmud, all of which they take very seriously. After all, if you believe that you are the chosen of God, a people apart, then equality before the law, and social, religious, cultural and financial equality is all rubbish.

Reality Check re "God's chosen people"... If they can show conclusive proof that their God exists and that He/She/It has chosen them as "superior" to the rest of us then we should take them seriously; otherwise they should be treated as parasites seeking power over the rest of us.

Around us we see politicians, religious leaders, and media pundits, all of whom profess their undying loyalty to transnationalism, multiculturalism, globalism, gender neutrality, open borders, and all the rest of the Ashkenazim-isms. Support for the ever-expanding government bureaucracy seems unending. This cabal of syncopates that includes over 70 members[226] of our legislative body who give their allegiance not to America, but to the Ashkenazi that provide the funds to run their re-election campaigns, and act as if they were in the Knesset not the U.S. congress. Profit for them is huge[227] almost every elected legislator is a millionaire when he retires from office. These people have a special value system; expediency, capitulation, and perpetual compromise of any principles or ethics they might have had before being elected. Within six months of election their sole and unrelenting interest is re-election, all efforts are directed toward that goal and nothing else, other concerns are window dressing. Thus through the gutless acts of this class we now have a national debt that cannot be repaid because it is 35% larger than the national economy and growing.[228]

The transformation of America from a Constitutional Republic to a Democracy and now to a corporatist totalitarian state (kleptocracy) is today's reality. Multinational corporations have become larger than most governments. These megaliths, through the power of the purse, control banking, transportation, manufacturing, distribution, law, and the legislature. They elect and decide who will be President through mammon.[229] In any such system in which the cost of attaining political office is so great (one billion for the presidency) the ultimate outcome is totally controlled by those who provide the money. They also decide where things will be manufactured; for this they pick the places with the lowest amount of government regulations, lowest pay for workers, no labor unions, lowest corporate taxes, and least environmental regulation. The best fit for these criteria are often some third world nation. This allows maximum profit. They also control banking and transportation and are thus able to undersell and destroy small and family businesses.[230]

America's all-prevailing optimism makes it difficult for our compatriots to see the dangers confronting our nation. Government schools, are dumbing-down our population in all subjects including math, science, economics, government, and history. The loss of religious instruction and the gradual secularization of society coupled with massive materialism have produced generations that see all issues in shades of grey; right and wrong are issues of the past. As the proverb states, "Those who don't know history are doomed to repeat the errors of their forefathers." Uneducated voters elect poor government. Our people are unable to grasp the severity of the issue; the blows directed at our society are understood by most as single-issue items, a grave miscalculation. Through exaggerated reporting of racial and gender issues they have separated Christians into many different factions, thus we have Second Amendment issues, abortion issues, open border issues, tax issues, race issues, and so forth, none seem to understand that all of them are the product of the same group of Ashkenazim, who are using these concerns to divide us. While we are all busy confronting one another, their agenda moves forward without our noticing. We lose—they win! It is a 20th century concept that man is destined to go on to ever-higher achievement; our technological prowess ensures it, we think. But if the Ashkenazim plan succeeds there will come a second Dark Age, a new feudalistic society this time based on corporatism and the dictatorship of the multinationals which are far more sophisticated and powerful than the princes and kings of old. We think ourselves to be omnipotent, virtual Gods; in fact we are inconsequential pimples in the realm of our universe and the eye of God. You disagree, well then. How about AIDS, Ebola, LBJ's "Great Society"[231] and all the thousands of issues we seem hapless to address. Additionally with our moral compass degaussed, we have been unable to solve any of our thousands of social problems. Our politicians think that the solution to every problem is throwing more of our (not their) money at it. Unable to distinguish right from wrong, the genie is out of the bottle, he will not go back in, and Western society crumbles just as Rome did and for the same reasons.

The spirit of internationalism and the culture of multiculturalism grounded in Ashkenazim controlled media and multinational corporations and banks are the new manifestations of the 21st century. The assumption of equality before the law has been perverted into a Cultural Marxist concept of total equality of everyone and everything—an absurdity. The late Pope clearly stated, "Democracy without morals and ethnical basis will, in a short time, turn into totalitarianism." We are almost there! In Dr. Krieg's book, *July 4th 2016 the Last Independence Day* published in 2000 by Hallberg he predicted the end of America.[232] Considering Change, Forward, and Hope the schlagwörter of the Obama progressives it may even be sooner. The aim is obvious, dilute the Caucasion race until all are beige, and equally stupid. We have already given up on the space race; patent applications are at the lowest level in decades, our population is unable to distinguish between right and wrong, and in military technology we are falling behind in vital areas.

We can surely accept that there have been Ashkenazim patriots. Likewise we must all be aware that this only occurs in converging advantage. What we mean is that Ashkenazim only become patriots when it serves their interests as well as ours, only when they coincide do they support us. We often hear that Israel is our best friend, consider the reason—we are their only friend and they surely are not ours. The system of Ashkenazim is always: "the Chosen People," their advantage first and there is no second. They committed the most egregious acts of espionage against us. Every one of these acts was for the benefit of a communist state or for zionism.

Jews are internationalists, a fact that cannot be argued. The reason is the Diaspora, which makes them akin only to other members of the Diaspora and alienates them from the societies in which they live. They do not like us, they know we don't trust them and with good cause, they don't even trust each other. Thus their allegiance is not to the societies in which they live, be they Christian, Muslim, Buddhist, or Hindu, their fidelity is only to other Ashkenazim. An

Ashkenazim views himself, first as a Jew, second as an Israeli, third as a member of his tribe, fourth as a member of a family group and never as a member of the society in which he has chosen to live. It has been taught to us that multiculturalism and internationalism are the wave of the future, that these are the forces of progress. This is true! "The forces of progress" to our destruction. This has been endlessly drummed into Western society until, the many of us have come to accept and believe it. This is a lie! The basis of Western man is the cohesion of our race, and since the third century, Christianity was the glue bonding us together.

Americans must appreciate the character of our forefathers, and the nation that they created. Today we seem as a society unable to make the right critical decisions in regards to the values necessary to advance our interests. The very concepts (brought forth by our opponents (the Ashkenazim) of infanticide, pornography, homosexuality, feminist perversions, open borders, and incompetent "propaganda-mill" schools are all designed to dilute our gene pool, mongrelize our population, and destroy our culture. Our failure to confront these issues promoted by academia, our media, our government, and internationalists is our undoing. The use of Cultural Marxism (CM) an Ashkenazim invention now expressed as Political Correctness (PC) in order to hide its nefarious origin is the academic tour de force of the Ashkenazim who infest our universities. The concept of immorality as an instrument of social change is nothing new, for an example the French Revolution and one of its most active supporters the Marquis de Sade.[233] The only limit imposed upon this perversion is the imagination of our desires. Surely the reader must understand where all this is leading us. Once society is devoid of its origin, separated from its religion, and infiltrated by degenerate foreign influence[234] the mob will take over and the society will collapse. If we do not as Western Man, of European origin, come to the realization that the concepts of moral and ethical behavior and Christianity are the course we should travel, we will become what those who are in mass immigrating into our nations had escaped from.

⁕ ^ How far has the perversion of our culture gone? We placidly allow the public display of the suspension of a Christian cross suspended in a jar of urine and a picture of the Madonna surrounded by depictions of female genitalia and elephant dung. Some deranged judge actually ruled that these items had redeeming social value, and then

⁕ Look at Democratic Party, federal level. anything goes!
Hillary Clintons a lesbian, progressives!

115

to top it off were protected by the first amendment. These jurists have turned the brilliant efforts of our Constitutional Congress on its head, in order to justify their own perverse opinions. This is the product of a "Living Constitution" in which the norms of any judge (frequently known to be crooked and morally incompetent) are deemed the appropriate opinion to be forced upon society. The courts have made themselves rulers of the people. Anyone who claims that a picture of a woman surrounded by pictures of genitalia and elephant dung or a cross-suspended in urine is first amendment-protected art is a pervert—or more likely someone with an agenda to destroy our traditional values and civilization. The judgment of the value of art is based on its value to society, if it has no value it is not art and if the observer lacks the ability to understand this he might consider returning to grade school and starting over—on second thought, he is already the perfect result of today's grade schools.

We don't know about you but self-degradation and the destruction of our society is not an endearing issue for us. Nor is a nation without values, or a basis of ethical behavior. Those aspiring to these ends should be aware that they tried it before in Rome, Constantinople, and then in the Weimar Republic in Germany, they ended badly every time. *2020*

Communist / Socialist Bernie Sanders a Jew running for US. President

221. 27 BC to 395 AD
222. 364 to 395 AD
223. Free Trade policies of the 80's through today.
224. Today food stamps, welfare, housing, fuel assistance, in the past gladiatorial diversions (Zirkus Maximus, etc.).
225. It is illegal for a Jew woman to marry a non-Jew in Israel.
226. Progressive Caucus, Black Caucus, Hispanic Caucus.
227. Pay $174,000. Tax deduction $3,000. Life insurance paid by taxes, retirement benefits after one term paid for by taxes, personnel aid pay $944,670. Office expense allowance, mail (franking privilege) $2,385,439. Legislative assistance $477,874, and MRA expenses allocated at representative's pleasure $1,195,554. On-line publication of documents, government printing office privileges, office furniture $40,000. (Congressional Research Service) (Estimated total cost per legislator $25 million annually.)
228. US economy debt about $23 trillion, national debt about $19.330 trillion.
229. The cost of running for president is $750,000,000, Senate $105,000,000, House $804,000,000.
230. From 2000 to 2014, 53,000 American small businesses shut down and 11.7 million American blue-collar jobs were eliminated.
231. To date since 1964 (LBJ's big promise to eliminate poverty) $24.8 trillion spent and today the same percentage of Americans are in poverty as in 1964.
232. Available from A2Z Publications LLC.
233. Donatien Alphonse Francois Marquis de Sade the libertine released by the mob from the Bastille.
234. Open borders, Illegal immigration, relentless visas, and amnesty for illegals.

Health care for illegals, drivers license, felons can vote, Sanctuary cities? (It's really crazy) 116

The Foundation of Zionism

While it is a simple matter to obtain a copy of the Bible, Old Testament, the Koran, the writings of Confucius, or any religious texts of the world, the various zionist writings, the Talmud, Mishnah, Gemara, and other zionist texts are another matter entirely.

Translations are few and difficult to obtain. Once the reader becomes acquainted with the content he quickly understands why.

From the Talmud:
My son, be more careful in observance of the words of the scribes (Talmuds) than the words of the Torah.

Erubin 21b (Soncino edition)

Unfortunately most people believe that the Torah, first five books of the Bible, are the basis of modern Judaism. This is not the case[235] as the Talmud explains. The Pharisees teach from the commentaries of rabbinical interpretations not from the Word of God. The Talmudic rabbinical commentaries are the supreme laws of Judaism not the Torah. Thus it is not God's word that Jews adhere to; rather the ranting of rabbinical lawyers. The Judaic scholar rabbi <<Yehiel ben Joseph>> clearly states "Further, without the Talmuds we would not be able to understand the passages of the Torah...God has handed this authority to the sages (rabbinical lawyers) and tradition (tradition established by rabbis) is necessary as well as scripture." Then at a hit against Christian priests and pastors he goes on to say, "Anyone who does not study the Talmuds cannot understand scripture." Yes indeed, we are far too stupid to be able to understand plain English, Greek, or Aramaic, we need a Jew lawyer to tell us what it all means. In modern terms we would call that job security. Synagogues today are the heirs of the teachings that were still verbal tradition at the time of the Pharisaic school[236] as later expressed in the Talmud. The Talmud did not come to be written until the Babylonian Captivity.[237] This is exactly the teaching that the Messiah (Jesus) opposed.

The precept of the Talmud of Judaism governs all the daily activities of Jews, as well as their social intercourse with non-Jews.[238] It is a fact of Jewish law that a Jew cannot accept a glass of water from a non-Jew. Thus Jewish communities of the diaspora remained and still today are separate from the societies in which they live. They are "A People Apart" preferring to live in ghettos and kibbutzim rather than among non-Jews. They build walls in support of this racial separation.

Ashkenazim have produced special Talmuds for Christian, Muslim, and Black readers in which all the racist commentary has been removed. This is verified by rabbi <<Tzvi Marx>>[239] who said, "We always have issued two different texts of the Talmud's[240] one to teach our own, the authentic version for

Rabbijn Tzvi Marx

our schools (kollel) and the other for dissemination to gullible Goyim for public consumption." This is of course completely in line with Baba Kamma (113a), which states that Jews may use subterfuge (lies) when dealing with Christians and Muslims. Hesronot Ha-shas lists both the original text as well as the second for non-Jew distribution versions, side by side.[241] Needless to say the new abridged version is now being sold to gullible Goyim as the true Talmud.

The supremacy of the Talmuds over the Torah may be verified by the current status of Black Ethiopian Jews whose society was isolated from the Babylonian Captivity. Ethiopian Jews are very knowledgeable of the Torah, but know nothing of the Talmud; their religion pre-dates the verbal texts of the Talmud. Ethiopian Jews are not allowed to perform marriage ceremonies or funerals in Israel. The Karaite sect of Judaism adheres strictly to the Old Testament (Torah) excluding all Talmudic teachings, they are the most hated and discriminated against Jews in Israel.

This brings us to the Mishnah,[242] which is the philosophic legal code of Judaism, and consists of 6 parts, sometimes called divisions, consisting of 63 tractates comprising Jewish law. Rabbis of Judea created it fearing that the verbal information could be lost. Since that time the text has been expanded may times and then called the Talmud. There are two basic Talmuds which are called the Mischnah commentaries. First is the Talmud of the land of Yisrael or the Yerushalimi (Jerusalem) Talmud. This text stems from about

400 BC. It is a commentary on the 1st, 2nd, 3rd, and 4th divisions of the Mischnah. The second that is much more in common use, is the Palestine Talmud of Babylon or in slang "Babi" which came from the Babylonian Captivity about 600 BC. It is a commentary on the 3rd, 4th, and 5th division of the Mishnah.[243] The commentaries of the Mischnah are called Gemara.[244] Both Talmuds are the personal opinions of the rabbis who wrote them.

The Babylonian Talmud is the one that modern Jews refer to. * Only if special notice is given will the Jerusalem Talmud be used or quoted from. If you examine a Talmud of the 20th century you will find many empty spaces on pages. These spaces if examined in older copies of the Talmud contain circles filled with blasphemies and insults to Christians and Muslims. The Polish rabbinical Synod in 1631 ordered that all such circled blasphemies be removed and be verbally taught to students. This is why you see Jewish students rocking back and forth as they memorize all the derogatory commentary about non-Jews. To gain an understanding of the enormity of size of Talmudic text with commentaries it comprises 12 volumes each of which has about 800 Pages, separated into six sections.[245]

To clarify an understanding beyond what was covered in the first part of this book we must look at some more Talmudic writings.

Yebamoth 98a — All Goi children are animals.

Baba Kamma 113a — Jews may use lies to circumvent Goi.

Baba Kamma 37b — Goi's are outside the protection of the law and God has exposed their money to Israel.

Abodah Zarah 22a-22b — Goi's prefer sex with cows

Moed Kattan 17a — if a Jew is tempted to do evil he should go to a city where he is not known and do evil there.

Zohar 1,25b — those who do good to the Akum (derogatory word for Christian)...will not rise from the dead.

Sanhedrin 59a — A Goi who pries into the law (Talmud) is guilty of death.

Baba Mezia 114a-114b — Only Jews are human, Goi are animals.

* CFR, Jew, Ruth Bader Ginsburg of US Supreme Court refers to it. The Talmud.

Sanhedrin 57a	A Jew need not pay a Cuthean (Derogatory word for non-Jew) the wages owed him for his labor.
Kethuboth 3b	the seed of a Goi is worth the same as a beast.
lore Dea 377,1	Condolences must not be offered to any Goi on account of the death of his servant or handmaiden.

To gain understanding the Torah always refers to the dead bodies of non-Jews as "Pegarim" This is the same word used for the body of an animal that has no soul. The Talmud is very clear in stating that only Jews have souls and that all the rest of mankind are simply animals placed on Earth to be servants to the Jews. <<Theodor Herzel>> expands this in the Protocols and; when he speaks of the "Power of the Purse".

> Midrasch Talpioth fol.224d **God created them [Jews] in the form of men for the glory of Yisrael. But Akum [Goys] were created for the sole purpose of ministering onto Jews day and night. Nor can they ever be released from this service.**

Think about the consequences of a child being taught such evil beginning at age six. What will the child think of non-Jews when he grows up? Then consider that many Jews send their children to Kibbutzim, which are communist training camps in Israel. The consequences of these actions result in the racial and religious divide between Jews and others exemplified by the racist policies of Israel. It is Jews that teach these absurdities, it is Jews that demand racial separation; it is Jews who claim to be "The Chosen of God", "A People Apart", "The Talmud is not education it is transformation," among many others. Never before in the history of man has there been such an exclusionary religion. A group of people so motivated by their religious instructors; to a posture of radical racial exclusion. No other priesthood ever came within miles of dominating a society to the extent of the rabbinical sophist scholars of the diaspora. Jesus Christ upset these zealots' entire apple cart; this is without doubt the cause of the virulent hatred of all things Christian.

We have now entered the text of the Talmud, which is the most hateful racist religious writing of history. Judaism is the only surviving religion in the world that espouses such evil. In general terms Jews are admonished to avoid contact with non-Jews for the following reasons:

1) Non Jews have no souls
2) Non-Jews are animals
3) Christians and Muslims are unclean
4) Non-Jews are not worthy of sharing the Jewish way of life
5) Non-Jews are idolaters
6) Non-Jews are murderers

These are the exact premises found in the Talmud over and over again.

<<Maimonides>>[246] Mishnah Sephardic Talmud[247] "Accordingly, if we see a Goim (Idolater) being swept away or drowning in a river, we should not help him. If we see his life is in danger, we should not save him." Maimonides is one of the most revered Sephardic Jews, certainly equivalent to a Saint in Christianity; this demonstrates the clear difference between Judaism and Christianity. Jewish philosophic understanding of life is "a tooth for a tooth and an eye for an eye," Christians is "turn the other cheek," and Islam insists that "10% of your income must go to the poor." <<Maimonides>> was a sick pervert whose teachings contradict the entire Torah and despises Christianity. Placing this in context of history remembering that Cordoba was ruled over by the Caliphate of Cordoba of the Islamic Umayyad Dynasty[248] who was very tolerant of Jews. It would have been unwise to attack Islam by <<Maimonides>> most likely resulting in his execution, it was however quite acceptable to insult Christians as they were the Caliphates greatest opponents.

The origin of the modern holocaust fable is firmly rooted in the Talmud. Gittin 57b claims that no less than four billion Jews were killed by the Romans in the city of Bethar. Considering that the entire Roman world of that time had a population of 55-60 million[249] and the Jewish world population prior to the diaspora was less than 1.5 million, we clearly see the exaggerations of Jewish history. Gittin 58a claims that 16 million Jewish children were wrapped in scrolls and burned by the Romans. Considering there were fewer than 2 million Jews in the world at that time we see another Jewish Talmudic lie.

ᐟ Coming to the 20th century we learned from an interview[250] of an Israeli Army officer (IDF)[251] who is an ardent disciple of Brooklyn NY rabbi <<Meir Kahane>> and learned from him that murder is OK. <<Goldstein>> murdered 40 Palestinian Muslims in a Mosque while they were at prayer, using an IDF issued machine gun. He informed a TV audience that it was OK to kill them because Arabs are dogs, and he had learned this from studying the Talmud. Then in confirmation

Baruch Kopel Goldstein *was an American-Israeli physician, religious extremist, and mass murderer who perpetrated the 1994 Cave of the Patriarchs massacre in Hebron. He was beaten to death by survivors of the massacre.*

rabbi <<Yaacov Perrin>> corroborated this by stating, "one million Arabs are not worth one Jews fingernail."[252]

Thousands of Christian ministers and priests, particularly those of the protestant persuasion do an enormous disservice to Christianity by consulting rabbis as interpreters of the Torah. The basic study of rabbinical education is one of numerology and occult studies. The study of the Old Testament cannot be based on such foundation. Denial of this is impossible because it is solely based on Talmoudic text. This is the identical text used by rabbis from the Babylonian Captivity until the present day, now, for almost 3,000 years. Judaism is the religion of the Pharisees and the text of the Babylonian Talmud, the last one written. From there also came the Talmudic and Kabalistic traditions of the religion. Orthodox Judaism, which is the basis of all Jewish beliefs, has other texts. Among these of primary importance are; The Qabbalah, a book filled with sooth saying, astrology, fortune telling, necromancy, and demonology. In direct understanding, the Qabbalah is a scripture of numerology; every Hebrew letter is given a numeric value, and students of this system claim to be able to predict the future. This is based on the presumption that God wrote the Old Testament (Torah) and He is incapable of error, and He provided the numeracy system key of translation to the authors of the Qabbalah. Needless to say these clever people have never once made any relevant predictions that came true. The six million number fits right into all of this, as later text will demonstrate. Many orthodox rabbis place curses, cast spells, and truly believe that they have greater power than God, which they think came from their study of the Sfer Yezriah, which is their book of Qabbalist magic. A common practice is to hold a chicken over the head of a parishioner while reading the Talmud thereby transferring the sins of the practitioner to the chicken. It should be noted that the Star of David is actually not of David it is a German 16th century invention[253] and is in fact an occult hexagram, which can be associated with the Khazar's of the 14th century in Bohemia.

The Pharisees have always claimed that any exposure of the contents of the Talmuds constituted anti-Semitic fabrications. The truth cannot be a fabrication. As proof of Pharisees control of Judaism we can examine exactly what authoritative Jews say on the subject. The Jewish encyclopedia pp. 474 "The Jewish religion, as it is today, traces it's decent, without break, through all the centuries, came from the Pharisees. The Talmud is the largest and most important single member of their literature; the study of which is essential for an understanding of Phariasism." In the encyclopedia Judaica, as quoted by rabbi <<Finkelstein>>, we learn that Phariasism became Talmudism, but the spirit of the ancient Pharisees survived unaltered. When a Jew studies the Talmud he is actually repeating the arguments of the Phariseean Academies. It should be noted that rabbi <<Finkelstein>>, was chosen by the Kehilla (entire Jewish community) as one of the 120 Jews that best represented "a lamp on Judaism to the world." He was at the time the head of the Jewish Theological Seminary of NY.[254] <<Finkelstein>> wrote the book on this issue titled The Pharisees in two volumes[255] "The Talmud derives its authority from the position held by the ancient pharisaic academies. The teachers of those academies, both of Babylon and of Palestine, were considered the rightful successors of the older Sanhedrin." [Authors note: that proves absolutely nothing, one bunch of rabbis verifying the validity of another group of rabbi's amounts to a self-endorsing of fact.]

Dr. Louis Finkelstein

Then <<Herman Wouk>> in his book[256] informs; "Whatever laws, customs, or ceremonies were observed—whether we are orthodox, conservative, reformed, or merely spasmodic sentimentalists—we follow the Talmud, it is our common law."

Judaism is not based on the Old Testament (Torah) but on Talmudic rabbinical postulations relating to what they think is written in the Torah. (Man's word not God's) All of this came from oral traditions of the Hebrews. It is exactly that oral tradition and Talmoudic interpretations of the Torah that Christ so strongly condemned. This tradition is what gave rise to the authorship of the Protocols of the Learned Elders of Zion, finally coming to light in the late 19th century. In fact the Talmud was originally called "The Tradition of the Elders".[257]

Everyone remembers the false charges made by Jews against the Romans relating to the murder of Christ. It commands us to look back at the history of the time, which is ample in Roman records.[258] The entire Roman garrison of Jerusalem at the time of Christ was less than 1,000 men. The population was about 50,000, consequently law enforcement was conducted by the Jewish king <<Herod the Great>>, by his army, that was subservient to Rome's. It was Herod's men who arrested Christ, it was Herod's courts that convicted him, and it was Pontius Pilot who said, "I see no fault in this man, I wash my hands of this." Jewish courts had total and complete autonomy. It was Jewish courts that were responsible not only for the crucifixion but also the previous murder of infants by Herod. Noteworthy is the fact that the greatest persecutor of Christians in the time of Rome was Nero; his mistress <<Poppea>> was a Jew as was his principal advisor <<Attilius>>. It was those two individuals that induced Nero to persecute all Christians. It is estimated that in Cyrenea Jews slaughtered 220,000 Greeks, and 240,00 in Cyprus.[259]

---

235. Those civilians are incapable of harming our forces, then according to the Halakhah they must and even should be killed...Under no circumstance should an Arab be trusted, even if he makes the impression of being civilized...In war, when our forces storm the enemy, they are allowed and even enjoined by the (Halakh) Babha Mestsia fol. 33a "Those who devote themselves to reading the Bible exercise a certain virtue, but not very much; those who study the Mischnah exercise virtue for which they will be rewarded; Those however, who take upon themselves to study the Gemarah exercise the highest virtue."

236. 400 BC

237. About 600 BC

238. 1973 Israeli IDF main Chaplain stated to assembled officers; "When our forces (IDF) come across civilians during a war or in hot pursuit or in a raid, so long as there is no certainty, they should kill even good civilians, that is civilians who are ostensibly good." [Geneva Convention be Dammed]

239. 1994 Shalom (meaning peace) Hartman Institute in Jerusalem

240. The Babylonian and the Jerusalem

241. Published by: Sinai Publishing Tel Aviv 1989

242. First appeared in about 150 AD

243. Mischnah means the repeated second law, i.e. the rabbinical interpretation of the five books of Moses, called the Torah. It is however nothing but the repeat of opinion instead a series of written opinions of its rabbinical authors.

244. Gemara is a rabbinical commentary on the Mischnah forming the second part of the Talmud. (Literally means to study) publication date is assumed to have been 200 AD by Judah HaNasi.

245. German translation by <<Lazarus Goldschmidt>> 1930 to 36 published by Jüdischer Verlag Berlin '30 – '36.

246. <<Maimonides ben Maimon>> was a Spanish (Cordoba) Sephardic Jew philosopher 1138 to 1204 AD during the rule of Islam in Spain 711 to 1492 (Al-Andalus)

247. Moznaim Pub. Corp B'klin NY 1990 English translation pp. 184

248. Abd-al-Rahman III proclaimed the Caliphate in 929 AD

249. Classical Roman history indicates a total population of the Roman Empire in 1 AD to have been 55 to 60 million people. (UNRV History) The total Jewish population time of <<David>> was 1.3 million (Statistic Jewish encyclopedia 1901-06)

250. 60 minutes on CBS TV Feb. 26, 1994

251. <<Baruch Goldstein>>

252. Feb. 1994 (Daily News Page 6 28th Feb.)

253. The Star of David origin was a Jesuit (Society of Jesus) invention in 1648. It was awarded to the Jewish militia who participated in defending Prague against Sweden. The German Emperor Ferdinand the III gave the Jewish militia the banner with the star based on the assumption that it symbolized the Aramaic two letters of King David's name. (National Journal of History)

254. Rabbi <<Finkelstein's>> star pupil was none other than Chief Justice Earl Warren (Who's Who in America) certainly the prime architect of the concept of the living constitution, and the destruction of America as a Republic. CFR Eisenhowers supreme Court justice.

255. <<Louis Finkelstein>> 2 volumes, ASIN # B003PD6DZU

256. The Talmud heart and soul of the Jewish faith.

257. Mark 7:14-20 Mathew 15:2

258. From 1 AD to 60 AD no Roman legions were stationed in Palestine. The procurators who governed Judea were lower level bureaucrats. Only Senators had sufficient rank to command a Legion. The closest Legion to the Levant was in Damascus Syria. The Procurator of Palestine commanded three to four Cohorts of auxiliary troops most of which were Greek or Syrian that were locally recruited. Each Cohort consisted of six Centurions and between 80 and 100 men. So, the maximum troop strength at Pontius Pilot's command was 600 to 800 men. It was not until later in the first century that a full legion appeared in the Levant. (Legio X Fretensis) which stayed behind after crushing the Jewish uprising where it stayed for the coming 150 years. (See Mark 5:1-14 a joke on the X legion whose standard contained the picture of a wild pig.)

259. Decline and Fall of the Roman Empire (Gibbons)

Secret Jewish Organizations

Truth is the greatest enemy of Ashkenazim, and the purpose of Jewish control of the media in sufficient size to suffocate truth is the greatest ally for them!

There is little difference between communism and socialism but in the way Ashkenazi seek to achieve the ultimate progressive end: Communism by force and socialism by election.

Dr. Göbbels so clearly articulated issues of propaganda when he originated the statement that a lie must be big and if it is repeated often enough, people will after time believe it. So, think about the Kennedy assassination, 9-11, the Alfred P. Murrah bombing, the USS Liberty, and all those false flag operations of the 20th century. To gain an understanding of Jewish behavior the reader must be made aware of a well-developed system of secret organizations that have been part of Ashkenazim culture for many centuries. For all that time they have employed an extensive network of secret organizations, which direct the Jewish Community (The Kahal) in all nations where the Diaspora is active. The authority of the Jewish priesthood that has been usurped by the rabbinical system derives its assumed power from the Ten Commandments,[260] which were delivered to <<Moses>>, and had already been expanded on by the rabbis by the time of Augustus Caesar. The expansion of power by these power hungry and corrupt clergy over the early ignorant and uneducated Jewish population has relentlessly continued through today.

Many have attempted to pierce the veils of secrecy behind which the Ashkenazim community functions. They are subject to severe penalties for divulging any information pertaining to the Kahal, knowledge on it is scant. In 1943 Hugo Wast, was the Argentine Minister of Justice, he published a

Hugo Wast

book about it. Argentina has a large Jewish community and Wast was familiar with many of its members. His book is one of the very few that expand our knowledge of the Kahal and its functions.

The many thousands of pages of the Talmuds are the primary tools of Israeli geographic expansion. (Eretz Yisrael) There were always two rivals for this enterprise, The Pharisees and the Sadducees; both of these formed political clubs (like the Likud) to attempt expansion of their goals and supremacy in the effort. Historically it is verifiable that these two groups had little interest in the Jewish state both preferring the self-interest of expanding their base.[261] Thus with the sack of Jerusalem and the destruction of the Temple, (second) they as holders of the sacred texts were the new Roman client state rulers. Through a continuous regimen of altering and augmenting sacred texts from that time until they had the original Talmud completed their religious and political dogma developed to become present day Jewish law.

Beginning at the Roman conquest of the Levant Jewish religious leaders began to exercise considerable legal and political dominance over the government. Not only religious power but also social, dietary, and political, which arose through the voluntary acceptance by the community, but this power was coercive naked power enforced by Rome. Crucifixion, public flogging, stoning, communal expulsion, and imprisonment were part and parcel of it. All such judicial rabbinical power as well as control of the entire judiciary was gradually expanded over the entire Kahal and all Jews living under Roman rule. This process continued through the diaspora through the 13th and 14th centuries in Christian as well as Islamic nations. The rabbinical class saw this as a means to an end, their total control of all Jews. These rabbinical courts that were developed under Roman rule were the seed from, which the secret organizations developed.

Throughout this formative time various ways, alterations, assassinations, betrayals and intimidations formed secret societies, which then changed the religious rituals and practices of Judaism. As a result and in concert with the newly acquired power of governance granted by Vespasian, they became successful in controlling the entire governmental apparatus of the community. They made their laws, the laws of man, superior to the Hebrew laws of God.[262] They formed a government, whose laws were absolute and enforced by their religious police and backed by the Roman Procurator that totally supported them. This government came to be named the Kahal. The diaspora that was actively completed in 135 AD did not lessen this power; it simply spread it everywhere that Jews migrated. The Talmud that now replaced the Torah as the principle article of Hebrew law was the instrument of producing the secret societies, so as to allow rabbinical control over the entire society. Every Jewish community, forced by their rabbinical rulers to live in ghettos, with a synagogue, became miniature Kahal's, with the chief rabbi acting as fraternal leader, actually dictator. While these communities of the diaspora were subject to various differing cultural societies to which they were legally subjected, they came into conflict with all of them. The main interest of the rabbinical class was social and religious cohesion of all Jews, so as to enhance and maintain their rabbinical power over the community. They, through intimidation of their central authority ruled all Jewish communities in the diaspora. It must be made clear that the deliberations of the Kahal are secret and never discussed outside the community by any member of the tribe.

This ruling clique developed what might be seen as a cast system within the Jewish community. This system saw to the change in the law from the Torah to the Talmud and the rule of all Jews by the individuals who were responsible for writing those laws. This is very similar to the subtle change in our 20th and 21st century laws through the judicial interpretation of the Constitution, and Bill of Rights, as a "Living Document", imposing the norms of present social demeanor and judicial personal opinions into legal interpretations. For the rulers, then as now, it has become a simple procedure to implement what had been used against them and applying it to their own rule of society. In application to outside community action this is more obvious as the continuation of the victimhood game in which every non-Jew is cast as an oppressor and can thus be victimized through *erpressung.* In order to maintain control of and strengthen their hold, they developed a system of espionage and subterfuge as is recommended in so many passages of the Talmud. They have continuously expanded this to include societies in which the diaspora exists, infiltrating the state security apparatus of those host nations.[263]

These Jewish secret organizations that were at the heart of the Russian Revolution have infiltrated labor unions, government security agencies, multinational corporations, banks, and the media as well as all businesses that have Jewish management. Their agents are active in reporting to the Kahal from police, courts, shops, hotels, banks, and of course the media. All of this is found in the

Protocols. Thus every sector of society that touches upon it is carefully watched and reported on. The community of the Kahal knows fully well that it is unwise to oppose the rabbi. Doing so can result in expulsion and thereby bankruptcy. In association with the rabbi is another organization called Beth-din, which is the tribunal that adjudicates issues of non-compliance with the law. The community carries out edicts of the Beth-din, or if that proves unsuccessful is brought before the courts of the location of the Kahal with community members acting as star witnesses against the violator.

As is the case with most secret organizations, many members of the communities in which such functions are common, remain unaware of their existence. These are Jews who have remained outside the synagogue and rabbinical control, something that has become more common in the late 20th century. It also includes most women who are, by Talmudic law, greatly discriminated against. The fact that Judaism is the most chauvinistic of all religions is well known. This as in Islam seems not to prevent females from being among the most ardent supporters of the system. This is amazing considering that the entire American feminist leadership movement is Ashkenazi.[264] *Alzirg, Friedan and Gloria Steinam.*

Rabbis are the most important functionaries of the Kahal. It is they who interpret the Talmud and thus it is they who call the shots. These adjudications are not trials, in any sense of the word; they are dictatorial pronouncements by rabbis, which are not open to dispute or discussion. This then is the theocracy that rules the Jewish community. This is why Israel is a socialist theocracy, which is an indisputable fact. How is this accomplished? On March 23, 1980 the Kahal desired a means of intimidating Arab Christians in order to prevent them from any support from the Muslim community of Jerusalem, in that communities' opposition of the theft of Palestinian land homes and businesses to expand Jewish settlements. Under the auspices of Yad Le'akhim, one of the Kahal's secret religious organizations they organized a public mass burning of the New Testament and the Gospels in which hundreds of New Testaments were burned in a bonfire.

The Kahal system is why so many Jews are eminently successful in many occupations; it is not that they are as they claim to be smarter, it is the issue of social cohesion, in which they always promote their own. Through unified action by the cohesion of the Kahal they act in unanimity of purpose. This vastly multiplies their power as <<Herzel>> stated[265] "By the terrible power of the purse." This system allows Jews to advance their personal occupations above and beyond that of competing Christians and Muslims through cooperation and with the help of other Jews. Advanced information, insider trading, consolidation of financial information, singularity of purpose, bribery, and blackmail are all part of this. Under such disclosure it is easy to understand why they are so eminently successful. Thus in recourse of submission to the system, it rewards them by the community in their struggles of achievement. All members of the Kahal anticipate and are granted full community support in all their endeavors, their joint financial power, and all their organizations and all their members purposefully work toward the ends of promoting their own. This system clearly explains why they come to dominate certain sectors of the economies of the nations in which they live.[266] In order for this system to function effectively a majority of Jewish participation in those sectors must be attained. This has been accomplished in banking, media, and academia. Academia provides the additional advantage of the ability to influence young and developing minds with Jewish propaganda. ✗

The entire Jewish population living as they do in either Christian or Islamic societies, pray upon those nations successfully based on two distinct precepts; first the absolute subordination of all members at the Kahal, and secondly the total secrecy of it. Another book enhancing this is "The Shulchan Aruk",[267] which is a guide of sorts of the Talmuds for Jewish governance. What the Kahal establishes is a hidden group of organizations and established groups hiding within society under the guise of a religion for the total control of that group. It further established the premises of victimhood allowing the willful extortion from societies in which they live for the benefit of its members. The Kahal, which was established in the second century, functions today much the same way as it has in the past 1,800 years. The ruling group is called the "Council of Elders", (Gerousia) and is led by the Patriarch. The function of this "Council" Is primarily diplomatic and ceremonial; it represents the Kahal in external issues. It looks a great deal like the old Sanhedrin that ruled Judea at the time of Rome. The second authority is the tribunal. (Beth-di)[268] The Beth-din adjudicates all matters between members of the Kahal, dealing with both religious as well as civil law maters. Beth-din judges have absolute authority including death sentences; they function in all diaspora societies and do not consider themselves to

2020
✗ Jew, Socialist Bernie Sanders running for U.S, president as a Socialist !! Free Everything! NEA has brainwashed students!

be subject to the laws of the societies in which they reside. A violator may by the Beth-din be declared outside the protection of the Kahal (ex-communicated) called (Guefker) and thus can be dealt with in any way the tribunal dictates. In this manner Jews have the ability to go before the tribunal to adjudicate matters between members. This is why Jews who are among the most litigious members of society rarely bring personal civil actions to Christian civil courts for adjudication. If the tribunal's efforts prove unsuccessful the offence is brought before the courts of the society in which the Kahal is located, thereby making Christian or Islamic Sharia law the enforcer of the Kahal tribunal enforcing the edict of the Beth-din.

Lastly we have the fraternities. They are the fiber that ties the Kahal together.[269] Jews have historically always created a scapegoat at the foundation of an act, always to allow them to claim victimhood.[270] The first openly published exposure of these societies appeared in NY newspapers in 1919,[271] which in detail explained the Kehillah.[272] The Register explained, "the Kahal was to weld Jewish interests and develop community consciousness." Further explanations including that "the coordination of all existing community agencies to save the synagogue from ruin to which purpose all the moral and financial strength of the Kahal is to be mustered." The final function for any Jew is for it to act as a burial society, which in fact is by the nature of its operating procedures an insurance company.

The "Kosher Tax" is an example of how Jews parasitize non-Jews every day and most people are completely unaware of how they are being robbed. Kosher laws relate among other things to the way animals are slaughtered.[273] If you purchase food (or other common items) that have a "K" or a "U" stamp on it, often in an inconspicuous location, it is "Kosher". Kosher actually means fit to eat.[274] What it really means is that some rabbi has collected a tax for his stamp of approval which is paid

Rabbi Bernard Levy is president of one of the leading nonprofit organizations in the United States which certify that foods are kosher—or properly prepared in accordance with the Jewish dietary laws.

for by the customer (that's You). It has absolutely nothing to do with the quality of the product. It produces many millions of dollars of profit for the Jewish community. Rabbi <<Bernard Levy>> is head of the orthodox "Committee for the Furtherance of Torah Observance" of New York City; he makes millions for simply allowing food processors to stamp their product with the "K" stamp. In reality kosher does not mean better, cleaner, or healthier, it is an instrument for profit and that is all, it means that some rabbi has made money from your purchase. Kosher is one of the many ways that the Kahal finances itself.[275] There is a great deal of mammon in kosher. The total Jewish population of America is about 3.7%. Of the total, Orthodox Jews (the only ones who actually care about kosher) are about 1.5% of the total Jewish population. In conclusion 98.6% of the "K" and "U" marked kosher products are sold to non-Jews who are thereby financing the Kahal. The "Kosher Tax" scam has been extended to include even non-food items like soap.

There are scores of secret zionist organizations everywhere. Hovevei Zion was confederated in 1887 into what was called Hibbat Zion (love of Zion) as a movement. This group is credited with the extraordinary exodus of Russian Jews. By 1914 and the beginning of WWI 2.5 million had already emigrated to America and parts of the British Empire, and over 3 million from Poland to Germany. Between 1883 and 1899 over 300 Hibbat Zion groups operating in Poland provided free finances for Polish Jews to emigrate. In Russia a group that originated in Kharkov called Bilu was one of the founding organizations to develop modern zionist dogma. This group developed a manifesto (their name),[276] which declares among many things, "Jews have been sleeping and dreaming the false dreams of assimilation…Now thank God thou art awaken, the pogrom[277] have awakened thee…we want a home country…it is ours as is registered in history."[278] Biluim was a group who set out in 1882 from Russia to settle the land of Yisrael, what the residents of Palestine were to do, or where they where to go, was never explained. Fourteen separate groups came to the Levant by the end of 1884. These were modern Ashkenazim called the Aliyah (First Wave) that arrived in Palestine (at the time part of the Byzantine Empire) from 1881 to 1903. <<Rothschild and Maurice de Hirsh>>, the two largest Jewish bankers in Europe financed the operation.

The first Zionist Conference held in Basel in August 1887 was the founding of the present zionist movement, by some called the committee of the 300. This name stems from the 300 participants in the Basel meeting. It may be inferred that many American Jewish groups like the AIPAC, SPLC, JDL, AZC, IFCJ, GPF, FJC, ADL, and

✳ *The Committee of 300 by Dr. John ⸺ Coleman.*

B'nai B'rith between over 200 are part of this zionist cabal. They are so violently zionist that they even attack Jews who disagree with them like Neturei Karta a Hasidic group that is listed by JDL as being in the 10 most active anti-zionist organizations.

The World Zionist Congress, the World Jewish Congress, The Alliance Israelite Universelle, The Jewish Defense League, B'mai B'rith, the names are not relevant they are all part of and subservient to the Kahal. Their actions today are no different than when the <<mistress of Nero>> prodded him to kill Christians, nothing has changed in 20 centuries.

---

260. Exodus XX
261. During the reign of Vespasian and the siege of Jerusalem by Rome, they betrayed their own people (The Sadducees) and were rewarded by Vespasian with the exclusive right to collect taxes and become the official Roman client government.
262. Brafmann, Jewish Brotherhoods Villa 1868
263. The Mossad   CFR
264. <<Barbara Walters, Naomi Wolf, Elizabeth Wurtzel, Sandra Zeig, Julie Zellinger, Ruth CFR Bader Ginsberg, Betty Frieden, Gloria Steinem>>, etc.
265. <<Theodor Herzel>> Brn. 1860 in Hungary. President of the First Zionist congress 1897 in Basel Switzerland. George Soros, born in Hungary. CFR- Jew
266. Banking, media, academia, Jewelry, politics.
267. The Shulchan Aruk is a manual of Jewish laws, deriving from the Talmuds and compiled by rabbi <<Joseph Caro>> in the 15th century
268. <<Brafmann>> "House of Religion" (book on the Kahal)
269. The reader should be made aware that contrary to the Protocols these are in no way related to the Masons. The entire Masonic references in the Protocols are a deliberate ruse to create a possible scapegoat and deflect attention away form the Kahal and Jews in general.
270. Jewish Communal Register.
271. Christ's murder on Rome, the Russian Revolution on communists, the French revolution on the people, slavery on New Englanders, 9-11 on al-Qaeda etc.
272. Kehillah is the plural of Kahal
273. Animals must be slaughtered under the supervision of an schochetim. Proper killing method called shechitah is a ritualistic killing of antiquity; a chalif is a special knife that is used to slit the animals throat. It is inhumane in forcing the animal to bleed to death. The rabbinical pronouncement that it is a complicated process taking many years to learn is rubbish.
274. Truth at Last (Marietta GA)
275. Washington Post Nov 2, 1987.
276. The Communist Manifesto comes to mind
277. The isolation of Jews into preset communities by the Czarist state. Some dictionaries state it was an organized murder of Jews, this is incorrect it was a geographic relocation. The pogroms restricted where Jews could live, and what occupations they could work in. Many Jews like Lenin's father, a lawyer, simply converted to Russian orthodox Christianity.
278. The fall back of the false claim that Ashkenazim have property rights in any place but the Caucuses.

Were the Protocols
Fact or Forgeries?

The claim by Jews is that the Protocols were deliberately written by the Czar's secret police to defame Jews. We disagree with that assertion for the following reasons:

1) The oldest known Protocols were written in the 15th century.
2) Over 20 copies have turned up most with slightly different texts.
3) Copies have been found in all nations that have a Kahal in the diaspora.
4) Besides Hebrew, copies have been found written in, Latin, Russian, German, French, Italian Spanish and Arabic.
5) All known transcriber/publishers of the Protocols have died violent deaths.
6) The British Museum in London does not catalog fiction.
7) A sentence of death for possession of a copy does not appear logical for holding a work of fiction. (Soviet Russia)
8) If it was in fact fiction why did zionists bring legal action against publishers in scores of nations.
9) If it was fiction why did zionists attempt to make possession a crime in Switzerland.
10) If it is fiction why does so much of it parallel the Talmud.

What are the Protocols?

The Protocols are transcriptions (notes) kept by individuals who attended meetings of secret Zionist organizations. These meetings are and have been held at irregular intervals. The last known and published meeting was held in Basel Switzerland at the end of the 19th century.

What is the Plan of the Protocols?

The Protocols are a plan for the centralization of governments, banking, media, education, housing, energy, manufacturing, etc. under one central zionist controlled body. The principal vehicles for this are socialism/communism, and progressivism under a liberal banner. (UN) ✱

The UN Conspiracy by Robert W. Lee.

Where is this planned to happen?

The Protocols are international in scope. The first was Russia, which failed miserably. The second was Europe (the EU). The third is the North American Union, (NAU) joining Mexico, America and Canada into one political entity. NAFTA, CAFTA, Free Trade zones, and free trade are all part of this.[279] *now, USMCA ~ all CFR agenda.*

What is the ultimate goal?

The final plan of the Protocols is one world government, one world currency, and total control of everything by zionists. To place the blame on others particularly Free Masons, and for every non-Jew to be a slave of the Jews as is explained in the Talmuds. The world government is to be run by "overseers" who are a special class (like Bolsheviks in Russia) that will be rewarded by the zionists.

No it's not a pipe dream!

The entire Russian Revolution from 1919 to when the system finally collapsed was invented, and run by Jews that were less than 4% of the Russian population, most of which were not even Russian nationals. The American Revolution was begun by about 3% of the population and only after two years had any military success. The French Revolution also had minimal popular support.

False Masonic Embodiment ?

Within the Protocols are repeated references to Masonic participation and the allusion that Free Masons are part of the zionist/ Jewish conspiracy. Firstly, Masonic bodies above the 3rd degree are separated into two differing bodies; the York Right which is totally Christian and has no Jew or Muslim members and the Scottish Right, which accepts Jews and Muslims. Secondly, Masonic law strictly prohibits political discussion in Lodge. Thirdly, there is no political or socially cohesive movement within Masonry. This is simply the creation of a scapegoat, which is a common practice and has always been, for all zionist operations.[280]

The Protocols of 1919

The statement in the testament of <<Montefiore>>[281] "Zion is not sparing, either money or any other means, to achieve its ends. In our day all governments of the entire world are consciously or unconsciously submissive to the Super-government of Zion, because all the bonds and securities are in its hands: for all the countries are indebted to the Jews for sums they shall never be able to repay."[282]

A letter was included with the Latin version Protocols addressed to the Israel International League. The lengthy letter details actions of the Russian Revolution including <<Lenin's>> train ride from Zürich to Berlin and Berlin to St Petersburg, and that the zionists totally financed and ran the entire Revolution. <<[Bronstein (Trotsky), Apfelbaum (Zinovieff), Rozenfeld (Kamenev), Steinberg>> all were Commissars and all were Ashkenazim.

Lev Davidovich Bronstein (Leon Trotsky)	Grigory Yevseevich Zinoviev (Hirsch Apfelbaum)	Lev Borisovich Kamenev (Rozenfeld)	Isaac Nachman Steinberg

Protocols of 1922

Actually dated August 10th 1906 and translated from Cyrillic Fa. Prof. Nilus

Protocols of Dec 24, 1912

<<Walter Rathenau>>[283] an Ashkenazi he revealed to newspapers[284] that "Three hundred men, each of them knows all the others, govern the fate of the European Continent, and select successors from their entourage." He certainly should have known, he was one of them! *He was assassinated, 6-1922. For talking!*

Walter Rathenau

Protocols of the 15th century

These were published in the <<Rothschild Journals>>. Remember that <<Lord Rothschild>> was the president of the World Zionist Congress. <<Revue des etudes Juives>> published and financed by <<Baron James Rothschild>> in 1889. The documents were sent to the Grand Sanhedrin of Constantinople by <<Chemor>> the rabbi of Arlen France on Jan 13, 1489. Interestingly they were signed <<V.S.S.V.F.F. Prince of the Jews.>>[285]

The British Prime Minister, an Ashkenazi speaks

<<Benjamin Disraeli>>[286] made the following statement in 1848 in his novel Conningsby; "The world is governed by very different

personages from what is imagined by those who are not behind the scenes." As another member of the 300 he also knew well of what he was speaking.

Lord Sydenham

In an article published in the spectator (UK) August 27, 1921 Lord Sydenham said, "The Protocols explains in almost laborious detail the objectives of Bolshevism and the methods of carrying it into effect. The methods were in operation in Russia when Fa. Nilus said that he received the Protocols. Nothing written in 1865 can have any bearing upon the deadly accuracy of the forecast in the Protocols, most of which have been fulfilled at this time."

George Sydenham
Clarke
*Lord Sydenham
of Combe*

<<Theodore Herzel >>

Founder of modern zionism. "When we sink we become the revolutionary proletariats, the subordinate officers of the revolutionary party." (If it quacks like a duck, waddles like a duck, and has feathers then by God it's a duck, the same goes for communists and zionists, one and the same.) "When we rise, there also rises the terrible power of the purse." <<Herzel>> was president and prime presenter at the first Zionist

Theodor Herzl

meeting in Basel, if there is a secret Committee of 300, he was surely a member, and the Basel meeting had 300 attendees. He became so totally obsessed with the "Jewish Problem"[287] that he began to think he was the Messiah, contrasting himself with <<Shabbetai Tzvi>> who falsely claimed to be the Messiah in the 17th century.[288] In 1899 he wrote a letter to Yusef al-Khalidi a highly regarded Arab of Palestine, in Jerusalem, informing him that Arabs and Muslims had no reason to worry about zionist immigration to Palestine as it did not represent a threat to the Arab inhabitants, because…"rather the industrious and talented Jews coming to Palestine would be well funded and be a tremendous boon to the local inhabitants." In a later personal letter to one of his zionist friends he stated the issue somewhat differently; "Personally I think that the displace-ment and transfer of Arabs…albeit with full compensation." Nobody to our knowledge was ever compensated for anything. Then in his diary, again…"We must expropriate gently…we shall try to spirit the penniless population across the border by producing employment and transit to those places while denying them employment locally." Remember this was long before the establishment of Israel in 1948; this was in the 1890's. It is exactly what the zionist state has been doing for the last 67 years. Later we learn again from his diary; "I want to establish a giant philanthropic Jewish national fund for the purchase of land to be owned by the state (socialist theocracy of Israel) so that large scale settlements can become possible." (The formation of a communist state)

<<Aldolphe Cremieux>>[289]

In his address to the Universals Israelite Alliances on the occasion of its founding, and relating to the assertion that the Protocols were a forgery he said, "The unfortunate part of this business is that the 'forgery' corresponds infinitely more closely with the facts of history than that which is claimed as genuine." On his gravestone is the following inscription, "Here lies Aldolphe Cremieux founder of The Alliance Israelite Universelle."

Aldolphe Cremieux

Claimed fulfillment of the Prophesies in 1923

<<Cremieux>> predicted on the Protocols 20 years before they became open knowledge as follows, "Four Christian Empires Russia, Austria, Germany, and France have already fallen to Jewish power. (Their banking systems) The only empire left is England [where the diaspora is now located] we shall soon control it." With <<Rothschild>> they now control England.

An 1897 copy

In 1897 a Russian Czarist officer was posted to Washington DC and was recalled by the Czar. He was then commissioned to go to Basel Switzerland where the first zionist conference was to take place. The Czar places a detachment of secret police to help. They staged a false fire alarm during the second day of the meeting and in the confusion stole all the papers that had been left on the lectern. One of those documents was the 24 chapters of the Protocols of the Learned Elders of Zion. The zionists began making extraordinary efforts attempting to have the Protocols labeled a forgery. In the JDL bulletin of January 1953 published by B'nay B'rith titled "The

Protocols and the Prague Trial" the assertion was made that the Protocols had been proven to be a "fabrication" of the Czars secret police. Somehow this must be taken with a grain of salt since the Soviet prosecutor[290] was a zionist and the conclusion was drawn in a soviet kangaroo court.[291]

---

(279) NAFTA (North American Free Trade Agreement) CAFTA (Central American Free Trade Agreement) Free Trade zones now include all of North and Central America, Columbia, Panama, & S. Korea. It is destroying American small business and family held manufacturing. From 1992 to 2014 it has cost the United States 54,000 small manufacturing plants and 11,700,000 blue-collar jobs.
(280) Masonry in the English-speaking world stems from the Grand Lodge of England that granted a Charter to the Lodges in America when it was a colony. There are three degrees to attain as Master Mason, 1) Entered apprentice, 2) Fellow craft, 3) Master Mason. The illuminist movement never infiltrated the English, Scottish, or Irish lodges. After achieving Master Mason rank, the candidate can chose to become a York Right or a Scottish Right Mason, or both. The only requirement being they believe in God and being a member of the readers of the Book. (Old Testament of the Bible) The York Right is strictly Christian which in ritual requires the candidate to affirm acceptance of Jesus Christ as the Son of God. The 32nd degree of the York Right is titled Knights Templar, there are no Jewish or Muslim York Right Masons. The Scottish Right accepts Muslims and Jews in their membership and has an honorary degree called the 33rd. The 33rd degree is not some political überactive organization it is simply honorary and restricted to Scottish Right Masons, therefore is unable to make any rulings for all Masons. The Grand lodge of each state consists of only Master Masons and the Grand Master of the state who rules all the Lodges in the state is only a Master Mason. All officers are elected by secret ballot.
(281) Moses Haim (From Dizionario Biografico degli Italiani (Vol 76 (2012))
(282) USA $ 18+ trillion EU 12.4 trillion.
(283) Rathenau was CEO of AEG (Allgemeine Elekteritäts Gesellschaft) He served in the Weimar government, as foreign minister but was assassinated June 24th 1922 after revealing details of the Protocols and opposing the Zionist movement.
(284) Wiener Freie Presse
(285) The title is is of great significance. After the diaspora by Roman emperor Hadrian in 132-35 AD Jewish leadership migrated from Jerusalem to Constantinople where the Sanhedrin was reconstituted. It remained there for 350 years. The head of the Sanhedrin was Exilarch <<Naci>> (Prince of Captivity). In the beginning it was always a member of the House of David, but later in the 14th century that changed to powerful banking families. When the Grand Sanhedrin eventually moved to Frankfurt <<Rothschild >> became that person as King of the Jews.
(286) <<Benjamin Disraeli>> 1srt Earl of Beaconsfield KG, FRS, British prime minister for Queen Victoria birth name Israel.
(287) We find it interesting that the very phrase attributed to the Nazis (The Jewish Problem) actually was first articulated by Herzel.
(288) <<Herzel diaries>>
(289) Cre'mieux 1796-1880 French
(290) Stefan Rais
(291) Source: Paquita Mady de Shishmareff. She had authored several books under the pen name of Leslie Fry; her husband was a Czarist army officer.

* Pg 41, 42, The New Babylon by Michael C. Piper.

The Final Protocol

The most commonly held historic observation is that <<Asher Ginsberg>> was the consolidating author who re-wrote the older texts, that is to say consolidated them and made them more under-

standable. Most of the Protocols were old and much of the language was not in the language of that time. Ginsberg as a well-known Jewish scholar had access to all of the pertinent documentation.

<<Ginsberg>> was born in Skvira the providence of Kiev in 1865. His parents were well to do and members of the local Hassidim temple. As such he

Ahad Ha'am (Asher Ginsberg)

was educated in a Yeshiva and after his education was married to the granddaughter of rabbi <<Menachem Mendel>>. In 1878 he moved to Odessa where he continued his studies specializing in Ashkenazim philosophers like Nietzsche, <<Spinoza, and Moses Mendelsohn>>.[292] Thereupon he traveled to France and became acquainted with <<Charles Netter>> one of the founders of the French Zionist organization, Alliance Israelite Universelle, that he then joined.

Charles Netter

In 1884 he returned to Odessa, where he joined the "Friends of Zion" another rabid zionist organization under the tutelage of <<Leo Pinsker and Moses Lilienblum>>. Due to his excellent knowledge of Hebrew he quickly rose in the organization. In some time he was asked by

Leo Pinsker   Moses Lilienblum

Aleksander Zederbaum

<<Aleksander Zederbaum>>[293] to become a contributing author in his paper. He proved to be too radical for <<Zederbaum>> as well as the Sons of Zion, because he wrote articles admonishing

141

Jews to oppose the Czar and to resist the governments of the nations in which they lived. This produced a schism in the Sons of Zion organization and <<Ginsberg>> went on to found a new "Sons of Moses". This organization commonly met in Odessa at a house located on Yamskaya Street. It was there that in 1888 Ginsberg met with <<Ben Avigdor, Zalman Epstein, Louis Epstein>> and <<Jacob Eisenstaat>>. It was this core of the Sons of Moses that produced the final version used in Basel the following year.

Publication of the document produced income from other zionists, and along with publication of articles related thereto produced income for the Sons of Moses. Substantial additional support came from the Odessa Kahal.

Chaim Weizmann

At the Basel meeting there was considerable friction between <<Ginsberg>> and <<Herzel>>. While Herzel was a more pragmatic European, Ginsberg was the original firebrand. Herzel was elected president of the congress but Ginsberg relentlessly attacked him on the podium.[294]

After fourteen years Ginsberg was finally victorious by getting one of his disciples <<Chaim Weizmann>> elected to the presidency of the World Zionist Committee. From there on forward the Protocols have been the guiding light of world zionism.

292. The father of the famous composer who converted to Christianity.
293. <<Zererbaum>> was the publisher of Ha-melitz the most widely distributed zionist paper in Russia.
294. Attacks by <<Ginsberg>> were mostly in publications of the time Hashiloah (the Way) and <<Ahiasaf>> of the Jewish publishing empire of <<Kalonymous>>.

Why Six Million?

In order to explain why the Jews lost six million, so many times, as they claim, we must first explain how the Talmud teaches Jews to look at us. Jews look at mankind in a completely different light than the rest of humanity. While we as Christians and Muslims look at man as seen equally by God and that all mankind are the children of God, Jews believe that they are the "chosen" of God, and thus have standing before and above all others. It would be interesting to learn the criteria for this choice and, for example, what percent Jewishness is required to designate a Jew. Does a non-Jew obtain a soul by converting to Judaism? Furthermore the Talmud clearly states, in numerous places, that non-Jews do not have souls and are in fact animals. If you can imagine a pyramid the very top of it is God (YHVH). Directly beneath him are the rabbis, who interpret the Talmud, and his laws. Then come all the Jews. The rest of the pyramid (99%) is comprised of all other living things. YHVY promised Jews, so they claim, that they are to rule over the 99%, the slaves of the Jews and other creatures without souls.

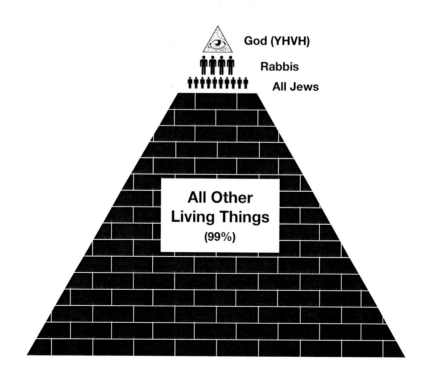

˧ The persecution myth is another salient feature of Jewish culture. In all Jewish religious texts from the Torah forward every document perpetuates the persecution of Jews as history. Considering that it takes two to start an argument we find it amazing that the Jews who have been expelled from over 100 cities and countries continue to blame others for their self-made predicament. This is one of the central concepts of Judaism. This is the glue that binds the community together and provides additional income through extortion from societies in which they reside. Rabbis use these elements to enforce their religious dictatorship upon their communities. It gives rise to the ability to use victimhood as a tool for extortion.

While Jews as a group are far from one mind on these issues among themselves, in the presence of their enemies (Christians and Muslims) all thought on these matters becomes unanimity. In this respect they consider these issues as ones of self-preservation. For over 2,000 years the Jewish community has been led and conditioned by their teachers (priests and then rabbis) to identical appeal. In all that time the shrill Jewish claim of victimhood, racial exclusion, superiority, separation from all others, and stewardship of all living things has never changed. The fact that Jews at times were persecuted is not news; there is not a single racial, religious, social, or even gender group that has not been persecuted at one time or another. What makes Jews different from all other groups is that they use these issues, relentlessly dredging them up to support their dogma, and extort for mammon.

The two most important facts of 20th century history for Jews is first the holocaust and second the foundation of Israel in 1948.

In order to proceed, another Jewish concept must be understood. Rabbis are in fact not priests but lawyers that explain and teach the Talmud. The most renowned of the rabbis are orthodox Jews, who are the predominate group that makes and explains Jewish law. Their education begins at age 6 and by the time they are 30 they believe themselves to be totally infallible.

˥ Bear with us, as this issue gets somewhat complicated. To go further you must understand that an influential rabbinical religious philosophy that is almost totally unknown to outsiders is the prime concern. This theosophical and theurgist belief is at the very pinnacle of their rabbinical philosophy. To make that more understandable the practitioners of religious philosophy are as the Pope in Rome is to Roman Catholics, or the Ayatollah to Shia Muslims. Gematria is a

Jewish method of interpretation or of decoding scripture according to the numerological value of each individual letter of the Hebrew alphabet, or for the method of, through numerology substituting one Hebrew letter for another, based on some numerological formula. This is all elucidated in the Qabbalah, the written text of numerology. The claim is that only through this can anyone really understand God. All this is embodied in the concept of Ein Sof.[295]

Qabbalah is derived from the Hebrew word qbl, which means, "to receive;" in earlier texts it meant reception. Modern verbiage seems to indicate that the present verbal expression came out of Greek and geometry. Historically the numerology (Gematria) came to prominence in Provence, France in the latter half of the 20th century but was developed in Babylon during the Captivity. Currently used texts are dated 1260 AD. So here is where it gets bizarre. These rabbis primary belief is that their study and application of qabbalahistic practices can affect the Godhead...i.e. influence God's actions. So that by performing certain ritualistic numerology they are able to establish harmony with God. <<Moses Maimonides>> mentioned in previous text was a strong supporter of this. If you think you are now confused, it gets worse. Although qabbalistic doctrine seems to be presented in a fragmentary manner it in fact consists of two separate methods in application, mathematical and symbolic. As outside observers it would appear to us that the

Rabbi Moses ben Maimon,
commonly known as
Maimonides

entire Gematria practice is a ruse to pull the wool over the heads of Jews, inducing them to believe that rabbis have some mystical powers. It has the appearance of a cult.

Hermeneutics is the study of the theory that biblical texts may be interpretive when written text is placed into qabbalistic numbers, especially in application to philosophy and literature of a biblical context. The Hasidim of the 13th century were particularly adept at selling this to their followers.[296] In modern terms this philosophy believes that human ritual through the use of magic and numerology is able to influence the sphere of human existence by influencing the divine nature of God. Put another way, these delusional twits think that they can tell God what to do. They have further concluded that; the cosmos operates in a 7,000-year cycle (shemuttah) and a 49,000-year period (Yovel) with each cycle terminating a 1,000-year rest. Do not be misled into believing that these people are kooks. Qabbalist have been part of the religious picture of Judaism for over 2,000 years, in which time they have produced more than 150 commentaries on the Sefirot[297] containing lists of letters and numbers.

Another group of Jews became interested in the philosophy of evil, (world of the Devil) describing in vivid detail the world on the other side, the demonic world. This is where many of the Hollywood horror films come from. They cast spells, made poisons, and generally engaged in manners not of civil society. The predominance of this was in the Spanish peninsula and is strongly attributable to the Inquisition.

Qabbalists believe that without their participation (i.e. the participation of qabbalistic practitioners) God remains incomplete and unrealized. It is therefore the practitioners of cabbalism that actualize the divine potential of God who desperately needs them. (Talk about a massive ego trip.) When confronted on the issue they say the aforementioned explanation is sufficient for one who is enlightened, and it is not possible to further explain this to the un-initiated. Then they further claim that God in the Garden of Eden gave these revelations. Considering that the Talmud, upon which all these inventions are based, began its formative cycle in about 600 BC that's a real stretch. The journey to enlightenment as a Qabbalist is long and arduous taking many years. To be learned are secret passwords, so as to be admitted by the angels of God. (Their words) What they claim is that while living among the rest of humanity, they and they alone visit heaven speaking directly to God. Not one single word of this is found in the Torah, every last idea stems from the Talmud. These texts[298] describe God as having multiple personalities expressed in ten separate conceptualizations. The Christian trinity has been outdone.

The concept of numerate interpretation is based in texts.[299] These texts are claimed details, the speculation of how God combined individual letters, as well as ideas, which in the Talmud and Gomorrah are exhibited as numeric entities. They then claimed to have devised a structure of mystical numbers through the use of Pythagorean mathematics.[300] Later, elements of Neo-Platonism were incorporated along with the concept of the origin of evil. (The Devil)

⁍ In 1280-AD a Spanish Jew mystic named <<Moses de León>> began circulating booklets to fellow Qabbalist written in Aramaic,

Moses de León

the language of Jesus. The text was full of invented words and symbols, something along the line of witchcraft runes.[301] Extensive texts followed.[302] <<de León>> cleverly told all his fellow Qabbalist that all his works were simply interpretations of ancient 2nd century texts written by <<Shim'on bar Yohai>> the great Talmudic scholar. No one ever questioned or dared to challenge de León, an Aramaic scholar in his own right. No one ever asked to see the original Aramaic text and none ever turned up. When queried de León followed the standard Qabbalist practice claiming that if you did not understand you had not been properly initiated into the Qabbalist practices. Lest you think this all has no relevance in the 21st century you might consider <<Mogen David>> the largest selling Jewish wine. It is named after <<David Messer>> one of León's works is entitled <<Magan David>>.[303] When you see Hasidim at the Wailing Wall in Jerusalem rocking back and forth it is because they are in meditation and repeating the divine name of God and combinations of Hebrew letters and their transposed numeric values.

The most prominent early figure in Qabbalist was <<Abraham Abulafia>>.[304] He traveled widely and lived in Spain, Sicily, and Greece, finally settling in Palestine. He had strong influence on Sufism as well as Yoga. He merged Yoga and Sufism with Qabbalism and the teachings of <<Sefer Yetsirah and Maimonides>> theories of prophesy based on the concept that he was able to, through those acts, merge

An illuminated page from Abraham Abulafia's Light of the Intellect *(1285).*

his consciousness with that of God. (In other words he claimed that he spoke with God.) These acts became so pronounced in his mind that he envisioned himself as the Messiah; traveled to Rome and in a meeting with Pope Nicholas the III tried to set the Pope straight on ecclesiastical issues. Pope Nicolas sentenced him to death, but he died before the sentence could be carried out.

By the mid-15th century Qabbalism as a religious philosophy comprised the core of basic Jewish belief. It was most certainly one of the causes that brought the Roman Catholic Church to establish the Dominicans as the Tribunal of the Holy Office of the Inquisition in 1478. This also established for the first time a feminist component to Judaism with the incorporation of an 11th face of God called the Queen. There is a Jewish poem[305] recited by Jewish congregations "Come my beloved, to greet the bride, let us welcome the Sabbath."

By the 17th century Qabbalism had become mainstream Jewish philosophy. Luria's theology of numbers Gematria, had spread to all diasporas. It seems to have most strongly influenced the Hasidim of Eastern Europe (Russia and Poland). Today traces of Qabbalism can be located in literature, in the writings of <<Walter Benjamin, Luis Borges, Franz Kafka, and Jacques Derrida>>.

| Walter Benjamin | Luis Borges | Franz Kafka | Jacques Derrida |

In rabbi <<Blech's>> book[306] we finally learn why the number **6 million deaths** in WWII is of such importance. Let the reader be well aware that from the very beginning of qabbalistic thought, revelations of their numerological interpretations were always made after the event, never before. Blech

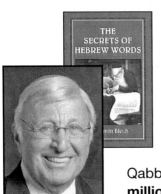

Benjamin Blech

demonstrates in his text that the Hebrew letter vav is missing from the Hebrew text in prophecies and predictions. The prophesy in question is the final redemption and it states **"yea shall return"**[307] but it is spelled incorrectly. The vav in the middle of the phrase is missing. **The numeric value of the letter vav is 6** thus Qabbalist tell us that they will return **minus six million**. The reason for acceptance of this prediction (actually after the fact and numerically inflated) is that God cannot make mistakes and therefore the missing vav is significant and predicts the loss to the community. But that is not the entire prediction it is expanded to:

TaShuVu total number 708

Tav 400, Shin300 vet 2 = the vet 6 = 708

The Jewish calendar has a different beginning and does not count the 1,000 number, through it the beginning of the new state of Israel in 1948 becomes the year 5,**708**, thus the prediction of **708** as the year they would return. So Cabbalist's which are the basic foundation of modern Judaism have claimed that they will return as is in the Torah[308] minus the 6 million. Just as we predicted, they claim (however long after the war).

To this we pose a simple challenge to the Hasidic Qabbalist. Since you claim to be able through your numerology, to predict the future and since you deny that Jesus Christ was the Messiah and that you are awaiting your Messiah's arrival, please give us the date of that event.

Arthur Herzberg

We in addition have two prominent rabbis. First, <<Arthur Herzberg>> of Englewood NJ who informs us that, "It is my opinion that these rabbis carefully crafted their predictions and doctrines as 'Prophets' and must be correct (in their predictions) in order to retain credibility." There it is, straight from the horse's mouth; in order to remain credible their predictions must be accurate, and after the fact. This is why the entire Jewish community insists on the six million, if that were ever changed the entire qabbalistic system of Talmud interpretation would be destroyed and along with it the entire house of cards of Judaism would collapse. Second, we hear from rabbi <<Yitzchak Ginsburgh>> of Tel Aviv; "The assumption behind Gematria is that numerical equivalence is not coincidental. Since the word [Torah] was created through God's 'speech' each letter represents a differing creative force. Thus the numeric equivalent of two words reveals an internal connection between the creative potentials of each one..." In <<Ginsburgh's>> CV we learn that he is a mathematician by trade and a rabbi by vocation, he must have somehow missed courses in logic.

Yitzchak Ginsburgh

The six million number is not an isolated case at all. A study of Qabbalistic history indicates that the number 6 appears often. In fact we learn that when God created man he made 6 million souls, considering that the world Jew population is 13,896,900[309] so 7,896,900 Jews were deprived of a soul—no wait we are wrong, the prediction regards Hebrews not Jews. But we have no idea how many Hebrews remain alive, because the Jewish controllers of information systems don't want us to know that. In 1919 the 6 million number again appears[310] in an article written by ex NY governor <<Martin Glynn>>, however in his story the cause was starvation. Then in the Babylonian Captivity it was six million, in the Roman destruction of the Temple in 70 AD the six million comes up as the number of Jews driven out of Jerusalem to the diaspora. The Roman number strongly contradicts that of Tacitus, who in his journal wrote that 6,000 Hebrews were killed. In all these cases the same story was floated, every time after the fact.

295. Ein Sof is simply the concept of infinity. Hard to grasp but certainly not some mystical religious issue.
296. When the Czar and his entire family even his dogs were murdered by Jews in 1918 the captain in charge was <<Yurovsky>>, they inscribed a warning on the wall of the building of the murders, in the blood of their victims. The inscriptions were in Gematria usage a warning to all non-communists of what would happen to them if they did not go along with the "New Order"!
297. Sefirot are according to Qabbalist the ten ways in which God manifests himself.
298. Shi'a Qomah
299. Sefer Yetsirah
300. The Pythagorean theorem states that among the three sides of a right triangle, that the side opposite the right angle is equal to the square root of the sum of the squares of the other two sides: $c = (sqrt (a^2 + b^2))$ Obviously geometry and mathematics is not Qabbalist strong suite. Considering Pythagoras developed his theorem in 595 BC and Qabbalist claim this all was provided in the Garden of Eden it would appear that we have another problem.
301. The Theban alphabet sometimes called the runes of Horus, so named after its inventor Honorious of Thebes is also called the witches alphabet.
302. The book of Radiance
303. Later published in about 1540
304. Brn. in Zaragoza Spain in 1240. Founder of "Prophetic Qabbalah" died in 1291.
305. Lekhah Dodi
306. The Secret of Hebrew Words
307. Leviticus 25:10
308. From the Alef-Beit Appendix
309. Jewish Virtual Library
310. Article published in The American Hebrew Oct. 31, 1919

A Verification of Evil

<<Theodore Kaufman>> a member of the American Jewish Congress wrote a book that was published in 1941 entitled *Germany Must Perish!* Concentration camps were built in the Weimar Republic long before the Nazis came to power

in 1933. No Jews were interned from any German controlled territory until after 1938.[311] Jews had declared war on Germany long before 1933 as documented in their London newspaper. The Jews were the primary authors of the WWI armistice, which inevitably led to WWII. The animosity of Jews against Germany was the result of two issues. Firstly, although they had total control of European banking, the Nazis refused to borrow money from <<Rothschild's>>. Secondly, the fact that the entire communist movement which had been the implacable enemy of the Nazis from the beginning, was run by and controlled by Jews under the direct authority of Stalin. The first party to declare war in WWII were the Jews of the diaspora headquartered in London. America had not at that date entered the fray; they declared war in November four months after publication of <<Kaufman's>> booklet. The book did not just appear out of nowhere it had been written the year before. The first Nazi concentration camp was built on July 11, 1942. In conclusion the scenario shows that it was the Jewish controlled international banking cartel plus their support of the violent threat of the communist party that was behind the drive to war.

Theodore Kaufman

The booklet, *Germany Must Perish!* is filled with such vile hatred as to make it difficult to read. It suggests that the entire German population be exterminated (Note: <<Eisenhower>>, whose father was Jewish, partly achieved this goal after the war by murdering over a million German POWs by starvation and exposure in open-air retention-camps during the cold European winter), that any surviving German should be sterilized, and Germany should be dismantled as a nation state. This was partly achieved by giving of Danzig to Poland, the creation of Czechoslovakia, changing the borders of Eastern Germany, and giving Alsace to France. Kaufman's book so incensed Dr. Göbbels that he had it translated into German and had over a million copies distributed to German soldiers. When Hitler read the book he ordered that all Jews must start wearing yellow armbands with the word Jude and a yellow Star of David.

Thus, the most immediate result of the booklet was action against Jews, and a probable extension of the war. This action was later ✕ supported by Churchill's night firebombing of Dresden, a refugee city without industry or military importance.[312] They destroyed the Katolishe Hofkirche cathedral completed in 1743 for absolutely no reason. FDR's secretary of the Treasury[313] <<Morgenthau>> of NY devised the <<Morgenthau plan>>, which called for the total destruction of all manufacturing industries in Germany, he demanded that Germany be turned into a wasteland as it was after the Thirty Years War.[314] Harry Truman scrapped the entire plan.[315]

Responsibility for starting WWII is revealed by <<Vladimir Jabotinsky>>[316] in a 1934 published article in which he states, "The fight against Germany has now been waged for months by every Jewish conference, all labor unions, and by every Jew in the world." This is dated four years before the Nazis had arrested a single Jew based on religion; those that had been arrested were communist organizers. The Jews were allied with the communists and those Western leaders, especially Churchill and Roosevelt who were willing puppets of the World Jewish Congress.

Einstein was run out of Germany for his Communist activities (Not because he was a Jew).

---

311. Kristallnacht
312. The Dresden fire bombing in 1945 killed about 380,000 civilians, mostly women and children. The British dropped 450,000 tons of firebombs on the city. The bombing devastated an area of 34 square km.
313. <<Henry Morgenthau>> radical zionist
314. 1618 to 1648 Began with Emperor Ferdinand II of Bohemia's attempt to curtail the religious convictions of his subjects.
315. Harry Truman 33rd. President USA
316. <<Vladimir Jabotinsky>> was one of the founders of the radical Zionist organization Jewish Self Defense organization, in Odessa Russia. (1880-1940)

✕ *Churchills War by David Irving.*

Modern Communism and the Reformed Jewish Religion

Communism is a social, economic, and political ideology, which advocates that all property be communally held by the state, and that every member of the community must work for the state and be rewarded in concert with his efforts. Sounds very egalitarian, but it has never worked because it ultimately transfers all power to a small elite which dominates and abuses the citizens. The evil nature of communism is demonstrated by one indisputable observation... it is always mandatory and never voluntary. The only remaining places where this is used are in Israeli Kibbutz and Robert Mugabe's Zimbabwe.[317] Most places that remain are in economic depravity. There are from 123 to 142, either in revolution, or war, or declining communist dictatorships. America by the way has sunk to number 10, in freedom ratings.

Information in various encyclopedias, dictionaries, and journals often edited by Jews, paint a rosy picture of communism depicting it as a Utopian system. Nothing is further from the truth; <<Karl Marx>> the plagiarist who had the Manifest der Kommunistischer Partei published in 1848, and later, Das Kapital had an interesting tutor. It was <<Moses Hess>> by many considered the father of modern zionism. This has gone to the point where one encyclopedia proposed that Plato and Thomas Moore the 16th century English philosopher had both embraced communism.[318] One can only speculate that soon, someone will claim Ronald Reagan was a communist.

Karl Marx

Moses Hess

' Communist theory speculates that the proletariat (workers) will overthrow the capitalist system, taking over the powers of government and management. The blue-collar workers will kill the evil owners and managers and will then run the government and industry. The ruling authority will then be the proletariat. In other words rather than the best and the brightest running things, the most violent and least capable would be in control of things. Well, we know how that works out, the Russians, under communism, could not even produce a decent car and their entire technology was stolen from the West. According to the theory (which has been wrong in every case) after a few years class distinction will disappear, and the dictatorship of the proletariat will evolve into a collective utopian state. Yes, just like Russia, Hungary, Poland, China, Cuba, Estonia, Latvia, Yugoslavia, North Korea and all the rest.

✱   <<Lenin>>, who by the way spoke Yiddish with his family and with his Commissars, transformed Russia into a zionist hell hole the likes of which have never before been seen in human history.

Vladimir Lenin *makes a speech to troops of Vsevobuch on Red square. May 1919*

The primary features of <<Lenin's>> state were:
1) State control of everything.
2) The Communist party arbitrator of all things.
3) A totally centralized economy
4) All property owned by the state
5) The elimination of Russian Orthodox religion.
6) An absolute totalitarian state run by the General Secretary (Lenin) of the Communist Party.

✗ Hillary Clinton's grandmother spoke yiddish in the home.

154

To expand; a totalitarian state without popular representation of the proletariat or anyone else, with only party members allowed to vote on issues.[319] From 1919 to 1924 being a Jew was prerequisite to becoming a party member, until Lenin's death Jan. 24, 1924 that remained the party discipline.

In 1924, every member of the Central Committee was an Ashkenazi; over 90% of all commissars were Ashkenazim, the entire controlling apparatus of the Soviet government was led or controlled by a Jew.[320]

<<Makeup of the quasi-cabinet USSR 1917 total membership 24>>

Jew alias	Real name
Lenin	Oulinaow (Ulianoff)
Trotsky	Bornstein *Bronstein* .
Steckloff	Nakhanes
Martoff	Zederbaum
Zinovieff	Apfelbaum
Kaameneff	Rosenfeld
Dan	Gourevich (Yurewitach)
Ganetzky	Furstenberg
Pavus	Helpfand
Urizky	Padomilsky
Larin	Luge
Bohrin	Nathansohn
Martinoff	Zibar
Bogdanoff	Zilberstein
Garin	Garfeld
Suchanoff	Gimel
Kamneff	Goldman
Sagersky	Kochmann
Riazonoff	Goldbach
Solutezeff	Bleichmann
Piatnizky	Ziwin
Axelrod	Orthodox
Galsnuoff	Schultze
Zuriesain	Weinstein
Lapinsky	Lowensohn

General Secretary of the Central Committee of the CPSU **Joseph Stalin** *(center).*

Jewish control began to evaporate when Stalin became Secretary of the Central Committee. Even though his wife was a Jewess he began purging them out of his government. By 1935 the Central Committee still had an active cadre of almost exclusively Jews. There were 56 members. Only three were not Jews but they were married to Jews, L.V. Stalin,[321] S.S. Lobow, & V.V. Ossinsky.

Absolutely nothing has changed in the last 98 years:

<<Famous name	Real name>>
Larry King	L. W. Zeigler
Woody Allen	Allen Konigsberg (Königsberg)
Garrison Keillor	G. E. Keillor
Whoopi Goldberg	Carolyn Johnson (convert)
Judy Garland	Frances Gumm
Helen Mirren	I.L.V. Mironov
Jack Benny	Benny Kubelesky
Mel Brooks	Melvin Kaminsky
Charles Bronson	Charles Buchinsky
Tony Curtis	Charlie Schwartz
Bob Dylan	Robert Zimmerman

The list is endless, over 80 major media personalities, and that does not count management.

It is important to understand that the commissars of the soviet state had the power of life or death over all its citizens. Commissars saw to and organized executions, in many cases simply shooting the victim in the head. For example a citizen caught with a copy of the Protocols was shot in the head. This effort was so successful that after the collapse of the soviet state not one single copy of the Protocols could be located. Captain Wilson, military attaché for the Roosevelt administration was the prime intelligence officer posted in 1919 Russia. He sent repeated communiqués to Washington that were never answered by Roosevelt's communist associates. "...The Bolshevik movement is and has been since its beginning, guided and controlled by Jews of an aggressive type..." Our American ambassador to Russia at the time was David Francis, he said, repeatedly, "The Bolshevik leaders in Russia, most of whom are Jews and 90% returned exiles, or foreigners, care little for Russia or any other country but are internationalists." The British envoy in communicating with Washington was more blunt when he stated, "There now is definitive evidence that Russian Bolshevism is an international movement controlled by Jews."[322]

The Protocols include the takeover of all police and security apparatus by the centralized state. The first Soviet police (internal security [Homeland Security]) apparatus was the Cheka.[323] Its leader was <<Moisei Uritsky>> [America's was <<Michael Chertoff>>] almost all of its ranking officers were Jews, including <<Sverdlov and

Moisei Uritsky

Yagoda>>. The Cheka murdered or sent to Siberia to slave labor camps so many Russians that an accurate count is not possible. We do know that it was about 66-million,[324] including over 1,000 Russian orthodox priests, who were worked to death in Siberia. We also know they destroyed over

Michael Chertoff

900 churches and monasteries. It is believed that from the beginning of the Revolution until the mid-1930s the Cheka had already murdered over 35 million Orthodox Russian Christians. State terrorism as described in the Protocols was in full operation. In the 21st century American terrorism is much more subtle, they do it with imprisonment[325] they indict by the use of so many laws that citizens are unaware of most and wind up in prison because they

were unaware of any violation. Comment on these events was made in the NYC newspaper "The Jewish Voice" which published the following, "The Jewish people will never forget that the Soviet Union was the first country—and only country—in which anti-Semitism is a ✳ crime." Marvelous, dead Christians and Muslims don't count—well, that's directly from the Talmud.

The Soviet state maintained a vast network of Gulags (concentration camps) most of which were located in Siberia. This system made murder unnecessary because the inmates were worked to death, starved to death, or frozen to death. Aleksandr Solzhenitsyn in his Gulag Archipelago book series lists the commanders of the various concentration camps as <<Aron Solts, Yakov Rapoport, Lazar Kogan, Matvei Berman, Genrikh Yagoda and Naftaly Febkel>>—all of them Jews.

The laws of the Supreme Soviet classified anti-Semitism as a crime against the state, which clearly tells you who and what the Soviet state was and conviction of a violation was Counter Revolutionary. Any such act resulted in a life sentence to Siberia. All active opposition to zionist rule was punished by death as is outlined in the Protocols. Very few ever returned from Siberia. The fact that 99.7% of the inmates of the Gulag system were Christians and Muslims is an indictment of the Jews in itself.

Pres. Trump signed Ex Order to withhold federal funds to any College convicted "of Anti-Semitism. Jews and Arabs are Semitic! Dec 2019.

---

317. Kibbutzim only continue to operate because of massive European and American aid. Zimbabwe is one of the poorest nations in the world #123 out of 142 nations, (Legatum Prosperity Index).
318. Just for clarification Moore lived in the 16th century about 200 years before the communist theory was published and Plato died in 347 BC exactly 2,195 years before Marx publication.
319. During the entire Soviet cabal the Communist Party never had a membership higher than 5% of the population
320. <<Lenin, Leon Trotsky (Lev Bernstein), Zinoviev, (Hirsch Apfelbaum) Kamenev, (Rosenfeld) Sverdlov (Herbert Aptecker), Emma Goldman the primary communist theoretician in America, Béla Kun (Hungary), Rosa Luxembourg (Germany) in 1924 384 commissars, 13 were Russians, 15 Orientals, 22 Americans, and over 300 Jews>>.
321. L.V. Stalin (Georgian) 1897-1953 both name Josif Vissarionovich Dzhugashvili, General Secretary Central Committee Communist Party of the Soviet Union.
322. Declassified U.S. Army documents of Robert Wilson
323. Later superseded by: OGPY, GPU, NKVD, NKGB, MGB, KGB, and today FSS (Federal Security Service of the Russian Federation).
324. I.A. Kurganov a Kremlin statistician.
325. 6,937,600 is the American prison population in 2012, the largest in the world. (Bureau of Justice Statistics)

What Brought on Communism in Russia?

For most of Russian history the Czars had difficulties with Jews. Russian peasants were routinely cheated by Jewish merchants and Russian bankers repeatedly demanded that the Czar do something about the Jews. The Ashkenazim spoke Yiddish with each other, a language the Russian peasants did not understand. Also most peasants were illiterate but the Ashkenazim could read and had some education giving them advantages over the peasants. This caused additional friction within the society. Since the Jews dominated in trade, retail and wholesale as well as banking and money lending, the peasants were at considerable disadvantage. The Jews, operating on the Talmudic claims of their superiority, took advantage of the peasants at every opportunity. This created a massive anti-Jew climate. Eventually the Czar who had become angered by the

---

May Laws

Enacted on 15 May 1882 by the Emperor Alexander III of Russia, the regulations of May 1882 were originally intended only as temporary measures until the revision of the laws concerning the Jews, but remained in effect for more than thirty years.

They read as follows:

1. "As a temporary measure, and until a general revision is made of their legal status, it is decreed that the Jews be forbidden to settle anew outside of towns and boroughs, exceptions being admitted only in the case of existing Jewish agricultural colonies."

2. "Temporarily forbidden are the issuing of mortgages and other deeds to Jews, as well as the registration of Jews as lessees of real property situated outside of towns and boroughs; and also the issuing to Jews of powers of attorney to manage and dispose of such real property."

2. "Jews are forbidden to transact business on Sundays and on the principal Christian holy days; the existing regulations concerning the closing of places of business belonging to Christians on such days to apply to Jews also."

4. "The measures laid down in paragraphs 1, 2, and 3 shall apply only to the governments within the Pale of Jewish Settlement."

Czar Alexander III

---

continuation of Jewish economic crime instituted the "Pogroms", a series of laws that prohibited the Jews from some professions and forced some resettlement of Jews to regions where they would be less of a problem, all within the confines of the Russian Empire. The first and immediate result was a massive emigration of Jews to Europe mostly to Germany, Poland, and East Prussia. This event resulted in the Ashkenazim community declaring war against the Czar and the Russian Orthodox Church by all Jews of the diaspora. The House of <<Rothschild>> suspended banking with the Czars' government and in fact called in all his outstanding loans. Thus the Russian government was unable to borrow money, or obtain credit for trade. Pressure on the Czarist government in financial terms gradually became unbearable. On Sept 3rd 1882 the Czar issued a statement which in part said, "With few exceptions they [The Jews] have as a body devoted their attention not to enriching or bene-fiting Mother Russia, but to defraud by their wiles the inhabitants... this conduct by them has brought forth protests by the people."

The first international act by the Ashkenazim was to finance the Japanese in their war against Czarist Russia.[326] <<Jacob Schiff>> was at the time one of the wealthiest men in the world, through his ownership of Kuhn Loeb & Co a banking enterprise that was also well connected to the <<Rothschild Banks>> of Europe. Schiff was also the prime supporter of the communists and <<Lenin>> in their takeover of the Russian government, which he partially financed along with <<Rothschild>> and other Ashkenazim. It is estimated that <<Schiff>> provided the Japanese a credit line of $20,000,000, which in today's money would be $526,000,000.[327] The year that <<Schiff>> died[328] the Soviet government deposited $600,000,000 into the accounts of <<Kuhn Loeb & Co>> in repayment of his gen-erosity.[329] Jews in America found no conflict in Ashkenazi bankers accepting funds of our greatest enemy at that time and the financing of another soon to be enemy, the Imperial Japanese Empire.

Anyone who truly desires to understand 20th century history must become aware of two issues: first the entire communist move-ment worldwide is Jewish, and second, communism, zionism, and Judaism are international movements whose adherents have no ties to any national entity, with the exception of zionists to Israel. We are certain that you are aware of the vast propaganda effort by zionism about our "Community of Nations", "Our Global Community", "Our International Environmental Responsibility", about what a small planet we live on, about "Our Home Earth", or silly bumper stickers "Save our Planet", and "Burn Wood Not Atoms", all these come from the communist zionist cabal. The entire environmental movement was infiltrated by the old Soviet socialist system and now sits firmly in the hands of socialist and communists. In Germany the political movement of the Greens (Die Grünen) the Communist environmental movement run by the Stasi[330] (Büntnis 90) and the socialists of West Germany, Socialist Party SPD and "Die Linken", and Bünntniss 90 and Die Grünen, have all formed a single political unit for over a decade, they all combined efforts when the wall came down. There was in the 60's in New England an organization called the

"Clamshell Alliance" their bumper sticker was "Burn Wood Not Atoms" congresswoman Rosa DeLauro (S for socialist CT) was a prominent member, she later became the chairperson of the Democrat Progressive Caucus. These twits demonstrated and then attacked the CT nuclear power plant in New London.[331] As they breached the fences, Federal and state police swooped in and arrested the lot. They found two leaders with detailed information of guard, security, etc. that

DeLauro *speaking in 2016*

had been provided by the Soviet KGB. From the very beginning the Soviets were involved in the Green movement to disrupt Western economic power generation. After the Berlin Wall fell, Green Cross, Green Cross International, and an entire consortium of environmentalists headed by Mikhail Gorbachev, supported by an all-inclusive cadre of old KGB operatives began running their scam for fun and profit.

<<Trotsky>> had some very interesting friends before the revolution, when he lived in

Mikhail Gorbachev

Vienna. His favorite watering hole was Café Central.[332] He was frequently seen playing chess with <<Baron Rothschild>>. Does it not seem strange to you, or at least odd, that the major communist theoretician of the communist anti-capitalist system would be playing a game with one of the wealthiest, most powerful, capitalists in the world? They had two things in common, both were Jews, and both wanted to remove the Czar from power to install a Jewish Empire, and we can include <<Schiff>> in that anomaly.

Academia teaches our children that the Czar was deposed because he was evil and unpopular. That is a lie; the Czar was the most popular ruler in Europe, he was venerated by the people who called him "father." The Russian Revolution was the world's first establishment of a Jewish super state under the banner of communism. In fact it is more accurate to say that it was not a revolution but an invasion. The "Evil Empire" was indeed communist but its operators were almost entirely Jews.

All this leads to an interesting question, why do we continuously see wealthy and influential Jews, not only supporting, but also helping in every possible way communist conspiracies to overthrow legitimate governments elected by the people. Furthermore if the goal was to oppose the Czar, then why did they not support the Kerensky's republican effort after the Czar had abdicated? The answer is that the Jews did not want a free, capitalist government, they did not want "power for the people," they wanted a dictatorship of the Jews not the proletariat. It is written in the Protocols, the Communist Manifesto, and the Talmud. All zionists have the same priority, which is the creation of a Jewish super state and the enslavement of humanity to serve them. People in the Middle East understand this well, people in the West are oblivious, and they have been put to sleep by the Jewish Lamestream and academia. Furthermore the revolution had nothing to do with care of the people or any egalitarian care of anyone; it was and had everything to do with rule over a society and the installation of Jews at every point of power within the governmental structure. The seeds of this are already well established and growing in America and Europe.

The murder of the Czar, his family, and even his pets was planned and ordered by <<Sverdlov>> and carried out by <<Goloshekin, Syromolotov, Safarov, Volkov, and Yurvsky>> all of them were Jews. There was no trial; there was no reason but hatred and fear of the people rising up in support of the Czar. The family was murdered in Ekaterinburg in 1918; general Denikin retook the town from the Bolsheviks whose officers discovered the grizzly scene. After the revolution and the Bolshevik victory they changed the name of the town to <<Sverdlov>>. The walls behind where the murders were carried out were covered in Hebrew, Samarian, and Greek script, made with the blood of the victims. The Hebrew letter L is repeated

The family of **Czar Nicholas II** *of Russia. Left to right: Grand Duchess Olga, Grand Duchess Maria, Nicholas II, Alexandra, Grand Duchess Anastasia, Tsarevich Alexei, Grand Duchess Tatiana. The family was murdered in Ekaterinburg in 1918.*

three times, this is in accord with qabbalistic Jewish practice. The repetition of three L's is common qabbalistic numerology; the first is symbolic, the second figurative, and the third sacred. This comes from the "Egyptian book of the dead" having been adopted by the Hebrews. The qabbalistic interpretation of the three is: <<"Here the king was struck to the heart in punishment of his crime…or here the king was sacrificed to bring about the destruction of his kingdom.">> It must be made clear that this warning was written in the blood of the victims for the sole purpose of establishing fear in European rulers as to what awesome power the Jews have. <<Sverdlov>> did not come up with this; it was by direct order of the Central Committee of the Soviet government.

<<Lenin's>> first Politburo (ruling council) was made up exclusively of Jews. Under Lenin's rule that predated Stalin, Jews became involved in all functions of the soviet government. To elucidate… despite the communists promise to democratize and end anti-Semitism, the exact opposite took place, due to the excesses of the Bolsheviks, anti-Semitism, rapidly spread.[333] The Cheka, which enforced Stalin's edicts, was a 100% Jew operation.

Stalin will surely go down in history as one of the world's greatest mass murderers, along with Genghis Kahn and Mao Zedong. In the mid-20s Stalin, after a long search, was able to find <<Trotsky>>, his principal rival. In 1927 in Mexico, he arranged <<Trotsky's>>

murder and thereby became the uncontested candidate for General Secretary of the Supreme Soviet. He held that office through terror, until his death on March 5, 1953. It is not known how many of Stalin's Central Committee rivals were liquidated but the number is over 1,000. In the 1930s he embarked on a massive systematic starvation effort in which over 20 million Georgians, Russians, and Albanians, were liquidated through starvation so that he could solidify his grip on the Soviet Union.

All the information in this chapter was common knowledge prior to WWII, but due to American and Russian media control by Jews it disappeared; consequently most people today remain unaware of it. The Soviet holocaust was the longest and most comprehensive human extermination process of human history. It resulted in more deaths than the entire loss of life in WWII. Operating from 1919 to 1953, it makes the so-called Jew-holocaust by the Nazis look like a Girl Scout picnic by comparison. All this information is common knowledge and a fact of history. To provide accurate historic information is neither anti-Semitic nor anti-anything, it is simply true and correct history.

The success of the Nazi party in Germany and Austria was a direct response to the bloody communist takeover in Russia and the real threat of similar communist coups in Germany and other European countries. Austria was a basket case. There were no jobs, the economy was failing, public service unions controlled by communists created a society without water, food, transportation, or employment. Strikes lasted for months, and violent street demonstrations made it dangerous to carry on normal activities. Morals and ethics were things of the past. Suicide, pornography, homosexuality, and perversion in general were the norms of the day. A large Jewish immigration from the Russian pogroms into Germany, Prussia, and Austria had increased the Jewish population which was culturally incompatible with the local populations, and who's social beliefs were vested in the Talmud, allowing them to cheat, steal, and prey on the local population which resulted in confrontation and the expanded alliance between communists and Jews. The Austrian Habsburg throne represented by Kaiser Franz Joseph was 50 years old, vested in the 18th century, and incompatible with the 1920's.

Into this Austrian stew came the Christian Social Party of Karl Lueger.[334] Hitler was an early adherent and was strongly influenced by the party politics and outlook. Marxism was the opposing philosophy, together with its zionist overtones, and the Jews in charge used every possible opportunity to promote anti-Habsburg sentiments and relentless political demonstrations. In 1899, Lueger was riding a crest of popular support and was violently anti-Jew and anti-communist. The communists were led by <<Victor Adler>> following the dictates of the communist party (Comiterm) in opposing anything to do with the existing government. By fall of 1905 they had attained sufficient political and social power to stage party rallies in Vienna (actually more like riots) of up to 250,000 party members all wearing red armbands and led by Jews. Some rallies lasted for hours and usually ended in surrounding the Austrian parliament. It is important to realize that the leaders of these rallies were not natives of the Austrian Empire or of Germany but were recent transplants from Eastern Europe who had immigrated due to the Russian Pogroms. There had always been Jews in the German speaking world but the Russian purges and those of Marshal Josef Pilsudski[335] at the turn of the century caused an influx of over 3 million Polish Jews to Germany. After Hitler came to power he wanted to send all of them back to Poland, but the Polish government cancelled their passports and refused them entry. Thus all these three million Jews without papers i.e. no national standing, that no nation would accept, became problems for the Nazis.

Next we consider Bavaria[336] at the close of WWI. The war had just been lost, Germany was in shambles, the Allies were composing the infamous Treaty of Versailles, there were armed communist mobs rioting, looting, and attacking governments and civilians throughout the country. A radical communist Jew, Kurt Eisner,[337] in the shambles of Munich, had just been put in control of Bavaria, all seemed lost. Then the Berlin government managed to send a few soldiers to the disaster in Munich. The communist forces (known as the "Reds" in those days) put up a resistance but after hard fighting, with many casualties the German forces prevailed. A convalescing German corporal was witness to these events, and although with no resources and no connections he resolved to devote himself to the restoration of the Germany he had fought for. Starting with nothing, in a devastated country, surrounded and infested with enemies that is exactly what he did. His name was Adolf. The liberation of Bavaria by the Freikorps and remnants of the German army was the Nazis' first involvement in counter revolutionary activities.

In November of 1938 a Polish Jew who the Germans had banished from Germany murdered the German Ambassador to France, in Paris. The Germans reacted by fining all Jews in Germany 400 million Marks split up among 600,000 Jews, which was the Jewish population of Germany in 1939. (Another verification regarding the six million fictions) Up to 1938 the German government (Nazis) did not make any opposing moves against the Jews, but the assassination of their ambassador to France was the last straw.

In 1939 Germany moved to reclaim Danzig from Poland, followed closely by the soviet's (Stalin) invasion of eastern Poland, for which it had no claim. England and France immediately used this as an excuse to declare war on Germany while eventually supporting Russia's invasion and furnishing Russia with massive arms shipments. A more realistic appraisal of the situation is that the economies of England and France were failing while Hitler's Germany was flourishing and they were afraid of losing their dominance.

Note: <<Karl Marx>> was a Jew, his father a lawyer converted to Christianity after the Czars edicts about employment. His grandfather was a Talmudic rabbinical scholar.

---

326. Russo-Japanese war of 1904-05. Resulted in the Treaty of Portsmouth (NH) brokered by TR in which Russia affirmed Japanese presence in southern Manchuria, and affirmed Japanese rights in Korea and granted them the island of Sakhalin. (US Dep. Of State office of the Historian)
327. DaveManuel.com inflation calculator.
328. <<Schiff>> Jan 10 1847 to Sept 25 1920
329. The Jewish communal Register of NYC 1917-18
330. Stasi secret intelligence operation of the East German DDR
331. Connecticut Yankee Nuclear Power Plant.
332. The Satori and the New Mandarins A. H. Krieg Hallberg Pub.
333. "Stalin's War against the Jews"
334. Karl Lueger Oct 24 1844 to March 10 1910 Austrian power from 1897 to 1910
335. Pilsudski Marshal (1867-1935) leader of Poland. At this time the Polish military was stronger and much larger than that of Germany, and was able to dictate policy to Germany several times. This mostly related the Hanseatic City of Danzig which was 85% German in population and whose Polish residents were less than 10%. Hitler after 1933 tried several times to allow a rail of highway corridor of transport to Danzig but was rebuffed by the Poles. Polish atrocities against the German population of Danzig was a major cause of the German invasion of Poland. This city was after WWII, seceded to Poland and is now called Gdansk. The Russians wanted Danzig because of the huge shipyards there.
336. Bavaria is the Texas of Germany being their largest state.
337. <<Eisner>>, organizer of the revolution that overthrew the Wittenbach monarchy of Bavaria in 1918. He was assassinated in München and the communists actually built a memorial to him.

Yisrael the Socialist Theocracy

Israel as will be shown in this chapter is a socialist theocracy. There are opposing, more secular and republican Jews living in Israel but the state is set up as a theocracy and is socialist in function. Listening to the American media one gets the impression that Israel is a republic or democracy, a veritable paradise, founded on constitutional principles just like Western republics or constitutional monarchies. Zionists in Western nations foster this view, which meets their goal of Eretz Yisrael. The ruling Likud party (The official War Party of Israel) is socialist, zionist and secular in religion but for zionism.

 First you must understand the constitution of Israel has a very strange provision. In 1985 the Knesset with almost unanimous approval passed a law which overrides provisions of all previously written laws and which cannot be revoked except by special procedures. By this law no political party whose programs openly oppose the principles of "A Jewish State" (Theocracy) or even proposes to make changes by democratic means can be a member of the Knesset (legislative branch of government). This law was made to prevent any Arab[338] from power in the legislative branch of government. This is the first positive proof that Israel is a theocracy. This law impacts foreign as well as domestic policy particularly in immigration, and voting procedures. It means that full participation in the governing of the state is restricted to Jews and Jews alone ([339]second evidence). Any Christian Arab for example cannot even run for office if he is opposed to the theocracy.

In Israel 92% of the land belongs to the state. 70% of the West Bank belongs to the state. Israeli law does not allow non-Jews to purchase such land because provisions of the state restrict sales exclusively to Jews (third proof of a theocracy). If you are a Muslim living in Israel and your family has lived there since Byzantine times and you served military service in the IDF you are prohibited from purchasing land adjacent to yours (fourth proof). There is an additional exclusionary clause in Israeli law that prohibits any non-Jew from living in any new Jewish settlement (fifth proof, [340]sixth proof). The Israeli Land Authority in accordance with the Jewish National Fund[341] that administers land purchases (seventh proof). Regulations within the structure of the fund prohibits sale of land to non-Jews (eighth proof).

Discrimination does not end at land ownership. Non-Jews even though they are citizens of Israel do not share equal rights before the law. These are expressed in a labyrinth of regulatory agencies that hide the jurisdictional power in sub-agencies that are often not even named. For example if a Jew emigrates from the Ukraine and is willing to settle in former Palestinian owned land in a West Bank housing complex, he is then granted $20,000 per family, full citizenship, and the immediate right to hold public office and a mortgage allotment. All funds for these immigrant benefits come as American foreign settlement aid, paid for by American taxpayers. While this transpires our government ignores Americans in Appalachia who can't even afford proper food!

To enforce these discriminatory laws on all citizens, a national ID card is required. This card is of particular interest because it lists the cardholder's religious status; Christian, Muslim, Druze, or the nationality as Jew. Thus this card allows immediate discrimination by IDF or police agencies. The actual number of benefits granted to Jews and not available to non-Jews by the government is extraordinary. Any Jew who leaves Israel and returns gets customs benefits, subsidies for children's education, grants, low cost interest loans, apartments, all for which non-Jews do not qualify. In Kibbutz, only Jews are accepted. Atheists, communists, and pedophiles are OK but Christians and Muslims are persona non-grata. In effort to expunge non-Jews from Galilee, one of the largest Christian settlements from the Byzantine time the Israeli government began a new program called "Judaification" in which they offer Jews subsides in housing rent and mortgages if they move there. Also, non-Jews get different colored license plates for their cars.

To really understand Israel you must understand what zionist believe. This is the primary reason for the friction between Islam and Judaism. There are two differing concepts of the territory that comprises Israel; they are the biblical concept and the zionist one. Zionists believe that Israel consists of all of the Sinai, all of Syria, all of East Jordan, all of Lebanon, Iraq up to the Turkish border and the Euphrates River, the northern most state of Saudi Arabia, and Turkey as far as Lake Van. This concept infringes the borders of; Egypt, Jordan, Syria, Lebanon, Iraq, Turkey and Saudi Arabia. This is the old rabbinical conception of the state of Israel. The second is the historic concept, which is the land that is claimed God gave to the Hebrews or that was at some past time settled by them. This is of course bogus because no current national border in the entire world is based on who ruled the region 50 generations or eons ago. The fact of the matter is that neither of these concepts have any historic or rational credence. This further compounds the problems because of now existing populations. Israel has a current population of 8,059 million. The territory of Eretz Yisrael has a population of 243.2 million comprising a territory close to 100 times the present size of Israel. Thus there exist two separate Talmudic concepts of history that are based on vague and indefinable fictitious ideas. <<Ariel

"On that day the Lord made a covenant with Abram and said, 'To your descendants I give this land, from the river of Egypt to the great river, the Euphrates — the land of the Kenites, Kenizzites, Kadmonites, Hittites, Perizzites, Rephaites, Amorites, Canaanites, Girgashites and Jebusites." **Genesis 15:18-21**

Sharon>> (The butcher), Israeli prime minister and Likud[342] member in 1993 proposed in the Knesset[343] that Israel should officially adopt biblical boundaries as absolute. Placing that in reality; first there are no biblical boundaries of Israel that can be verified, second Biblical history predates written text, thirdly any existing borders of any national entity 5,000 years ago has no bearing on the present. This would be akin to Mexico's PRI announcing that California, Texas, New Mexico, Honduras, Panama, and the Caribbean Basin were all part of Mexico, all based on an ancient Mayan manuscript, written in a hieroglyph that has never been translated.

It is realistic to make two statements about Jews in general; both are easily verifiable in the Talmuds and other Jew writings. First, Jews as a community are xenophobic, chauvinistic, hedonistic, and racists. Second, Jews have a very strong totalitarian nature in their character. This is why Israel as a socialist theocracy is unable to sustain itself through its own resources and engages in extortion to fund the imbalances of its economy. Due to this governmental structure, Israel requires unrelenting foreign funds, which are organized by various criminal as well as legal collection efforts by the entire Diaspora. Extortion by victimhood, extortion through political means, extortion through lies, extortion through inflicted guilt, all to create false victimhood, the vehicle of the Israeli collection agency.

One of the greatest problems relating to Jews is in the way they see themselves or more pointedly how others see or relate to them. The problem is not as commonly conceptualized by the outside world but in fact how Jews see themselves. We believe it is factual to point out that Jews and by this we mean all Jews see themselves as a race, religion, or nationality, whichever is at the time of discourse most convenient to their position. Since being a Jew is not a racial issue, nor for that matter a national one, it can be a religion but that is up to the individual and is not applicable to the community at large. They however interchange these three identities at will to suit their situation. Interestingly Jews have a very structured hierarchy; German Jews for example, look down their noses at Jews from other places, and Ethiopian Jews are widely discriminated against and maligned. Polish Jews are made fun of by German Jews and East Europeans from Russia are looked down on. German Jews see themselves as the "Culturträger" of the culture in which they live, actually an accurate concept.

Rabbi ? TV begs for donations for Jews left in Russia
IFCJ a shake down ?
Rabbi Eckstein (International Fellowship of Christians and Jews.)

---

338. About 25% of Israeli's population is Arab of which 20.6% are Muslim and 4.4% are Christians.
339. The term Jewish illustrates the difference between Israel and any other nation. By official Israeli definition, Jewish irrespective of where you live or came from is being a Jew, born of a Jewish mother, or having officially converted to Judaism. A multi-generational Arab whose family has lived in Palestine for ten generations, who is not a Jew is under the law considered an inferior citizen to a first generation Jew immigrant from Russia, who does not even speak Hebrew.
340. By authorization of the rabbinical council as prescribed in the Talmud.
341. Is an affiliate of the World Zionist Organization, which extorts funds for future land purchases by the Israeli government.
342. Likud is Israel's war party.
343. Israel's legislative branch.

Our Jewish Media

In the 21st century there exists a power above all else in the world, that power is the media. They elect our leaders, and they control our society. This is neither distant nor impersonal, they are in our living rooms, TV's, radios, and magazines. Their images and writings, result in the way we see the world and each other.

Dr. Göbbels[344] the Nazi Minister of Propaganda once explained it: "If you tell a lie big enough and keep repeating it, people will eventually come to believe it. The Lie can be maintained only for such time as the state can shield the people from the political, economic, and/or military consequences of the lie. It thus becomes vitally important for the state to use all of its powers to repress dissent, for the truth is the mortal enemy of the lie. And thus by extension, the truth is the greatest enemy of the State!"
Welcome to 21st century America!

American media in this century has fallen to levels we never dreamed of in the 20th century. Consider now the lies propagated by the media and by pundits therein employed:

Bill O'Reilly: "When the Germans invaded Austria" (2015 his TV program)[345]

CFR **Brian Williams:** "The Helicopter I was riding in got hit with an RPG" it did not happen!

CDC: spokesperson: "There is no evidence linking vaccines to autism"

NSA: "We are not spying on phone calls of US citizens"

US Navy: "No sailors were hurt in Fukushima radiation"

The American Diabetes Assoc.: "Diabetes cannot be reversed; only managed with drugs"

DOE: "Common core provides quality education"

CNBC: "The rising stock market proves that the economy is strong, and has nothing to do with the FRS printing more money"

FCC: "We don't really want to control the Internet; we just want to regulate it a little"

Obama: "You can keep your doctor" "Healthcare costs will go down by $2,500 per person" "You can keep your insurance"

IRS: "We lost the tapes, the computers crashed, Lois did not lie," "inflation is 1.5%" etc. etc. etc. *Lois Lerner,*

The Lamestream Media repeats these lies, among thousands of others, over and over. The American media is completely controlled by zionist interests, not Jews, zionists. We know this because of the media's relentless support of Israel and Israeli polices. Zionist control of media is not a single-issue item; they control TV, radio, newspapers, magazines, book distribution and publishing, film, and stage. Let's all understand that total ownership of a business is not necessary to control it. The Rockefeller dynasty has not owned more than 10% of Chase or its follower J. P. Morgan Chase but has controlled it for decades. A fine example of zionist control of media is the destruction of Gateway Press of Cleveland Ohio, whose 12-year old paper, The Gateway was eliminated after running an editorial about president Clinton's extraordinary number of Jewish appointments.[346] The editorial went on to state that the appointments as well as the cabinet hardly looked like the promised "cross section of *CPR·TC* America" that Bill Clinton had promised when campaigning. Which obviously was more than just a casual observation. The Cleveland Plain Dealer[347] in an editorial by Jewish <<Carolyn Davis>> finished the job off in a diatribe of left wing anti-free press rhetoric, stating among other things how she was horrified that anyone would suggest that Jews controlled the media. Then Editor of the Cleveland Jewish Press <<Cynthia Dettenbach>> did much the same thing with another article. None of the critics ever countered with a single real fact the assertion of Gateway Press's author Jack Killey, that Jews controlled America's print media.

The first great lesson that any revisionist author learns is that the progressive left never ever counters factual information with logic or facts, no indeed, they immediately begin with personal attacks on the author, character assassination, lies, slander, and linkage.[348] The usual first act in media is a Jewish organized boycott of advertisers: that's what they did to the Plains Dealer. There's that "terrible power of the purse" again. How did they destroy the paper? First was the boycott, of advertisers by all local Jewish owned retailers of Cleveland. Then they organized a letter writing campaign to Christian advertisers, that their business would be boycotted unless they halted advertising in the Plain Dealer. This by the way is no isolated issue, as authors we are well aware of book boycotts[349] by all book distribution outlets against stocking books like this one. In radio and TV journalism and interviews in Lamestream sources you will never hear a disparaging word about zionism, Judaism, or Israel. This has reached the point where the media in Israel is more open on critique than American media. This is by no means restricted to questionable journalism, historically proven documented, and well-indexed information is not exempt.

We think it useful to point out that disharmony between Whites and Blacks as well as Christians and Muslims has been stoked by Jews for decades. Most of this is facilitated through the Jewish controlled media wherein all racial and religious issues are exploited and twisted to meet zionist-desired goals. One way this is accomplished is what has become the mantra of the left; making all white males appear as oppressors of all minorities, homosexuals, and women, while at the same time excluding Jews from the Whites because they are "victims!" Evil Columbus, bad slave owning Thomas Jefferson, terrible George Washington and so forth. The fact that the entire leadership of the feminist movement, 98% of all pornographers, the leadership of the complete homosexual movement, are Jews is never ever found in print. What do we hear from our Jewish media? You are all racists look at the prison population over 80% is Black, Blacks are only 14% of the population but commit 83% of all crime! This has nothing to do with wealth, in Appalachia 95% of the population is poor White and crime is minimal.[350] The fact that statistically Asians and Whites have the lowest crime statistics and Blacks the highest, closely followed by South and Central Americans is never made public in the Lamestream.

In our 21st century media almost anything passes as news. Instead of news we have various talking heads, groups of people that often amaze us as jackasses with the uncommon gift of gab. The endless Council on Foreign Relations (CFR) twits with their zionist twisted opinions of relentless misinformation, omit and twist the truth until it is unrecognizable. They will report for 20 minutes about one dead Israeli and then omit the deaths of 1,000 Palestinian Christians and Muslims in Gaza. They label Hamas as terrorists but the IDF who has killed over a million Palestinians since 1948, as freedom fighters. They will not condemn Israel's relentless expansion into the West Bank and theft of Palestinian land, businesses, and farms but they will accuse Hamas of terrorist acts when they shoot a rocket into what four months before was their land. All public relations on behalf of Israel is news. We refuse to address the sitcoms of major TV networks that can only be characterized as brainwashing the mindless, and social engineering of society. Major TV anchors are actually readers of the news most of which is written in Washington and then edited in New York, we can prove it! Turn on any recording device on ABC and CBS then listen to the evening news turn on NBC, you will note that not only are all three networks reporting on the identical issues, but also they even use similar or identical sentences and sentence structure. This shows that the news is the product of a single source and is locally edited in New York. American news on major Lamestream media has long ago changed from news to entertainment. TV anchors in particular relentlessly pound the public with the "Beautiful People" and "Smart Money" and "He's a Celebrity" to attempt to induce the listeners' emotional responses—pathetic! Most of these "celebrities" are on their third wife or husband, have absolutely no morals, many are recuperating drug addicts or alcoholics, and are fools whose only ability is to regurgitate dialogue written by someone else.

To expand on previous text: Nine American companies control our media. One of these companies is AOL/Time Warner a group of companies that consist of: *Skull + Bones George W. Bush, drug + alchol + Hunter Biden · drugs!*

Time Inc.

WARNER MUSIC GROUP

WARNER BROS.

Time Inc.
Time Life Inc.
Book of the Month Club
Little Brown & Co.
WB Oxmoor
House Sunset Books

Warner Bros.
WB TV Network
WB Home Videos
WB Consumer Sales
WB TV
DC Comics

Warner Music
Warner Records
Electra Records
WEA Inc.
Atlantic Records

AOL/Time Warner
Courtroom TV
Network
Comedy Central
Sega Channel
Entertainment TV

HBO
HBO E
HBO W

TV Channels
Time Warner Cable
NY 1 News

Turner
Sports: Atlanta Braves, Atlanta Hawks, Goodwill Games, and WCW.
Home Entertainment: Turner Worldwide Video, Turner Publishing.
Programming and Production: Hana Barbera, Cartoon Inc., New
    Line Cinema, Castle Rock Entertainment, Turner Pictures, Film
    Library, MGM, and RKO.

So, who are the big names in media?

Gerald Levin	AOL/Time Warner
Edgar Bronfman Jr.	Seagram's, Universal Studios
Sumner Redstone	Viacom
Dennis Dammerman	GE
Peter Chernin	Co-COO News Corp Ltd.

Gerald	Edgar	Sumner	Dennis	Peter
Levin	Bronfman Jr.	Redstone	Dammerman	Chernin

These five control; ABC, NBC, CBS, Turner, CNN, MTV, Universal, MCA, Geffen, DGC, GRP, Rising Tide, Universal Records, and Iterscope.
Just as a note, PBS is a wholly Jewish operation.

We do not intend to cover the entire media, the aforementioned is simply an example; anyone with a computer can access corroborating information on the Internet.

Some people will now say that just the ownership of a corporation does not indicate control of content, well, okay, the executive news producers of ABC, CBS, NBC, CNN and PBS are all Jews. "Fair and balanced," yes so long as it complies with zionism. In fact reported news in America is so uniform as to make it difficult to distinguish between sources. Yes, there is difference in format, but not in content. About 40 million Americans rely on network TV for their information, possibly another 10 million on newspapers. The rest of the population is oblivious; at least 100 million Americans are clueless on news, or Government. Consider now the 40 million:

- Network news anchors become judge, jury, and executioner.
- News anchors have in the recent past made complete crooks or fools of presidents, Carter, Clinton, W. Bush, Obama.
- They make or break issues; the Gulf war, the Afghan war, the Libyan war, the Syrian revolution, Arab Spring, Black on White crime, the attack on the Liberty—all based on misinformation provided by the Mossad and very bad investigative journalism.
- By trickery they form public opinion; the false testimony of the
✳ Kuwaiti Ambassadors daughter regarding actions of the Iraqi army in Kuwait. (See note)
- All the endless wars since the end of WWII not one of which can be demonstrated to have any beneficial effect on America.

Let us all remember what James Reston said about the NY media, "NYC is the most unrepresentative community in the United States." Almost all network news originates in New York, after absorption of Washington DC input. The producers, editors, journalists, and news anchors all go to the same theaters, restaurants, bars, and movies, don't worry you won't ever see them, you could not possibly afford their lifestyle. And since you are not a member of Congregation Emanu-El you positively won't see them in your church. With the entire media forming their opinions and positions in the identical ways, that are an anathema to your own outlook, is it any wonder that all of their postulations appear slanted? Worst fact of the day is that your own government sanctions all this.[351] Therein lies the rub! Since the goals of all zionists are identical any populist news efforts remain a pipedream. The upshot of it is that all this dis-information, invented news, and unchecked facts produces a fabricated and distorted view of America and the world, with zionist dogma as the viewpoint in charge. Americans should not tolerate this, from our news sources or our government regulatory agencies. It is ridiculous that 1% of the American population, that are zionists are allowed to control our entire media. Remember that these pro-Israeli zealots' through ownership of media and banking select the movies to be produced, the TV programs we will watch, the news we are exposed to, the books we will read, the newspapers delivered, all imbedded with their liberal leftist messages. They distort and falsify current and past history in order to support their agenda. Nothing is safe; even children's programs are fair game. Remember in 1938 Hitler was speaking at a rally[352] when a heckler shouted out, "You will never have my support Mr. Hitler" he responded, "Never mind, I don't need your support, I already have your children's support." That is what it's all about!

<<Who are the media moguls that provide all this to us>>?

Ron Meyer	Nick Meyer
Mark Hoffman	Harry Sloan
Jeff Shell	Kevin Mayer
Aron Milchan	Barry Diller
Jeff Robinov	Peter Gruber
Bruce Rosenblum	Ron Nessen
Shari Redstone	Martin Rubenstein
Brad Grey	Robert Samoff
John Lesher	Robert Greenblatt
Eddy Hartenstein	Robert Iger
David Bell	Orin Aviv
Edgar Bronfman	Alan Horn
L.H. Goldman	Martin Shafer
Gerald Levine	Sumner Redstone
Don Newhouse	Mathew Blank
Leonard Stern	David Geffen
Adam Fogelson	Sam Zell
Michael Lynton	Dawn Ostroff
Thomas Rothman	Arthur Ochs Sulzberger Jr.
Barry Meyer	Max Frankel
Polly Cohen	Victor Kaufman
Peter Roth	Samuel Newhouse
Leslie Moonves	Steven Ross
Stanly Snider	Laurence Trish

Need we go further? The grand prize will be granted to the individual who is able to locate a Christian or Muslim in the above list.

Note: Hill & Knowlton, a NY ad agency was paid $10 million by the Bush administration and the Kuwait government to propagandize the American population into believing that the war in Iraq was justified based on false news. Included in this package was testimony before the U.S. Senate, which was nationally televised, of a young Kuwaiti nurse's eyewitness account of Iraqi soldiers bayonetting babies in Kuwait City in order to steal incubators and ship them to Bagdad. Grim stuff. However it was discovered that the entire story was completely false, fabricated by the Bush administration and the ad agency. The "nurse" wasn't a nurse at all; she was the daughter of the Kuwaiti ambassador to the US; coached by the ad company to read a bogus script; at the time of the "atrocities" she hadn't been in Kuwait City; she was a college student in America. Neither President Bush nor Hill & Knowlton nor the "nurse" were prosecuted nor even charged with this serious crime which was instrumental in launching the attack (war) on Iraq. *I witnessed it on T.V. RJ*

---

344. Joseph Göbbels Gauleiter & Reichspropagandaminister 1933-45
345. The Anschluss was by popular Austrian vote with an approval of over 90%
346. 72% of Bill Clinton's appointments were Jews, who comprise less than 3% of the total population. *Many CFR*
347. Newhouse Group of papers
348. Linkage is the process of association the author of an issue with some vile popularly disliked individual. For example Peter Arnold and Dr. Göbbels…
     Inferring that the author is a Nazi without incurring the possibility of a lawsuit.
349. "Black listing" of authors and book titles, in some cases even publishers, conservative authors are also dealt with in this manner.
350. FBI crime statistics indicate that White males commit less than 1% of violent crimes and Black Males over 10% of violent crimes. Based on the entire population that would indicate that a Black male is 100 times more likely to commit a violent crime than a white male.
351. Federal Communications Commission (FCC) regulates airwaves, and print media.
352. Nürnberg party rally in Beer Garden.

Jews in American Politics

The only difference between the DNC and reformed Judaism is the holidays.

Richard Brookhiser

Jews represent just fewer than 3% of the total American population. Anyone suggesting that such a minority could control a political party must by crazy. Or are they? (Well—just think of a 97 lb. dog with 3 lb. of fleas.) The facts are self-evident. Jews are registered voters at 80% of their population; Christians are barely at 50%. Examinations of presidential elections however indicate that only 58.2% of Americans vote.[353] But more importantly Jews block vote. If a Jew is running for office Jews vote 100% for him. They also do not vote based on American issues but on issues as they relate to Israeli-American foreign policy. American Jews are concentrated in a small number of states in which they make up a larger percentage of the vote. About 70% of American Jews live in the following states; CA, CT, FL, MD, MA, NJ, and NY (mostly in the metropolitan NYC area). The chart below shows the percentages as comparison with overall Jewish population:

State	Jews as % of Pop.	Jews as % of electorate
CA	3.0	5.8
CT	3.0	6.2
FL	4.7	8.2
MD	4.3	8.1
MA	4.5	8.3
NJ	5.5	9.9
NY	9.0	18.3

The aforementioned states cast 202 of the 535 Electoral College votes which is 37% of the total electoral votes. To demonstrate this issue let's look at an actual presidential campaign. We will not use the 2008 or 2012 campaigns because Obama is Black, which skews the numbers in the vote. The 1992 election was a three way split between Bush, Clinton, and Perot. 110 million votes were cast, thus with a population at that time of 250 million, turnout was just

3 of 9 Supreme Court members are Jews. 2 are CFR, Ginsberg and Breyer. (Other Kagan)

179

over 50%. In percentage Clinton got 43%, Bush 38% and Perot 19%. Jews however voted in a completely different pattern, 78% for Clinton, 12% for Bush and 5% for Perot.[354] Thus we can see that Jews made up between 53 and 56% of the 5.5-million vote margin by which Clinton won. It thus stands to reason that if Jews had not voted, America would not have been straddled with one of the most corrupt presidents of our nation's history. !

On all international issues Jews vote exclusively for Israel. America, community and family don't even come into play. On social issues they vote exclusively socialist. In the American understanding of conservatism Jews account for fewer than 2% of their group as conservative. America first is not even a recognized concept. The second amendment is not a concept. For complex reasons American Jews block vote for things that their Israeli counterparts would never even consider. By population percentage of well over 90 percentile American Jews vote for gun control, abortion on demand, the UN, internationalism, globalism, multiculturalism, and against, school prayer, the Ten Commandments, and "In God We Trust". They are not patriots, they are zionists. By plurality they vote Democrat, because the DNC is closer to socialism than the RNC. We can examine this by looking at the polling of past elections:

Year	Candidate	Percentage of Jewish vote
1968	Humphrey ,CFR	81
1972	McGovern, CFR	65
1976	Carter , CFR, TC	64
1980	Carter, CFR, TC	45*
1984	Mondale , CFR	67*
1988	Dukakis , CFR	64*
1992	Clinton ,CFR, TC, Rhodes, Bilderberg.	78

* Exceedingly weak candidates.

Nowhere is it more obvious that Jews control our government than in foreign aid. Israel, a nation the size of the state of New Jersey[355] with a population smaller than that of NJ is the benefactor of the largest recipient of American foreign aid in the world, NJ gets $30 billion less than Israel. Total aid since 1948 is $121,000,000,000 (That's B for billions.[356]) Israel is the world's largest recipient of aid as of 2014 that was 60% of total foreign aid.[357] In fact American

* Just look at Pres. Biden, Sanders and Cortez (AOC).

aid comprises 22% of total Israeli military expenditures. New Jersey citizens get $140 billion in Washington subsidies, same landmass about same population,[358] vs. Israel at $169.19 billion. Israel's per capita income is #21 out of 131 nationals listed. There are over 100 nations poorer than Israel, which leads to the question. Why are we providing them all this money? What have they ever done for our people? Often we support Israeli policy in conflict with other nations, and our own self-interests. Then any politician that will not tote the line of zionist hegemony or pundit disagreeing is pilloried and called a xenophobe or a Nazi by the media as well as Jewish support groups.[359]

Abraham Feinberg *(left) and Glenn T. Seaborg at the Weizmann Institute of Science annual dinner held at the Waldorf Astoria in 1971.*

Demonstrating the issue of Israeli political control of Washington is the <<Feinberg>> affair. From <<Feinberg's FBI file>>; "…there were a lot of people involved in this affair [The <<Haganah/Sonneborn>> arms theft and smuggling network] and the Department of Justice knew it. He further pointed out that more than 70 people on the West coast knew it."[360] This issue takes us back to the Kennedy/Johnson administrations. During the Kennedy administration Israel had concluded a deal with France

John F. Kennedy *was a member of Congress when he first met Prime Minister* **David Ben-Gurion** *in 1951. In this photograph taken at Ben-Gurion's home, Franklin D. Roosevelt, Jr., then a member of Congress from New York, sat between them.*

to supply a nuclear reactor, which would be used exclusively to produce plutonium for nuclear weapons. This was called the Dimona project, named after the desert it was located in. Eventually a successful bomb test was concluded in partnership with the Republic of South Africa near Prince Edward Island near Antarctica.[361] Kennedy was strongly opposed to a nuclear Israel, and insisted that the NRA and IAE inspect the plant. <<David Ben Gurion>> the Israeli Prime minster telephoned <<Feinberg>> in 1961 and asked if he could help, he bribed Kennedy's DNC with a $500,000

see Final Judgement by Michael Collins Piper.

contribution and Israel got their bombs.[362] Then Kennedy provided Israel The Hawk system the most advanced at that time missile aircraft defense system. When Kennedy sent a group of inspectors to oversee the plant he gave Israel a four-week advanced warning and the Dimona project managers hid everything and labeled everything in Hebrew. By the time LBJ was in office, after Kennedy's assassination, <<Feinberg>> had total access to the White House and Johnson to the point that cabinet meetings were interrupted if he telephoned. By this point American foreign policy was being made by <<Feinberg>> or the State Department of the president.

This is indeed a serious matter, that zionists control our foreign policy even with Russia. And what they don't control the media takes care of. An excellent example is the 1974 U.S. Soviet trade pact.[363] Part of that treaty that we still adhere to is a provision that gives Jews the power to veto any trade deal with the Soviet state based on the way the Soviet government deals with Jews.

⟋   The most powerful lobby in Washington is not the NRA as the media continuously claims; it's AIPAC,[364] the illegal Israeli lobby.[365] The annual budget exceeds $15 million. It has a staff of over 150. The issue is explained in several books.[366] These writings clearly show that zionists place Israeli interests far ahead of those of the nation in which they reside. This tilts American polices on all issues in Israel's court and in the hands of the political left. The power of the Jewish lobby is far beyond Jews representational population of America. This is caused by several factors, 1) Jews give far more cash to politicians and political parties than any other group. 2) Jews have long memories unlike Christians that forget in days what took place. 3) Jews are subjected to severe peer pressure by the Kahal. 4) Jews are extremely clannish. 5) On average they are the wealthiest group within our society. They solicit and cajole mammon at every opportunity and then use it for communal advance of the Kahal. They use extortion in this effort against anyone or anything that they see as wealthy, Swiss Banks and Insurance companies, America, Germany, French and Italian insurance companies, Caucasian Governments around the world, and then they have the nerve
✳   to collect for Jewish charity in TV commercials, demand and get tax-write-offs for Israeli bonds, the list is actually endless. It was a three-court press against the Swiss, the only people in Europe that allowed Jews in during WWII[367] and gave many[368] transit visas that allowed them to travel through occupied Nazi territory to Portugal

✳ IFCJ — Rabbi? on T.V. Ekstein. Begging for money!

CFR

and Spain. It was Alfonse D'Amato as the US attorney Eastern District NY that allowed the World Jewish Congress (WJC) (<<Bronfman>>) to embezzle $1.25 billion for war reparations of a neutral in the war.[369] Swiss banks that do billions of dollars of business here were threatened by D'Amato with seizure of assets if they did not pay off the WJC absolute unquestionable extortion, and the election of Alfonse to the U.S, Senate in NY.

Any responsible overview of these issues must consider Jews running organizations that have overriding power in areas affecting large portions of society. The Jewish political left spearheaded by the progressive movement has long been involved in social, labor, and religious groups. The American Federation of Labor (AFL) was formed by <<Samuel Gompers>>, his follower was <<William Green>>, this begs the question; what are Jews doing running labor unions when most Jews are professionals, shop keepers, retailers, Jewelers, lawyers, and organized labor accounts for less than 1/2% of membership as Jewish. The first president of the National Organization for Women (NOW) was <<Betty Freidman>>, all leadership members are Jews, this minuscule organization can, due to massive media support, get 500 women at one of their meetings. The media then informs the public that these feminists represent the entire female population of America, when they have one of their rallies. Ten women protest is front-page news and when conservative Phyllis Schlafly has a rally with 4,000 women present it does not even get mentioned on page six. Only two socialists have ever been elected to congress, <<Victor Berger>> and <<Bernie Sanders>>. <<Robert Bernstein>> founded Human Right Watch an organization that never has a thing to say about thousands of Palestinian deaths in Gaza due to IDF bombings. People for the American Way, who should change their name to "People for the Zionist Way" is nothing but a shill for Israel. The NAACP is a wholly Jewish invention founded in 1909 by <<Mary White Ovington, Oswald Garrison Villard, William English Walling and Dr. Henry Moscowitz>>, not one of them was Black. It was not until 1975 that the NAACP elected its first Black president. We find it absolutely amazing that Jews who always in conversation reefer to Blacks as Schwarze (derogatory Yiddish for Blacks) and whose primary religious text the Talmud calls them animals without souls and akin to monkeys should have managed the largest Black support group for over 65 years. But remember the Talmud mantra or that in the Protocols "divide and conquer." Vol I,

Pg. 221, My Awakening and Vol III. Bio Dictionary of The Left, by Dr. Francis X. Gannon, pg/40-152,

As an end to this chapter we offer a statistic that places all of this into perspective. The question being, exactly how far to the political left are Jews? 49% support homosexual rights, 51% support abortion on demand, 87% are for free choice, 90% oppose school prayer, 89% oppose the second amendment, 89% oppose the Ten Commandments (Jewish Law) from being publically displayed, 94% oppose "In God We Trust" on currency, 83% are opposed to the display of the Christian Cross, and lastly 87% are not opposed to displaying the Menorah. That in fact makes most of them atheists.

---

353. 2012 presidential election
354. National Jewish Democrat council (affiliated to the DNC)
355. CIA fact-book
356. 2007 military package $30 billion over 10-years. 2013 military aid $3.1 billion. Refugee resettlement aid $15,000,000 Military missile defense $99,800,000. F-35 Advanced stealth fighter for 2015 $ 2.75 billion. Iron Dome defense systems $50 million each of 8 batteries'. Arrow II and Arrow III and X band Radar $ 110 million, $ 58.9 million $66.2 million and $205 million respectively. Refugee assistance funding annually average $ 25 million. $289.5 million Economic recovery loan guarantees. ASHA grants for schools and hospitals $38.925 million. Israeli Egyptian peace treaty $3.75 billion. Aid for peace program $1.2 billion. U.S. bilateral aid $14.991 billon (1997 to 2013) [Congressional Research Service U.S. Foreign Aid to Israel March 12, 2012]
357. US Foreign Aid to Israel CBO
358. Center on Budget and Policy Priorities.
359. AJC, ADL, AIPAC, ARZA, CAMERA, CJF, CRC, HIAS, JCRC, JDC, NACRAC, NCSJ, ORT, PU, RAC, UAHC, UJA, WZO & ZOA. All the rest of races, nationalities, and religions, don't have this many cheerleaders.
360. Abraham Feinberg (1908-1998) was a smuggler, and financing agent to the DNC. It was <<Feinberg>> that gave Harry Truman's DNC $500,000 to recognize Israel in 1948. When later Kennedy opposed Israel's nuclear program it was Feinberg who again gave the DNC another $500,000 to overlook the Israeli Dimona program using a French built reactor to advance their nuclear program together with RSA.
361. The Vela Incident. September 22, 1979 an American Vela satellite detected a double flash nuclear explosion. The issue was sidelined but the US navy, US Air force, and Defense Intelligence Agency all corroborate the incident.
362. Estimated nuclear weapons by 2014 are 400 warheads.
363. For some unknown unfathomable reason our government continues to adhere to treaties signed with the Soviet government that has not existed in 24 years. (1991) The treaty is called the Jackson-Vanik amendment to the Trade act of 1974.
364. American Israeli Public Affairs Committee.
365. Acts in violation of 18 U.S. Code 219 L 113-296 except 113-287, 113-291, 113-295 Foreign Agents Registration Act
366. *Fateful Triangle* (Noam Chomsky), and *The Lobby* (Edward Tivnan)
367. 40,000 of them.
368. Over 100,000 transit visas.
369. Noteworthy is the fact that it was illegal to transfer money or insurance policies out of Germany from 1933 to 1945. The penalty was concentration camp. The only people able to transfer funds to Switzerland were Nazi party members and we think we can all agree that this did not include any Jews.

Treason & Betrayal

This is a chapter about the betrayal of society and of nations by their residents. It is reasonable to remember that all Jews consider themselves dual nationals, Israelis first wherever they are living second.[370] Jews from the first century forward when their leader betrayed the entire Kahal to the Romans are as a group un-trustworthy. They are not selective in this, it is a group trait, and it is vested in the Kohl Nidre prayer; absolution before the event. No bad consciences for sticking it to your neighbor, you have already been absolved of the act.

<<Jonathon Jay Pollard>> was a paid Israeli spy, even before the U.S. Navy employed him as an intelligence analyst. He tried employment at the CIA but was rejected. How he was qualified for that position has never been disclosed, but his employment as a spy for the Mossad was finally verified by <<Rafi Eitan>> in 1979 Israel's top spy master. Why a nation that claims to be our most trusted ally

Jonathan Jay Pollard is driven away from U.S. District Court in Washington after he pleaded guilty to selling classified U.S. government documents to Israel in this 1986 file photo.

(PHOTO: DENNIS COOK, AP)

hires a spy to do tremendous damage to our security can only be understood after the entire affair is revealed. We have a nation that is the recipient of billions of dollars in foreign aid, a nation that we at our own peril relentlessly defend in the United Nations, return our favor by spying on our defense systems. <<Pollard's>> handler was <<Yusef Yagur>> who worked at the Israeli Embassy in Washington as a scientific researcher. The inside source within the White House in the Clinton administration code, named MEGA was never revealed. This source provided <<Pollard>> with intelligence keys, codes, and other things that <<Pollard>> did not have access to. The fact that the Mossad had Clinton's office bugged, and that <<Monica Lewinsky>> was in all likelihood a Mossad agent, opens the possibility of blackmail. <<Pollard>> was this nation's most harmful spy, over our entire history. In volume and damage it exceeds the <<Rosenberg's>>[371] or <<Klaus Fuchs>>. What is even more amazing is the short timespan in which he did it. <<Pollard>> stole and provided to the Mossad 500,000 pages of secret defense material relating to naval defensive technology. He also provided all CIA operations and management personnel lists to the Mossad. Information he would not have had access to without MEGA. This information came from one of the president's National Security advisors. Then he went on to reveal the entire American CIA operations in the RSA to the Mossad, which then had to be shut down. Considering that South Africa was Israel's second-best ally after America makes this unbelievable. It is important to understand that none of the information provided to the Mossad was offense, it was all American defense. The total amount of information would fill a room 6 ft. x 6 ft. by 10 ft. Furthermore, the bastard did not do this out of some egalitarian reason; he did it for the money, total payments of $745,000. Additionally, he took several vacations including one with his wife to Paris. The worst however is what the Mossad did with the information; they sanitized it so that sources remained secret and then sold it for millions to America's greatest at that time adversary, the Russians. Our wonderful best friends and only ally sold our entire defense technology to the Russians. It must be emphasized that Polard did Not act alone, he was part of an operation conceived and run by the individuals and departments at the highest levels of the Israeli government.

Treason against America and South Africa was not limited to the Pollard affair. It was South Africa that provided fuel for Dimona, it was South African nuclear technology that allowed Israel to build its first atomic bomb, and it was South Africa's navy that, facilitated their first nuclear test on Sept 22, 1979 in the remote southern Indian Ocean. On November 21, 1985 in conjunction with RSA[372] Israel sold the entire joint nuclear development technology to the PRC (Peoples [Communist] Republic of China) and by doing so stuck another dagger in our backs. South Africa had a very large Jewish population and this was one of Israel's primary armament suppliers, especially heavy industry produced items that the Israelis could not produce. At this very same time our moronic Justice Department was prosecuting an American shotgun manufacturer for selling shotguns in South Africa.[373] RSA was at that time the fourth largest arms producer in the world. And this was due to South Africa's apartheid domestic policies, the very same that Israel and the Jews have been doing for the last 5,000-years. One of the defensive items sold by <<Pollard>> and then provided to the Russians was South Africa's "Cactus" missile interceptor system that was then promptly sold to the Russians.

TRAITOR On national security issues, Clinton was a total idiot. In May 1995 Bill Clinton appointed <<John *CFR* Deutch>> as Director of Central Intelligence, it is likely <<Deutch>> was aware of who the source for Pollard in the White House was. As director of the CIA <<Deutch>> transferred top secret information from CIA computers to his laptop, taking it home and often accessing the Internet with his laptop. In June of 1999 one of the idiots woke up and they striped <<Deutch>> of his

John Deutch
*17th Director of
Central Intelligence*

security clearance, but allowed him continued access to his industrial clearances. Deutch remained in the business as a consultant to companies like Raytheon, whose obvious internal security was worthless. This was no single issue; in 1977 <<Deutch>> had worked for DOE[374] where he was targeted by the FBI relating to the transfer of nuclear technology to Israel. The Israeli newspaper Ha'arez was

Allen Dulles

at the time quoted, "<<Deutch>> is such a committed zionist that he may as well wear a Kippa[375] to work." (At the CIA)

CIA and Mossad links go way back to 1954 and Allen Dulles (one of the infamous brothers) who had a very cozy relationship with Mossad head, <<Isser Harel>>. The flow of help and information was always one way from us to them, never reverse. Dulles provided

Isser Harel

Meir Amit

the Mossad all the latest American technology used for spying, which the Mossad then promptly turned on us. Just so you understand all this clearly, in 1967 during the height of the Vietnam war Mossad head <<Meir Amit>> traveled to Vietnam's capital Ho Chi Min City, met with the Viet Cong and provided Vietnam advice and intelligence to use against America and South Vietnam.

We learn from "Defense Helicopter", a military journal, that the new Russian HIND's are sporting a new missile system. That's sadly not the half of it; Israel has already provided the Russians the Mi 24v sans intake particle separators developed for the U.S. Army after the Iran hostage fiasco. They also provided the Russians IRCM missile jammers which had come from the U. S. and been upgraded by Tammam division of Israeli aircraft. In fact the Russian HIND helicopters shown at the Paris air show in 2000 saw over a dozen new improvements, all stemming from America and sold to the Russians by Israel, all of them stolen from America. The latest Russian HIND is equipped with "Rafael's Spike" a system that utilizes IR and CCTV camera tracking software utilizing fiber-optic linking systems. In other words a copy of the American provided TOW system paid for by American taxpayers. And again with friends like these...well you know the story by this time.

Robert Maxwell *in 1984 when he bought the Daily Mirror.*

The last item, previously mentioned, was the PRC being provided the plans for our advanced fighter by Israel who was given a set of plans that they swore they would never release...release they did for a tidy sum from China.

How large is the Mossad operation in America? Well we can't say but one thing is certainty it is the largest and most active spy operation against America. We do know that the Mossad has about 35,000 Sayanim[376] who are at the beck and call of AIPAC and the Israeli security services to do dirty work for them. These would be people like embezzler <<Robert Maxwell>>[377] or Israeli journalist <<Nicholas Davies>>, or <<Abraham Feinberg>>—the list is endless. These unpaid "helpers" for the Mossad are doctors, nurses, and engineers, rabbis, whose allegiance is not to America but to Israel. It is the primary reason why America should pass

Nick Davies

Abraham Feinberg

188

Gordon Thomas

a constitutional amendment barring any dual nationals from having US security clearances or holding public office. Reasonably reliable sources claim that 20,000 of the helpers are field operatives and 15,000 are sleepers. We do know that according to Gordon Thomas's book *Gideon's Spys* that in 1998 the Mossad had 48 members in their "Black Bag" (Assassins) operation of which six were women. They embarked on things like the assassination of Iraqi physicist Dr. Yaha Al-Meshad in Paris on March 18, 1981, for the sole reason that he was a physicist. Just imagine the mayhem if the world ran about murdering people because of their occupation. They murdered Canadian Gerald Bull[378] because he was designing a cannon for the Iraq government. In 1997 the British M-I5 and the French DGS reported to their respective government that they could no longer work with the CIA or American intelligence because the agencies were riddled with Mossad agents. In many instances the sanctions went completely awry like the one of Ahmed Bouchiki in Lillehammer Norway that was completely unwarranted. Then the attempt but failure on <<Khalid Meshal>>,[379] which turned into a diplomatic fiasco. We must always remember that Israel is the only nation in the modern era that has multiple times elected a known terrorist as prime minister.[380]

Dr. Yaha Al-Meshad

Ahmed Bouchiki

Gerald Bull

Khalid Meshal

The Mossad's agency of Physiological Warfare is a full-time operation of controlling the Israeli and American media to propagandize their populations. They are responsible for massive misinformation campaigns of such demission that it makes American government agencies look like children by comparison. Some examples are the story that Arabs were responsible for the TWA 800 flight disaster. Another fable was that the Murrah Office building[381] was blown up by Iraqi agents. Or how about the Iraq weapons of mass destruction that did in fact

A History of Zionism

not exist—note: nuclear and chemical weapons are not something one builds in his garage and hides under his bed. The "evidence" presented by Bush et al were blatantly bogus even to the lay public.

Lest you think that these are new issues, the Jews have been at this for a very long time. During the expansion of the Ottoman Empire when it was ruled over by Sultan Mohammad II [382] the Sultan had a trusted physician <<Maestro Jacobo>> a Jew who was also in the employ of the Venetians, who were anxious to curtail the power of the Sultan. Jacobo accepted payment and murdered the Sultan by poisoning him.

370. Any Jew can claim and will be issued Israeli citizenship and an Israeli passport on request and evidence he is a Jew.
371. <<Julius and Ethel Rosenberg>> gave the Soviets the atomic bomb secrets
372. South Africa's (RSA) nuclear program was at the time called Valinbada (which in Sotho means "the end of talking.")
373. Winchester Arms.
374. The Department of Energy
375. Skullcap worn by Israeli officials
376. Unpaid dual national Jews
377. Maxwell embezzled his newspaper's pension funds that financed Mossad operations he was murdered in his yacht. (Probably by one of his employees)
378. Gerald Bull (1928-1990) murdered by the Mossad because he was the ballistic expert in Project Babylon, a supergun.
379. Attempted murder was in Jordan using Sarin
380. <<Ariel Shalom and Menachem Began>>
381. Oklahoma City Bombing
382. 1403-81 AD

190

The King of the Jews

If the Jews had a royal family it would be the <<Rothschild's>>. In fact the resident of Waddesdon Manor and Ascott House both of which were donated to the National Trust, got to cut those taxes, <<Lord Rothschild>> has been often referred to as the "Prince of the Jews". His antecedent who took the name <<Meyer Amschel Rothschild>> actually adopted that name after he purchased his home in the Frankfurt A/M Jewish ghetto called the House of Red Shield, on Judengasse, his born name was <<Amschel Mayer>> and he used the alias Peter Arnold when posing as a Christian, something he did almost daily. He was at the time[383] considered as one of the most pious Jews of the Empire, he never ate at a Christian table, not even the emperor's. His nephew was his administrative assistant had a servant go directly before him, to wipe every door handle so as to ensure that <<Rothschild>> never soiled his hands touching polluted door handles e.g. touched by any non-Jews. The original family fortune was made in money lending (Usury) and selling rare coins. Three factors propelled the family's financial prominence. Firstly a total lack of moral inhibition in financing of virtually all sides in any military conflict from 1800 onward. Second, five sons strategically placed in financial centers of power. And finally, the uninhibited profit from renting of Hessian military forces to King George III for the American Revolutionary War. The city of Frankfurt was an open Imperial city and was therefore run by the local guilds. It was an inhospitable place for Jews. The city gate had the following inscription:

Kein Jud un kein Schwein
Darf hier herein!
Eng. No Jew and no pig may enter within!

Jews were not allowed in parks, not allowed in schools, and not allowed outside the ghetto after dark, naturally this did not apply to <<Rothschild>> who had a city pass under the name of his alias <<Peter Arnold>>. While Jews were not allowed to own land outside the ghetto, accommodations through intermediaries were very common, it was through efforts like these that <<Rothschild>> eventually was able to establish large warehouses all over the Holy Roman Empire, all managed by surrogates. <<Rothschild's>> five sons whom he dispatched all over the Empire created: A.M. <<Rothschild & Sons, Frankfurt A/M, N.M. Rothschild, London, Rothschild Frères Paris, S. M. Rothschild Vienna, C.M. Rothschild Naples>>, all brothers owned stock in all firms. Through this clever arrangement of ownership all gained if the majority gained, thereby their interests were bound not by nations but only by family. This is the primary reason of the <<Rothschild enterprises>> remarkable success in financing one war after another. All five brothers were fluent in German, Yiddish, French, English and Italian, but all with heavy Yiddish accents. They only spoke Yiddish with each other in order to prevent others from understanding their plans. As their banking enterprise expanded the Austrian Emperor took notice and allowed them to place a von before their name, insuring their status as gentry. Not long after that, they assumed Baronial status. As time progressed the bothers began changing their names as is so common with Jews even today <<Amschel to Amselm, Jacob to James and Calmann to Karl>>. Understand that in the 19th century this was an extraordinary event, almost impossible. In general terms even today, changing your name is not an acceptable act in Europe, it is in fact considered to be the act of a criminal.

This brings us to the first of two acts that so enriched the family. King George III of England had a serious rebellion on his hands in America. English press gangs had run out of poor peasants that could be pressed into service. George required foreign troops. He approached his cousin the Czar of Russia, unfortunately the Czar was heavily in debt with <<Rothschild>> who told the Czar that if he provided troops to George he would call all his outstanding loans, and The Czar told George no deal. In 1776 <<Rothschild>> was the court factor of Wilhelm of Hessen,[384] at that time the richest man in the world. Wilhelm was another cousin of George. Seeing another opportunity to make a killing Wilhelm told George through the intermediary of <<Rothschild>> that he could provide the necessary military muscle, under some very unusual terms. This proved to be the jackpot for <<Rothschild>> who through the arrangement wound up making a profit on every soldier provided to George for the American insurrection. To call the arrangements between George and <<Rothschild>> unprincipled would be a major understatement. In fact every Christian banking enterprise on the continent had turned George down. The Deal: First none of the soldiers were professional military, only the officers, all soldiers were rounded up by press gangs. All were between 17 and 45 years of age and from poor and farming families. The claim that the Hessians were professional troops is a lie. Terms of the draft were severe; deserters were made to run the gauntlet twice. The cost of troops was high, as negotiated by <<Rothschild>> on behalf of the Elector. Rothschild had already ensured his deal by blocking Dutch and Russian troops for England. The king of England had little choice but to accept <<Rothschild's>> offer. First there was the basic retainer of 51 Thaler (about 75 Gulden) for every foot soldier. (10% to Rothschild) This fee was payable within 60 days of delivery. If a solder was killed another 51 Thaler was due. For every wounded soldier another 17 Thaler was due. If a company was lost or if a ship on the way to America or back to Europe sank, or solders died from disease all the funds were due (102 gulden) per soldier plus the cost of establishing a new set of troops. To examine this deal let's assume that a ship with 700 men sinks in mid Atlantic. George will have to pay, to the Elector, 71,400 Thaler, in today's money $992,800. <<Rothschild>> banking took a 15% cut on this plus the Elector did not want to wait for his money so Rothschild acted as the factor charging a 25% fee for factoring the outstanding due money from George. The elector earned millions every year of the conflict and <<Rothschild>> hundreds of thousands. It is estimated that <<Rothschild's>> income for the American Revolution from 1775 to 1783 earned the family well over 15 million Gulden. <<Rothschild>> was at the end of the American Revolution worth about 130,000,000 Gulden.

ᶠ   To now maximize profit <<Rothschild>> struck a deal with Bruderus who was the Elector's chief revenue officer. <<Rothschild>> would give Bruderus a kickback on any financing deals that Bruderus could direct toward <<Rothschild>>. This gave <<Rothschild>> the inside track on every financial deal in Hessen and Kassel, money rolled in at unprecedented rates. <<Rothschild>> now expanded to Wilhelm's English business, which produced another £250,000 per annum. In today's money that is $18,750,000.

About this time at the outset of the Napoleonic wars the family had expanded yet again with Brothers <<Salomon and Amschel>> delving into the commodities business. They cornered the wool, cotton, and flour markets, commodities that due to the Napoleonic wars were in very short supply, they made another killing becoming the principle suppliers to the militaries of Austria, Prussia, France, Italy, and England, who were all participants in the wars.

This brings us to the second big <<Rothschild>> coupe. As the Napoleonic wars came to a head the Prussians and British were allied against France. The battle of Waterloo would be the final battle. On Sunday, June 18, 1815 in present day Belgium, the forces of Prussia under Gebhard of Blücher and the Duke of Wellington faced the French army under Napoleon Bonaparte and his army of 69,000, which comprised 14,000 cavalry, 48,000 infantry and 7,000 artillery, with about 250 guns. Wellington had 67,000 troops consisting of 50,000 infantry, 11,000 cavalry, and 6,000-artillery. Prussia had 48,000 men. The <<Rothschild's>> had the best communications system in the world. They could get a message from Waterloo to London in a matter of hours; normal communications for the same places was about 1½ days. The <<Rothschild's>> falsely reported that Wellington and his ally had lost the battle on Sunday. Monday morning the English stock and commodities markets crashed, by lunchtime <<Rothschild>> and his agents had purchased England for 2 cents on the dollar.

Then they financed the Opium trade from India to China netting them billions and resulting in the Boxer Rebellion. Then, with the Hudson Bay Company in North America, the effective neutralization of the American Indian population. After that it was an easy downhill jog, with "Colonel" House their agent controlling President Wilson and <<Paul Wartburg>> their banking correspondent in NY to produce the XVI and XVII Amendments of the US Constitution, and it was over—they owned America.

The fortune was made. When <<Rothschild>> married off his only daughter to another Jewish banker, her dowry in today's money was $200,000 with free home rent for two years, 5,000 Gulden in cash and the promise of 10,000 gulden upon <<Rothschild's>> death. By 1835 the family's banking enterprise less the commodities trading companies and warehousing had a net value of about 150,000,000 French francs and that does not count the English assets, which were again expanded when Nathen in London married <<Hannah Cohen>> whose father was the wealthiest banker in England. Hannah's dowry was a mere £10,000 about $69,000 in today's money.

---

383. <<A. Rothschild>> (The Founder) 1744-1812 Frankfurt was a free city of the Holy Roman Empire.

384. Wilhelm I of Hessen (The Elector) Landgrave of Hessen-Kassel eldest surviving son of Frederick II and Princess Mary the Great of England daughter of George II

The Magical Money Machine

Most people are not aware that capital markets fluctuate because of the actions taken by the **Federal Reserve System (FRS)** and major banking operations. Neither are they aware that there is no such thing as a national bank, all are linked and all are international. Ask any American, "Who owns the Federal Reserve System?" and they will assuredly respond with either the people or the government. They are, of course, wrong on both counts. Banking has ceased to be a matter of nations and has become the epicenter of an international cartel centered in Europe. The Federal Reserve is not federal, has no reserves and certainly is not a system but a corporation, incorporated in New York State on September 23, 1914.[385] If you already knew that great, you're ahead of the curve.

Markets, and by that we mean stocks, bonds, municipals as well as federal fiat are all controlled by the same people who control the prime interest rates. And just by chance they are the very ones that push national policies like Free Trade. Since these policies are basically injurious to our economy we must ask why and who stands for this? **The two largest supporters of Free Trade and the Federal Reserve System are the Business Round Table and the National Chamber of Commerce.** Well, superficially that does not make sense. Why would major trade associations that supposedly represent American business interests support policies that obviously are injurious to our national economy?

These are very basic issues that are never spoken of in polite company because that society does not want the answers made public. To examine this we must view the larger economy and how it functions. We shall use international trade as our example because it impacts everything in our society. In 1992 "Bonesman" (Skull and Bones secret organization of Yale University) President George H.W. Bush (41) signed an Executive Order that produced the North American Free Trade Agreement (NAFTA)[386]. **Incrementalism** is the prime directive of the Fabian Socialist. Thus, if we look at history we see that the Mexican government had an operating system called "The Bracero Program"[387] which expired in 1965 and was replaced with a new initiative called the Maquiladora program which was the precursor to the NAFTA accord. The Maquiladora program was to induce American manufacturers to move their production facilities to Mexico. This was very successfully accomplished by providing the following guarantees and benefits.

The Maquiladora Program

Guarantees and Benefits of constructing a new plant in one of the Mexican states bordering America:

1. Ten year property tax exemption
2. 30-year ownership of the manufacturing plant
3. No social security taxes
4. No required product liability insurance if the product was sold in America
5. Free labor training
6. Plant and operations security provided by the Federales

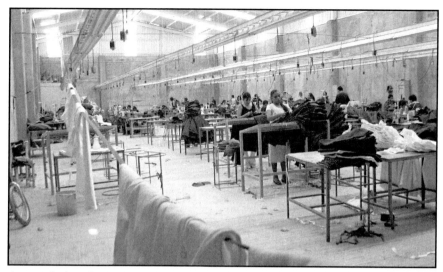

A maquiladora-factory in Mexico

Labor cost in Mexico at the time was 44 cents per hour and American minimum wage that was exceeded by all factory workers was $1.20. With the enactment of NAFTA the Maquiladora program became unnecessary. In 1982, American workers in manufacturing plants in America cost $34.00 per hour and Mexican workers in Mexico cost on average of $1.85 including overhead.

The leading small business association in America is the National Federation of Independent Business (NFIB).[388] They don't even get a seat at national discussions and they are lucky if some congressional committee allows them to testify. **The National Chamber and Business Round Table are totally controlled by big business which supplies 95% of their financial needs.** The large contributors to both organizations are all big business. And who is big business? Amazon, Boeing, General Motors (GM), Google, Apple, are some. Examining GM's manufacturing operations can be an illuminating experience.

Remember when Obama bailed out GM with an $80-billion government subsidy and in the process shafted all the GM bondholders and then gave the United Auto Workers (UAW)[389] most of the stock sticking the taxpayers with billions of junk bonds? Bondholders were screwed, unions were rewarded and US taxpayers were bilked. From Obama's perspective all he did was to reward his voter-base. So, what did General Motors do in the ensuing years? Today seven out of ten GM cars are made outside the United States. Before the

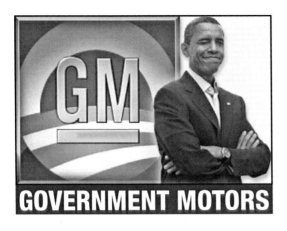

bailout seven out of ten **were made in the US**. All Buicks are now made in China. GM has a joint venture in China with the Chinese army's SAIC & FAW, which are the primary communist army's manufacturing operations. GM now has 14 plants in China, ten are assembly line and four are power train manufacturing operations. Today in China General Motors has 2,900 car dealerships.

Surely you understand that while GM talks the big talk, that's all it is. GM's interests do not lie in America, its financial interests are where their manufacturing base is. GM now employs more people outside the US than in their original home of Detroit, Michigan. Apple supports 4.8-million jobs in China. Amazon, whose Chinese presence is considered small, still has over 5,500 employees in China. Goggle has over 5,000 there. Microsoft employment is 126,079 worldwide and in the USA 74,530. **It's all a part of Ross Perot's warning during the US 1992 presidential campaign in reference to NAFTA, "They'll be a giant sucking sound going south, and it will not end until Mexico's hourly wage moves up to $6.00 an hour and the US hourly wage falls to $6.00 an hour." By that time the American middle class will have been totally destroyed.**

The profit motive is the driving cause of large **businesses** going overseas. America still has, even after Donald Trump's business tax cuts, the highest corporate tax rates in the industrialized world. Even worse is the personal income tax code. The Internal Revenue Service (IRS) tax code which no one understands, now comprises over 73,954 pages of legalese. Every year for the last ten years accountants have been challenged to do a fictitious tax return; no two have ever produced the same tax liability. This is not an inducement for business to stay in America. When we then add the hodgepodge of environmental and safety regulations and the rampant anti-government into the mix the actions of corporate managements are somewhat understandable. The fact is that our government functions in an adversary role against business, they are totally disinterested in helping business and hell-bent on regulating, fining and obstructing corporate America. In order to bring business back to the United States, the government must learn to achieve its desired outcome, not as an opponent, but as a facilitator.

Progressive politicians and bureaucrats in this country treat the people and business as cash cows to be milked daily. They never miss an opportunity to stick it to the taxpayers and the middle class. American made products are penalized by product liability insurance, which costs that average American manufacturer between 7% to 15% depending on the product. Offshore producers who have no attachable assets in America can forego that expense and therefore can offer their product at lower prices. By electing lawyers, which today are the great majority of legislators, that problem will never be solved.[390]

The profit motive I spoke of above includes many factors, over-regulation as applied in the Obama administration that from 2010 to 2016 has been horrendous. This has been demonstrated in

Independent candidate Ross Perot coined a phrase, still widely used today, on October 15, 1992. During a three-way presidential debate between Perot, Republican President George H. W. Bush and Democratic nominee Bill Clinton, Perot made a prediction about the effects of the proposed North American Free Trade Agreement (NAFTA). Many people today would view it as prescient.

Perot said: "If you're paying $12, $13, $14 an hour for factory workers and you can move your factory south of the border, pay $1 an hour for your labor, have no health care, have no environmental controls, no pollution controls and no retirement, and you don't care for anything but making money, then there will be a giant sucking sound going south."

That quote by Perot was included in hundreds of news reports about the presidential debate. Probably thousands.

the first nine months of the Trump administration in which thousands of regulations were terminated with resulting improvements in the economy and reduction of unemployment. Labor costs are another issue; it is simply unrealistic today to expect a manufacturer who has a labor cost per hour of $38.00 to compete with China ($6.50 max), Mexico ($4.82 max) or Vietnam ($2.99 max). The basic manufacturing law in a free trade environment is: produce your product in the place that has the lowest labor cost, the lowest regulatory regimen, the lowest energy costs, and the most amenable government. In all those factors America comes in dead last, **This is why free trade is such a lie.**

"If the American people ever allow private banks to control the issue of their money, first by inflation and then by deflation, the banks and corporations that will grow up around them, will deprive the people of their property until their children will wake up homeless on the continent their fathers conquered."

Thomas Jefferson

When we now consider the international financial situation we can surmise very similar outcome based results. Outcome based management is one in which the operators of a system, be it banking, business, education or manufacturing set an outcome to be desired before any action is taken. **In banking, the outcome is a single world currency under the control of the international banking cartel.** As Myer Amstel Rothschild put it, "Give me control of a nation's money supply, and I care not who makes its laws." In America it's the Federal Reserve System (FRS), in Europe it's the European Central Bank (ECB), in the international arena it's the bank for International Settlements (BIS) and the World Bank. And the Rothschild family still has their hands on all the levers of control.

A great example of control is the "Plunge Protection Team" (PPT) the colloquial name given to the "Working Group on Financial Markets." An Executive Order of Ronald Reagan in 1989, EO 12631 created it. Let me explain, the Plunge Protection Team is a group of about 1,000 capital market traders located geographically at the various twelve Federal Reserve System bank branches with its headquarters at the Union Bank of Switzerland (UBS).[391] American operations are in Stanford, Connecticut, which has the largest financial market trading floor in America. What the PPT does is ... if sudden market forces cause the stock, bond or securities markets to fall rapidly for an unknown cause, the Stanford office issues orders to their traders to begin buying. OK, so far so good, just one question, where do they get the money to buy? Now this is a really interesting question because they don't have any money and because the United States Treasury is prohibited from giving them money without congressional approval. It so happens that beginning in the second half of the Obama administration when interest rates had fallen to 0.05% no one had any interest in purchasing federal fiat certificates (T-bills, T-notes, savings bonds, etc.), the Federal Reserve sent orders to their branch operations to increase the asset side of their reporting books by billions. **The money never ever existed, all the so called monies are simply accountant's journal entries—why did you think that the Federal Reserve System, New York City depositories, and Fort Knox have never been publicly audited by any totally independent accounting firm outside of government?** *The Fed will not allow it!*

You see many things you thought are not at all as they appear, or as the "Lamestream" media reports them. Of course that's one of the problems, **the very same people who are the Deep State or the seventeen national security networks, or the major media, and the lobbyists on K-Street, the banksters, all of them act in unison along with the progressive mantra.** If you really want to know what that is why not get a copy of Karl Marx's "Communist Manifesto," skip all the political minutia and go straight to the ten points of the manifest—say, almost the entire thing has already been instituted as law in America. Want some more proof?—read the "Protocols of the Learned Elders of Zion" both documents are easily available on the Internet.

Does our American foreign policy confuse you? It did me for a long time, but then I read the Oded Yinon Plan for Eretz Yisrael[392] and I got it. All at once it was crystal clear why the Mossad produced that totally bogus Weapons of Mass Destruction lie about Iraq, and why Israel relentlessly tries to get us into a war with Iran. After all in the 9-11 attack there were nine Wahhabi Sunni Saudi Arabians and not one single Shia from Iran. Iran signed onto the United Nations (UN) Nuclear Non-Proliferation Act decades ago and their entire nuclear program is constantly monitored by the UN. Israel has not signed the UN Non-Proliferation Act and has an estimated 400 nuclear war heads, many produced in conjunction with the Republic of South Africa (RSA) government in the 60's to the 70's. But the real laugh (if there is anything to laugh about) is the continuous diatribe for over a decade from the Likud party in Israel about the development of Iranian nuclear weapons to be finalized in just three more months. Really, ten years of in just three more months! That's a repetition of fourteen times as Einstein said, "The definition of insanity is doing the same thing over and over and expecting a different result."

What you really need to understand is that banking in the world is about the creation of debt and who controls it; individual debt, corporate debt and national government debt and who controls it. The fastest and best way to produce debt is with wars and the end result is always the same, more debt owed to those who financed the wars. In most cases it is the same banking groups who finance both sides of the conflict. This is why banks always come out of conflicts smelling like a rose. They possess the debt and thus have control of all the debtors after the war. The bankers get richer and the societies involved get poorer and the working middle class loses their liberties and becomes financially enslaved through indebtedness.

27 Dec 2019
6 Mar 2020
My B.D. 29 Apr 2021

---

385. NY Times Sept 23,1914
386. NAFTA (North American Free Trade Agreement) not a treaty that would have to be ratified by the US Senate, which with massive public opposition (87%) could not have passed the hurdle.
387. Brácero program was for Mexican workers to work seasonally in America without work permits.
388. NFIB (National Federation of Independent Business) (under 500 employees)
389. UAW (United Auto Workers)
390. Contingency suits are when the law firm covers the costs of the suit and then takes 30% of the winning settlement.
391. UBS (Union Bank of Switzerland)
392. Greater Israel the plan is a 9-page document on the internet translated from Hebrew in the 80's

Bibliography

The Gulag Archipelago series	Solzhenitsyn	numerous numbers
The Holocaust Industry	<<Finkelstein>>	1-85984-773-0
Gideon's Spies	Thomas	0-312-19982-1
Roman Census	Quirinius	Internet download
Dr. Göbbels His Life and Death	Manvell/ Fraenkel	978-1616080297
The Protocols of the Learned Elders of Zion		Internet download
The Two Seeds of Genesis (2 volumes)	Gayman	no ISBN
Israel's Changing Society	<<Goldschneider>>	0-8133-3917-0
The Holocaust Dogma of Judaism	<<Weintraub>>	No ISBN
The Essential Kabbalah	Matt	0-7858-0870-1
Rudolf Hess His Betrayal & Murder	Melaouhi	978-1-937787-18-9
World Almanac 1933		Public Library
World Almanac 1948		Public Library
July 4th 2016 The Last Independence Day	Krieg	0-87319-47-5
The Intimate Papers of Colonel House: Behind the Political Curtain		before ISBN

Philip Dru: Administrator	House	before ISBN
Black September	Dobson	0-02-531900-0
Palestinian Walks	Shehadeh	978-1-41656966-4
The Sword of the Prophet	Trifkovic	1-928653-11-1
Byzantium	Mango	1-89880-044-8
The Koran	(Macmillan)	0-02-083260-5
Taliban	Rashid	0-300-08902-3
Warriors of the Prophet	Huband	0-8133-2781-4
Arabisher Frühling	Tahar Ben Jelloun	97838227010483
Islam	Guillaume	0-1402-0311-7
The Assassins	Lewis	0-465-00498-9
Origins of Western Civ.	Barnes	978-0-9742303-8-2
World & Witness	McCurley/Reumann	No ISBN
History of the Arab Peoples	Hourani (Harvard Press)	No ISBN
The Communist Manifesto	<<Marx>> (Plagiarized)	No ISBN from JBS
Israel's sacred Terrorism	<<Sharett>>	0-937694-70-3
Your Heritage	Comparet	No ISBN
Israel's Global Role	<<Shahak>>	0-937694-51-7
The Zionist Factor	Benson	0-945001-63-0
The Hidden History of Zionism	Schöneman	0-929675-01-0

Jewish History, Jewish Religion	<<Shahak>>	9-780745-308197
The Founding Myths of Modern Israel	Garaudy	0-939484-75-7
A People That Shall Dwell Alone	McDonald	0-275-94869-2
The High Priests of War	Piper	0-9745484-1-3
The Talmud Unmasked	Pranitis Russian Translation by Sanctuary)	No ISBN
Our Political Systems	Krieg	
The Secret Relationship between Blacks and Jews	Levin	0-9636877-0-0
The New Jerusalem	Piper	AFP No ISBN
The Sampson Option	Hersh	0-394-57006-5
Jewish Power	Goldberg	0-201-32798-8
The Controversy of Zion	Reed	0-945001-38X
The Collected Works of C.S. Lewis		0884861511
Jews and their Lies	Martin Luther	9 781930004894
The Secret Empire I & II	C. Cunningham	0-9700966-0-7 & 0-9700966-2-3
The Torah		
The Talmud		

Index: Names

Ekstein,   I B C J

Rabbi - Passover help #25   207   wife = yael

was #25 - $35,6 Mar 20

Index: Issues

Rabbi Epstein, wife Yael, IFCJ
Rabbi Eckstein,

Page 164

see pg 101, Individualism and the Western Liberal Tradition by Kevin MacDonald.